The Witches' Almanac

50 Year Anniversary Edition
An Anthology of Half a Century of Collected Magical Lore

CONTAINING pictorial and explicit delineations of the
magical phases of the Moon together with information about astrological
portents of the year to come and various aspects of occult knowledge
enabling all who read to improve their lives in the old manner.

The Witches' Almanac, Ltd.

Publishers   Providence, Rhode Island
www.TheWitchesAlmanac.com

Address all inquiries and information to
THE WITCHES' ALMANAC, LTD.
P.O. Box 1292
Newport, RI   02840-9998

13-ISBN: 978-1-881098-77-5 Softcover
13-ISBN: 978-1-881098-78-2 Hardcover

ISSN: 1522-3184

First Printing July 2020
Hardcover Second Printing December 2020
Softcover Second Printing February 2021

Printed in USA

Established 1971 by Elizabeth Pepper

Preface

Centuries of arcane lore add up to the witchcraft experience. Despite the vast storehouse of knowledge that fills the world's libraries, both public and private, most magic remains in the oral sphere, rigorously preserved secrets handed down reverently from one generation to the next.

The study of Witchcraft is the understanding of nature and the ability to tread its path with confidence as a surfer is able to step on and off a wave at will, using its energy and force as long as he can accept its immutable direction.

The theory and practice of Witchcraft is possible only to those who truly believe but to them it becomes an unsurpassable art in which nature is neither master nor servant but an invincible ally in whose harmony all things can be achieved.

To the true skeptic nothing is possible, nothing can be taken on faith alone. His subconscious slumbers beneath the earth like a dormant seed before the warm sun melts the insulating snow, nurturing its quest for awareness.

The scientists have had their day and once again the Olde Religion is coming to the fore. The bankrupt religious and political philosophies of the past twenty centuries, with their unceasing battle against the forces of nature, have only served to prove how impotent is the alliance of man and machine.

But the winds of change are blowing and once again the individual is about to assert himself. As so many times in the past, Witchcraft will illuminate the darkness.

CONTENTS

Contents

⟶ CONTENTS ⟶

CONTENTS

The Names of Familiars

The Familiar Or Animal Companion to Witches is peculiar to the British Isles and America.

In 17th Century England the naming of a familiar was important enough an event to call for an Esbat—a meeting of the Witches' Coven.

Some of the name the Witches chose for their animals have been culled from their trial records and are listed below.

Amie	Panu
Bessie	Pigene
Collyn	Prettyman
Elimanzer	Priscill
Elva	Robert the Rule
Fancy	Robin
Fillie	Rorie
George	Rug
Gibbe	Sack and Sugar
Grissel	Sanders
Hoult	Sathan
Inges	Sparrow
Jacke	Susan
Jarmara	Tewhit
Jezebell	Tibbe
Lightfoot	Tom
Littleman	Tyffin
Makeshift	Vinegar Tom
Mak Hector	Wynowe

Bell Book And Candle

Ring the bell, light the candle and open the Book of Shadows; the ancient preface to an act of magic. Later, this simple ceremony would become distorted into a rite of exorcism. But in the beginning, it belonged to the cult of the wise… the Witches.

If you would learn to cast an enchantment or work a spell, remember the prime requisite is complete confidence in your ability to do so. The words and actions are mere formalities. The magic lies in the strength of your will and power of your mind. These are fire charms and must be performed alone.

To Attract a Lover

Crumble dried leaves of laurel and scatter them over live coals. As they burn, firm your will and bring the face of your beloved to your minds eye. Chant…

Laurel leaves,
Burnt in fire,
Draw to me…
My heart's desire

To Rid Oneself of the Pain of Unrequited Love

Kneel before a roaring fire. As you hold a handful of dried vervain leaves, concentrate upon your intention. Throw the herb, all at once, on the blaze and repeat…

Here is my pain,
Take it and soar,
Depart from me now,
Offend me no more.

To Gain Control of Another's Will

Take the dried leaves of St. John's Wort, enough to make a generous handful. Strew them over the fire as you say alout…

It's not the herb that I now burn,
But _____'s heart I mean to turn,
May he no peace nor comfort find,
Ere he bend to me in soul and mind.

Witchery

A witchboard is one of the basic tools that you can use to help achieve some of your desires. Almost any piece of wooden board will serve, irrespective of size, as long as it has been unused and free from any joins, joints, metal (screws, nails, etc.)

With something sharp—stone or slate—draw a circle on the surface of the board and then a triangle inside the circle so that each point of the triangle touches the circumference.

The witchboard should be kept beside the bed, near enough to be seen conveniently at all times, and can be used as the focal point for whatever it is you are seeking. When you have decided what it is you want – money, a lover's attentions, a letter, a business contact- take pen and paper and write it down in as few words as possible.

Next, pin the sheet of paper to the witchboard *without touching the pin*. Hold it between a pair of wooden matches or wedges of paper and hammer the pin into the board with a mallet, or other piece of wood.

Finally, go to sleep with the witchboard beside your bed and don't touch food or water before sunrise. Whatever it is you witched for will come to you within a few days.

Making a Magic Wand

The wood of hazel or box elder trees is most suitable for a magic wand which must be made solely by the person who intends to use it. The piece of wood should be reasonably straight and long enough to reach the ground.

First strip off the bark and then insert into the end of the bough a steel knitting needle or stout piece of straight wire. Next determine the direction of magnetic North (with a compass) and bury the elongated rod in the ground facing in that direction.

After two months, dig it up. It will have absorbed the magnetic force of the Earth and will be ready to use.

To Summon Winds

In a foot length of light rope, tie three knots. Untie the first for a gentle breeze, the second for a fresh strong wind, the third for a storm and tempest.

The Way of Witches

"If you would know more of the way of the witches; their rites and practices, then study children at their play. In their innocent games are preserved the very essence of the old way."

"Witches, Witches, without bother, Chance to meet and know one another."

THE CAT

AS FAMILIAR

By Amanda Martin

Although its origins are in the East, the domestic cat was well established in the western world long before the dawn of the Christian era. Britain, for example, probably owes it earliest knowledge of the cat to the Phoenicians, who sailed to Cornwall to trade for tin. But if not them, the cat surely found its way into every corner of Europe in the wake of the invading Roman legions.

While the link between the cat and the occult is often credited solely to its deification by the Egyptians, it is of interest to note that the chariot of the Norse Goddess Freya was traditionally drawn by two grey cats. Perhaps the truest reason for the link may be found in the ancient Celtic belief that a cat's eyes are the windows through which human beings may explore an inner world.

Whatever the origin, cats and Witches have enjoyed a long association. Nocturnal creatures of evil repute, they suffer together the consequences of falsely inspired fear along with a trait of being called "she" regardless of gender. Both provoke unreasonable hostility by merely being true to their own nature. But misfortune alone does not hold them together. An archetypal kinship and a deep, genuine affection are evident in most cat-Witch relationships. It comes as a surprise to many who assume that the cat is remote and aloof to see it behave like a friendly puppy in the company of the Wicca.

Not every Witch is a cat lover, nor is every cat qualified to be a psychic aide. But you would do well to engage one as a familiar spirit. Let instinct alone guide your choices. Breed, color or sex are not determining factors. The potential familiar will possess a mystic quality to be inwardly sensed rather than outwardly seen.

For establishing strong personal ties, it is not sufficient merely to observe the ancient ceremony of mixing a drop of your own blood in its first saucer of milk or of eating together from the same plate which is said to "strengthen the psychic bond between ye"; such rituals cannot replace time, patience and acts of kindness which lead to mutual love and respect.

Here, from an eighteenth century *Book of Shadows* are instructions for the training of the cat to occult use:

"To be performed every evening, at the same time, in the same place... Adapt the cat to sit close by you, facing the same direction you face which shall be in the place where the moon will rise. Stroke gently but firmly with love in your hands until it purrs and your breathing are heard as one sound. Now you and the cat posses the same will, your eyes will see as its eyes see, and your thoughts will travel together. The time has come to work spells and cast enchantments for power is doubled through the agency of your familiar.

Birds AND FEATHERS

Fallen feathers of wild birds were once read as auguries. At molting time in late summer, the wise would stroll into the countryside to collect as many as the eye could spy. Color was an important matter. A grey feather meant peace of mind, whether it fell from a nuthatch or a catbird. A black one was a sign of death or disaster and probably added to the unfortunate reputation of the crow. The reading of the feathers, while most often of a personal nature, could foretell the weather pattern ahead. A multitude of feathers foretold of an early autumn, while a scarcity indicated a period of Indian summer was at hand.

Feathers figure in many occult usages. A wreath of chicken feathers placed on the victim's bed warns of harm in the practice of Voodoo. The custom of sending a white feather to one who has betrayed a trust was observed in the film *Four Feathers*. The exotic peacock feather bears ill will; the curse of the evil eye. But not all feathers are omens of bad tidings. A red quill brings good luck, and a blue one promises success in love. Present a traveller with a feather of good will and his journey will be a pleasant one. A charming old gesture is recoded: the custom of securing a feather to a package when it was sent by messenger – possibly one of the earliest forms of gift wrapping.

The Language of Feathers

Red: *good fortune smiles upon you*
Orange: *a promise of delights to come*
Yellow: *beware of false friends*
Green: *adventure awaits*
Blue: *love will enliven your days*
Gray: *peace of mind*
Brown: *good health*

Black: *ill tidings or death*
Black and white: *disaster aversed*
Green and black: *fame and fortune*
Brown and white: *joy and mirth*
Gray and white: *your wishes come true*
Blue, white and black: *a new love*
Purple: *exciting journey soon*

The Bath

HERBAL AND RITUAL

BY THE FLICKER of candlelight, inhaling the fragrance of pungent incense, ease into a full tub of very warm herbal bath. You are about to give yourself over to an ancient ritual of cleanliness and purification. After scrubbing with a pure soap, close your eyes, relax your muscles section by section from head to toe. Focus your closed eyes at a point in the center of your forehead. Remain in the ritual bath from 15 to 20 minutes.

You will emerge with your physical senses extended in a disciplined way, calm yet energized, with increased awareness of the subte forces.

The water may be prepared in a variety of ways. A sea salt bath is an ancient method for general tonic effect... add one pound iodized sea salt to the bath water. For a pine needle bath, boil one pound pine needles and cones for a half hour, leave for 13 hours to infuse, strain and use a gallon amount for each bath. Flowering herbs may be used, either prepared by infusion as for the pine needle bath or tied in a chessecloth bag and added to the bath water. Hyssop, chamomile, lavender, bergamot, rosemary, thyme, lemon verbena are traditional. While still wet, rub your body well from head to toe with pure oil. The ritual bath has prepared your body and spirit for the ceremony of an exquisite act of magic, holiday observance or love.

The Gift

IN A TIME when conscientious mind-benders control the world of children's books, it isn't surprising to find the old-time fairy or folk tale neglected. Today's concerns seem to be the building of reading skill and the imposing of correct social attitudes. Both are commendable; but what of nourishment for the fancy and the spirit? Myths and legends handed down from one generation to the next, long before the advent of the printed word, still have great value. Enriching childhood, they form the notions of good rewarded and evil punished. The spirited stories awaken imagination and quicken the young mind to see beyond mere appearance to true value. In a guileless way, they serve their purpose and delight at the same stroke.

For the student of Witchcraft the ancient tales provide an excellent source of information. Although her name was changed to fairy god mother, the bestower of gifts was in fact the wise woman of the village—the Witch. Here she is in an old illustration: pointed hat, wand and the power to make Cinderella's dream come true.

Briar Rose, or Sleeping Beauty, reveals the age-old Wiccan custom of wishing upon a child a special gift.

Once upon a time a King and a Queen gave a christening feast for a long-awaited first child. To the celebration the royal couple invited seven fairies (or Witches) of the kingdom in the hope they would bestow upon the infant princess special gifts as was their custom.

Unfortunately they had neglected to invite one rather bad tempered fairy. Angered by the slight, she arrived at the feast in a rage. As the fairies began to give their gifts the wisest of the seven waited, hidden behind the cradle, for she feared the wrath of the bad tempered one.

Beauty was the present bestowed by the youngest fairy; it was granted by the next; the third offered grace, the fourth, virtue; the fifth, a lovely voice; the sixth, a smile to win all hearts. Then the bad tempered fairy arose and pointing her ivory wand like a spear at the royal baby, she cried out: "While still in her rosebud youth the King's daughter shall prick her hand with a spindle and fall down dead!"

Hearing this the company despaired but the wise fairy stepped forward and said: "Although I cannot undo what has been done it will not be quite as she said. Your daughter will prick her hand with the spindle and fall to the floor but she will not die. Instead her, sleep will last for 100 years and from that sleep, when her dream is over, a king's son shall awaken her."

Here is the inevitability of a Greek tragedy, yet the promise of a happy ending. In Witchcraft, you see, hope is believed to be the most singular of human attributes.

Illustration by Margaret Evans Price from ONCE UPON A TIME. Copyright 1921, 1949 by Rand McNally & Company.

Gerald Brosseau Gardner
(June 13, 1884–February 12, 1964)

IN 1951, in England, the last law against Witchcraft was repealed. This meant that, after centuries in hiding, witches could once again come out and practice openly. Yet they had learned to be cautious; they remained hidden.

One man, at the time, belonged to a Coven that he felt was possibly one of the last in existence. Before that too disappeared, he wanted to give the public the witches' side of the story—to show what witches *really* did and believed, as opposed to what people had for so long thought them to do and believe. That man was Gerald Gardner.

Gerald had been born into a well-to-do family of Scottish ancestry. From as early as he could remember Gerald suffered from asthma. Because of this he spent most of his life abroad, in climates sunnier than that of England. His earliest reading was the works of Florence Marryat, the Spiritualist. From her he developed a firm belief in the survival of the spirit after death. Form the many native tribes, with whom he came in contact in the far East, he accepted the idea of many local gods and spirits.

Gerald got his first job working on a tea plantation in Ceylon, at the age of sixteen. Spending much time in the jungles, associating with natives, he learned of their beliefs and magical practices. In 1908 he moved on to Borneo and the headhunting Dyaks. From there he went on to Malaya. From plantation work he went into government employ, first—in 1923—as an inspector of rubber plantations, and later as Principal Officer of Customs. Wherever he went, whatever his job, he never ceased his study of native customs and magical beliefs. He studied anthropology; he indulged in archeology. His first major book, KRIS AND OTHER MALAY WEAPONS, became the standard work on the subject and established him as a world authority. His researches and excavations—discovering the site of the ancient city of Singapura, for example—led to his receiving an honorary Doctorate from Singapore University. His reconstruction of ancient sea-going ships are to be seen both in the Singapore Museum and the Victoria and Albert Museum, London.

It was not to be until his retirement, and final return to England, however, that Gerald came into contact with Witchcraft *per se*. Through a chain of circumstances he discovered the existence of a witch Coven in the New Forest and, after a certain waiting period, was initiated into it. He was extraordinarily happy—his interest as an anthropologist/folklorist was very definitely stirred—and he was extremely excited. He was excited, firstly, to find that Witchcraft was still alive and, secondly, to find that it was *not* Satanism and anti-Christian mumbo-jumbo, but that it was a religion in its own right dating from pre-Christian times. His first impulse was to run out and tell the world it was wrong! He was not allowed to do so.

Gerald continued to travel. He was able, through his experience and learning, to find many, many parallels with Witchcraft in other societies and civilizations. He came to recognize the origins of many things within the craft that the average witch accepted without question. He even found instances where, over the centuries in hiding, obvious errors had crept into the rituals—errors obvious to one of Gerald's background, though not to others.

In 1949 Gerald was permitted—rather grudgingly, by his High Priestess, Dorothy—to publish a book called HIGH MAGIC'S AID. This was written (very entertainingly) as a novel, but gave a truer picture of Witchcraft than had been shown until that time.

Dr. Margaret Murray, the famous Egyptologist and Anthropologist, had by this time stumbled on the fact that Witchcraft was a religion having no connection with Christianity. She had shown, in her book GOD OF THE WITCHES, that it stemmed from the days of early Man's belief in animism. This had prompted other scholars to examine her theory and, in general, agree with it. It was not until 1954, however, that there was to be any confirmation of the theory.

In 1954 Gerald was finally allowed, by his Coven, to publish WITCHCRAFT TODAY. A factual book—perhaps the single most important book on the subject—showing the true side of Witchcraft; telling as much as might be told to an outsider. With its publication Gerald was surprised and delighted to start receiving letters from other Covens dotted about Western Europe. Each of them had thought that perhaps *they* were the last surviving Coven, but were so happy to hear of Gerald's.

By this time Gerald had opened the world's first museum of magic and Witchcraft, housing his fantastic collection of religio-magical artifacts from around the world. He had long since achieved the degree of High Priest within his Coven and was now very much regarded (unofficially, of course) as the "Grand Old Man" of Witchcraft!

Yet things were far from easy for Gerald. Looking back from today some people (many of them "pseudo-witches") claim Gerald was simply out of money! This was far from the truth. What he did took a great deal of courage, and also *cost* him money. To claim to be a witch at that time was to invite people to throw rocks through your windows; to be slandered; to be ridiculed. Yet all this Gerald endured, for he felt that someone had to give the true picture of Witchcraft. No one else was willing so he went ahead. Today's witches—even the "commercial" ones—owe Gerald a great deal.

The Coven which Gerald originally joined was a Celtic group (as in Christianity there are various denominations, so in Witchcraft). In later years Gerald went through the rituals and corrected them, where errors had crept in. He brought them back to what was probably their original form. Later followers of these rituals then became known as "Gardnerian" Witches, after Gerald. A better name might, perhaps, have been "Purists". However, since the name does honor Gerald's work, it is a good one.

In the late winter of 1963/64, as Gerald was returning home from Lebanon, he died at sea. His body was taken ashore and buried, at Tunis, the following day February 13, 1964. Witchcraft—"the Craft"—lost a great man.

STREGERIE, ITALIAN WITCHCRAFT

By Leo Louis Martello

Italian Witchcraft is based on many traditions, from Sabine, Etruscan and Greco-Roman Hermes to those of the multi-racial blend of Sicilians. Diana, identified with Herodias, is known throughout Italy as "Queen of the Witches." The book *Aradia, or Gospel of the Witches* by C. G. Leland, published in 1899, translated the legend of the daughter of Diana and Lucifer, called Aradia, and born to teach Witchcraft to humanity.

In ancient times people came from all over the world to worship at the Temple of Demeter, in Enna, Sicily, to celebrate her daughter Persephone's resurrection from the Underworld to become Goddess of immortality and souls. In this same town there Is a Catholic Church that has a Madonna with a female child. Its sculptor belonged to *la vecchia religione* (the old religion) and in this way paid tribute to his Goddesses of Demeter and Persephone. Even today the Sicilians revere the female

deity (Madonna) more than the male (Christ). Most Italian-Sicilian Catholic churches are built upon former pagan worship sites.

Diana, as Goddess of secrecy and sorcery, was worshiped by runaway slaves, outcasts, the oppressed, night people, and those who were anti-establishment. Often called Luna, since she was the Moon Goddess, they congregated in the forests night and paid her homage. These victims of oppression could not turn to a Christian or Roman God but they did have their Goddess. Unlike many Northern races the Italians have always revered the Goddess, and when the country became Christianized this was transferred to the Blessed Virgin.

In *Treatise on Witches* (1547) by Paulus Grillandus, he writes that the witches "think that Diana and Herodias are true Goddesses, so deeply are they involved in the error of the pagans." In his *Demonomagie* (1818) Horst

writes: "In the indictment of witches it is generally stated that—, the party accused, acted with (worshipped) Diana and Herodias. It is very remarkable that we find this among the declarations of public Church council—that of Ancyra in the middle of the fifth century—just as in later witch trials. It was asserted that certain women imagined that they flew by night through the air with Diana and Herodias. But as this was spoken of at the Council of Ancyra as a well known thing, the belief must be much older, and I do not doubt that there exist much earlier historical records of this, which are unknown to me."

Etruscans worshipped the trinity of *Tina* (Roman Jupiter, Greek Zeus) *Thalna* (or *Cupra*) forebearer of Hera or Juno; and Menrva (Pallas Athene, Roman Minerva). Tina was the God of thunder and lightning; *Cupra* was Goddess of marriage, protector of women, who later changed her sex, and *Minerva*, majestic Goddess of wisdom and patroness of the arts. Prior to the Roman take over there was a temple to each of them in every city. Note too that there is one God and two Goddesses, or more precisely, one God, one Goddess, and and one who supposedly changed sex from female to male.

Author Leland was one of the first to point out that Witchcraft is the remnant of an old religion (*Aradia*, 1899), taken up by Margaret Murray in her *Witch-Cult in Western Europe* (1921) but dealing only with the Horned God, and popularized by Gerald B. Gardner in his *High Magic's Aid* (1949 under pseudonym of *Scire*) and his *Witchcraft Today* (1954).

Gardner later demoted the Horned God of anthropologist Murray's research and elevated the Goddess. The underground la vecchia religione has existed for centuries in Italy and in Sicily. Some even became Catholic priests in this way were able to warn their craft brothers and sisters when danger threatened.

On April 23, 1969, 10,000 witches of Rome went on strike to get Social Security benefits. The Italian Union of Magicians meets in Palermo, Sicily, regularly. Every town in Italy has at least one local witch. There is a secret society of ancient *strege* in Sicily allied to a Maltese underground. The *L'Amanaca Barba Nera* (Black Beard's Almanac) is an annual bestseller in Italy. Stegeria...Italian Witchcraft...up till now a secret-silent force is making itself heard throughout the country and the Church is greatly alarmed. Like Mount Etna, the world's oldest active volcano, the Old Religion threatens to erupt once again spreading its pagan lava over all the Christianized country.

THE ABDUCTION OF PERSEPHONE
Woodcut from Ovid's *Metamorphoses* (Paris, 1539)

THE LEGEND OF PERSEPHONE

Persephone, daughter of Demeter, the Goddess of fertility, was gathering flowers with her companions in a sheltered valley "where spring is everlasting." There she was seen by the king of the Underworld, Pluto, who was examining the foundations of Sicily, fearful that earthquakes might have opened the Earth's crust and let light into his dark realm. He loved the maiden at sight and bore her away in his chariot drawn by black steeds to his kingdom of the dead beneath the earth.

Ovid, Metamorphoses, V

When Demeter learned that Persephone had vanished, she sought her daughter throughout the Earth. But there was no trace of the girl, and in her sorrow Demeter neglected to watch over the crops, casting a blight over the whole land. At last Arethusa spoke from her river and told of seeing Persephone being carried off to the Underworld.

Demeter begged Zeus to have Persephone restored to her. The king of the gods "agreed that her daughter should go down for the third part of the circling year to darkness and gloom, but for the two parts should live with her mother and the other deathless Gods." And so each spring, when Persephone arises, pleasant weather comes and living things begin to grow on Earth after the dark winter.

Homeric Hymn to Demeter

But it is always a condition of these nocturnal assemblies that upon the crowing of the cock everything vanishes.

—Henri Boguet
An Examen of Witches
(1590)

Witchcraft being by nature one of the secretive arts it may not be as easy to find us next year. To make sure we know where you are why don't you send us your name and address?

To: The Witches' Almanac, RD 2, Box 200, Pine Bush, N.Y. 12566

Detail from William Blake's painting of Hecate. Tate Gallery, London.

HECATE

Goddess of the Cross-roads is the term sometimes given to Hecate, whose three-fold aspect as Queen of Witchcraft dates back to classical times when she sometimes merged or was associated with Selene, the moon, in Heaven; Artemis, the huntress, on Earth; and Persephone, queen of the Underworld.

In the third century A.D. Hecate was portrayed by Apollonius with triple heads—those of a horse, a snake and a dog—and later Greek pictures and statues were placed at crossroads (themselves centers of ghostly activity and Witchcraft) so that the Goddess could watch all three paths simultaneously.

Originating in Caria, southwest corner of Asia Minor, Hecate seems to have been forgotten by early Christian times although memories of her as Diana survived. Ovid has Medea invoke her.

"O Night, faithful preserver of mysteries, and ye bright stars, whose golden beams with the Moon succeed the fires of day; thou three-formed Hecate who knowest our undertakings and comest to our aid; ye spells and arts that wise men use."

Hecate who has been called the Goddess of the Dark of the Moon is reputed to appear as a terrifying apparition to wanderers who meet up with her in the night and her aid is often enlisted by sorcerers and necromancers. Dogs howl at her approach.

*Hark! Hark! Her hounds are baying
through the town.
Where three roads meet, there she is
standing.*

In a familiar scene from Act III of Macbeth, Shakespeare recounts the stormy meeting on the blasted heath where the three witches meet Hecate and she berates them:

*Have I not reason, beldams as
you are,
Saucy and over bold? How did
you dare
To trade and traffic with Macbeth
In riddles and affairs of death;
And I, the mistress of your
charms,
The close contriver of all harms,
Was never call'd to bear my part,
Or show the glory of our art?*

Wheel of Hecate

Emblem of eternity of Witchcraft and a mystic symbol used in invoke the Dark Goddess from ancient times.

Arms Against Psychic Attack

Psychic forces can be generated by intense emotion. Hatred channeled by power of a strong will is a dangerous weapon. In revenge when clearly visualized with firm intent is liable to become a hostile reality. The victim of a psychic attack usually experiences at the outset an odd feeling of futility. Dejected spirits lead to unreasonable panic and as pressure mounts, physical well-being is placed in jeopardy. It becomes increasingly difficult to think or act rationally in this condition and many surrender without a battle. But there are means by which a psychic assault may be deflected before it has time to develop.

The first rule of defense is to relax the body. Match the siege with the cunning of nature. If you have ever had occasion to restrain an animal you know how it will seem to go limp in your grass. The intent is to better judge the captors concentration. The moment your attention waivers, the creature will struggle free. In similar fashion, a tree or plant will bend with the wind rather than try to hold firm against it. If you have reason to believe a psychic attack has been directed toward you, as soon as possible purify your body in a full tub of warm salted water. Follow with an anointing of oil on the four head, shoulders and breasts in the sign of the pentagram while chanting:

> *In the name of mercy,*
> *With the power of fate,*
> *Pray attend me now*
> *While my need is great.*

the ceremony of stilling the mind completes the ritual and directs a barrier only a cone of power could penetrate. The outer circle formed with objects belonging to you. They may range from close to bric-a-brac but all should hold special significance for you and have been touched often by you. Sit on the floor in the middle of the circle with your knees drawn up to your chin. Grasp your legs with both arms and lightly rest your head on your knees. Close your eyes and repeat allowed any rhyme or lyric you know by heart into the words lose their meaning to monotony. Remain in this attitude of contemplation until your mind is free of thought.

To maintain protection you may wish to burn the sacred herbs of hyssop, rue or vervain. Many where and amulet or hold a talisman as a safeguard. There are some who prefer to identify their attacker and answer in kind but as this requires a great emotional investment, the game is seldom worth the candle.

This is a German folktale collected by W.J. Wintemberg in Canada. It appeared in 1906 in the *Journal of American Folklore*, Philadelphia: American Folklore Society, 1888 to the present.

An Alsatian Witch Tale

The Witches held monthly festivals. In Alsace the chimneys of houses are very wide, and it was through these they left the house without being seen. At a certain farmhouse there were two women—mother and daughter—who were Witches. With them lived an inquisitive young farmhand. He had noticed that something unusual is taken place in the house every month, so one night he hid in the kitchen and watched. About midnight the women came and stood before the fireplace, beneath the chimney, and after anointing themselves with an oil which the Germans call *Hexenfett* (i.e., Witches' fat), uttered some magic words, and up they went through the chimney. The young man then emerged from his hiding place, and seeing the vessel containing the oil, he anointed himself to see what effect it would have on him. He had scarcely pronounced the mystic words when he went up the chimney with a suddenness that was surprising, and when he reached the ground he found himself astride a large black sow which carried him with great speed across the country. They soon arrived at a broad and swift flowing river, but this did not hinder the onward advance of the sow, for it cleared the broad expanse of water in a single bound. The young man looked back, and admiring its leaping powers he said to the sow, "That was a long leap you made," but as he spoke the spell was broken, the sow disappeared, and he found himself in a strange country many miles from home.

CASTING *shadows*

In the beginning all arcane knowledge was transmitted orally. The novice Witch learned by heart the chants, spells and rites required to perform an act of magic. As the world became literate, grimoires and books of shadows were born. Grimoires are books of ceremonial magic—texts produced during the 14th, 15th and 16th centuries. A book of shadows is the private journal of a Witch. Adages, maxims, poetry and secret thoughts as well as the properties of the sacred herbs, spells, incantations, charms, potions and philtres copied down by hand might be found in a typical book of shadows. No rule govern binding, number of pages or contents. Each volume reflects the personal taste and essence of its author.

Here are three spells drawn from individual books of shadows kept during the 19th century. In reciting an incantation, remember that the tempo should be far slower than that of ordinary speech. The desired effect is one of quiet emphasis and certain intent.

TO MAKE A WISH COME TRUE

With a thorn prick the symbol of the waxing moon in a short, broad candle of pure beeswax. Light the candle and with eyes fixed upon its flame, concentrate on your wish as you chant:

> *Gracious Lady Moon*
> *Ever in my sight*
> *Kindly grant the boon*
> *I ask of thee tonight.*

Blow out the flame but hold the memory of its light in your mind's eye for as long as you can. A way to make your wish come true will reveal itself.

TO MAKE LOVE GROW

Plant a bulb of onion in a clay pot that has never previously been used. As you cover it with earth, thrice
repeat the name of the one you love. Then daily, morning and evening thereafter, say over it:

As this root grows
And as its blossom blows,
Made my true love's heart be
Gently turned unto me.

TO IDENTIFY AN ENEMY

In a one foot length of scarlet yarn, tie 9 knotts as you
say:

These knots I knot,
To know the thing, I know not yet,
That I may see,
The one who is my enemy.

Sleep with the charm under your pillow and a vision
of the person who means you harm will appear in
a dream.

The Dance of Death (1538).　　Hans Holbein the Younger

Life is a jest, and all things show it,
I thought so once, and now I know it.
JOHN GAY, 1688-1732

The Witch (1532).   Hans Weiditz

The Old Ways

By Paul Huson

What is it that calls to us from all ancient things: tangled woods; mossy lichened stones; secret gardens like Avalon and Lorien; forgotten paths and long lost secrets? These things possess a power which flows from their very oldness itself.

I would say—but then I am prejudiced—that it is the call of the Old Ways, living paths of myth, fable and legend. Mankinds's dreams, if you like, your roots and mine. All ancient things partake of this mysterious ability to stir ones soul. C. G. Jung, the depth psychologists, attributed it to the workings of the Unconscious Mind; anthropologist refer to it as Numen or mana; poets call it inspiration. Witches have a better name for it, I think. They call it Magic.

Lay out a deck of tarot cards and you will feel it breathing out from behind the pale hands and faces of the actors in the tarot play, once Gods and Goddesses, now funny little puppets, quaint and hieratic but still very potent. Or open any book of mythology for that matter, tales of wonder and lost cults, of Morgan and Arthur, Math and Gwydion, the Tuatha De Danaan, Aradia, or even contemporary myth—J. R. R. Tolkien's Middle Earth reverberates with the power of the Old Ways—and you will find it there. These are the bibles of our hidden gospel.

All things wild and free in nature also reflect the workings of power; the Sun and the Moon; stars; stones; rivers; springs; Fire and Water, Earth and Air; plants too, trees and especially herbs, these also are vehicles of power, being wrapped in myth and legend all these centuries, only awaiting the rightly performed word or deed to awaken them to magical life again.

"... by the Virtue of the Heavens, of the Stars, and of the Angels who preside over them; by the virtue of stones, herbs and animals; by the virtue of hail, snow, and wind..."

conjures Solomon's famous cabalistic rune.

Yet behind the ceaseless interaction of the elements, rise and fall of stars, rotation of the seasons, birth and death of the year, lie those things which join our actions to theirs, the great common denominators, the eternal play of birth, love, death, and birth once more, enacted by the unseen Old Ones, lost Gods today, but once simply primordial powers. To many of us they are just the Lord and the Lady. Whether we care to call them Hu and Cerridwen, Bell and Toevohe, Pan and Diana, Lucifer and Aradia, Watto and Andred, Cernunnos and Habondia, or even, yes, Sweet Jesus and Mary—for so they were frequently renamed during the Middle Ages—the archetypes are the same.

Be our observances traditional or discovered, handed down within a family or closely knit group bound with oaths of secrecy, or lit upon in the pages of a book or within the fabric of a dream even, provided they elicit the deep response, that unmistakably shiver of wonder and awe, then they are of the Old Ways. Deep will call to Deep, power will come down, as surely as iron follows the lodestone, and no one, neither Master nor Lady, nor Priest nor Priestess, nor King nor Queen, self-appointed elected or initiated, may gainsay us or them. For at their most fundamental, before ever they were organized into any cult framework, the following could be said of these rites:

"... No special class of persons is set apart for... (their)... performance... The rites may be performed by anyone, as occasion demands. No special places are set apart for the performance... there are no temples... The rites are magical rather than propitiatory... the desired objects are attained not by propitiating the favor of the divine beings through sacrifice, prayer and praise, but by ceremonies which... are believed to influence the course of nature directly through a physical resemblance between the right and the effect."

These are not my words but Sir James Frazer's, whose *"Golden Bough"* along with Jacob Grimm's *"Teutonic Mythology"* and Robert Graves's *"White Goddess"* are our bibles.

So if you truly seek knowledge of the Old Ones, then turn to the Sun and kiss your hand to the Moon; be aware of the Sky above your head and the Earth beneath your feet, her bounty, her herbs and all living things. Above all, observe the Seasons and the Tides. It isn't in human institutions that the true secrets of vision and power are to be looked for, but only in the inwardness of your own being as reflected in Nature.

Why go elsewhere when you have what you seek so close at hand?

And for witches,
This is law —
Where they enter in,
From *there* must they
withdraw.

THE GIFTS OF

Aradia

The legend Aradia came to light just before the turn of the present century when Maddalena, and Italian witch, delivered to Charles G. Leland a manuscript called the *Vangelo della-Streghe*, or the *Gospel of the Witches*. Leland assumed the material had been set down from oral narration of tales and traditions reaching back to Etruscan times. Realizing his book *Aradia* would find but a limited audience, Leland noted in the preface, "there are few indeed who will care whether there is a veritable Gospel of the Witches, apparently of extreme antiquity, embodying the belief in a strange counter-religion which has held its own from prehistoric time to the present day." And nearly seventy five years would pass before the lore Leland regarded "as something to say the least remarkable" would begin to receive the attention and appreciation it deserves.

Among the conjurations, spells and invocations of the *Vangelo* we find the allegorical tale of Aradia, born of the mating between the lady of darkness (Diana) and the lord of light (Lucifer), destined to teach the secret art of witchcraft to the children of Earth. Upon those she favored were bestowed certain symbolic gifts.

To know success in love.
To bless or curse with power friends and enemies.
To converse with spirits.
To find hidden treasures in ancient ruins.
To conjure the spirits of priests who died leaving treasures.
To understand the voice of the wind.
To change water into wine.
To divine with cards.
To know the secrets of the hand.
To cure diseases.
To make those who are ugly beautiful.
To tame wild beasts.

The Saga of Mother Shipton

The tiny Yorkshire town of Knareborough (pop. 11,000) in the north of England was already well known to historians by the fifteenth century. In 1086, spelled Chenacrsburgh, was listed in that early compilation of English habitations, the Domesday Book. The stone castle, built in 1070, sheltered, a century later the four knights who had murdered Thomas Becket, Archbishop of Canterbury, after King Henry II wished aloud that somebody would rid him of "this turbulent priest."

Near the castle in 1380, the English patriot John of Gaunt (Ghent) into whose mouth Shakespeare put the words: "This royal throne of kings, tis sceptered isle…" is reputed to have killed the last wolf in England. And to the castle, in 1399, John of Gaunt's son, Henry of Bolingbroke, sent the deposed King Richard II after seizing the throne and declaring himself King Henry IV.

Between 1206 and 1400, in fact, there were ten other royal visits to Knasburg—as it was then called—all for the purpose of hunting deer. The Royal Forest of Knasburg was a regal preserve, one of the biggest in the land, and the venison it yielded graced many a medieval table. Today of that vast forest one tree alone remains, preserved carefully for sightseers in Harrogate, six miles to the west.

But one event of the 15th century was to put Knaresborough on the map for hundreds of years to come. This was the birth in a cave beside the River Nidd in July 1488 to one Agatha Sontheil of a daughter named Ursula. She was unfortunate in appearance but early displayed a quick intelligence and unusual energy. Her mother's lifestyle and wanderings had caused enough talk in the district for her to be tried (and acquitted) of witchcraft and so it was perhaps inevitable that when Ursula was born there with those who said it came about through Agatha's liaison with the devil.

Ursula's childhood was without recorded incidents, however, and at the age of 24, she was married to a carpenter, Tobias Shipton, from a nearby village. She was soon to be known both to her contemporaries and to history as Old Mother Shipton and until her death at York in 1561 was visited by folks from far and wide who wanted to hear her prophecies.

At first Mother Shipton's predictions concerned merely local matters—whether or not somebody would recover from an illness and so on—but soon her prerecognition extended to natural and historical prophecy, often being couched in verse of subtle ambiguity.

When the Cow doth wive the Bull,
Then, priest, beware thy skull!
For one great Court to pass
*   shall bring*
What was ne'er done by
*   any King—*
The poor shall grieve to see
*   that day;*
For they who did Feast
Must Fast and Pray—
*   Fate so decrees their overthrow*
For Riches brought Pride,
*   and Pride brings Woe.*

The "Bull" in that first was Henry VIII who ruled during most of Mother Shipton's life, and the "Cow" was Anne Boleyn whose opposition to Catholics eventually resulted in the execution of Cardinal Fisher, the dissolution of the monasteries and hence the ending of much charity and help for the poor.

The bulk of Mother Shipton's prophecies, and the reason for her lasting fame, referred to events that came to pass long after her death, but in 1530 a celebrated clash between the seer, by then living in York, and cardinal's Wolsey achieved national attention. Her prediction that the Cardinals, then on his way north, would never reach York so angered the celebrated theologian that he vowed that when he did so he would

have the old crone hanged as a witch. He was actually at Cawood Castle, within side of the city, when he made the threat. But that same night the Cardinal was summoned back to London by the king and, taken ill on the way, fulfilled Mother Shipton's prophecy by dying in Leicester Abbey.

Eventful as were the years of Mother Shipton's life culminating in the accession of Queen Elizabeth ("a maiden Queen full many a year/shall England's warlike sceptre bear...") the years that followed were crowded with dramatic incidents that she appeared to have foretold:

Great London's triumphant Spire/ *Shall be consumed with flames of fire* could refer only to the burning of St. Paul's steeple in 1561...*More wonders yet! A widowed Queen/ in England shall be headless seen* (Mary Queen of Scots, executed 1587)...*Between Calder and Aire/ Shall be great warfare* (two Yorkshire rivers between which a Civil War was fought in the 17th century)... *The Crown then fits the White King's head/Who with the Lilies soon shall wed* (Charles I, robed in white for his coronation married the French king's sister, the lilies being the arms of France).

There were numerous other verses, most of them referring to obscurer events in English history, and long after her death people kept becoming aware of them. Samuel Pepys, for example, records in his diary that when Prince Rupert sailed up the Thames to find the

Great Fire of London raging he said: "Now Shipton's prophecy is out!" This was in 1661, exactly 100 years after the old lady had died leaving the prediction behind her that the master of a ship would sail up the river to find London devastated.

Best known to mother Shipton's admirers today are several verses which begin

Carriages without horses shall go
And accidents fill the world with
woe...
Around the world thought shall fly
In the twinkling of an eye...
The world then to an end shall come
In Eighteen Hundred and Eighty
One.

The verses go on apparently to predict such 19th century phenomena as the Crimean War, the Klondike gold rush, the building of the Crystal Palace, ironclad ships and horseless transport, and they have been reprinted and quoted endlessly.

But although the present-day custodians of her Knaresborough cave reprint the verses in toto (changing the end of the world to "Nineteen Hundred and Ninety One") in their "carefully collected and compiled" biography, another author, Arnold Kellert says in the *Knaresborough Story* ($2 from The Advertiser Press, Paddock Head, Huddersfield, Yorks) that they are a posthumous forgery.

They were composed, Kellet maintains, by Charles Hindley of Brighton who admitted his authorship in a letter to a publication called *Notes and Queries* on April 23, 1873.

Nevertheless, Mother Shipton's fame and her drawer as a Knaresborough tourist attraction continues in the 1970s. Our visit last spring was before the season officially opened but even then sightseers were clamoring to enter the closed gates

and visit Mother Shipton's cave.

The popular view that Mother Shipton was a repulsive old crone dates from a drawing printed in an edition of her prophecies in 1663, more than 100 years after her death. This woodcut of a medieval seer may be closer to a true likeness.

Walpurgisnacht

ON THE BROCKEN

Douce Collection, Bodleian Library, Oxford

From the earliest time the Brocken, highest peak of the Hartz mountains in East Germany, has been a site of mystery and magic. The beautiful region of the Hartz was held sacred by the Saxons, and May Eve the spectral forms of the gods were believed to make these mountains their meeting place.

When May Day became the feast of the Christian saint Walburga (Walpurgis), its eve (Walpurgisnacht) and the Brocken retained their Pagan identity. A Witches Sabbat, famed throughout Europe, continued to honor the old gods on May Eve. As late as the 1930s, costumed celebrants ascended the sacred peak on Walpurgisnacht.

War and political partition have now denied us the sight of the magic mountain for over forty years, yet its rocky heights remain vivid in memory. The great blocks of granite we knew as the "Sorcerers Chair" and the "Witches' Altar" must still stand on the Brocken's lofty summit. No doubt that the crystal clear water of the spring we called the "Magic Fountain" continues to bubble forth their over 3000 feet above sea level. And the anemone, the sorcerers flower, will bloom again this spring high on the rugged wind-swept slopes of the Brocken.

CHORUS OF WITCHES

On to the Brocken the witches are flocking—
Merry meet—merry part—how they gallop and drive,
Yellow stubble and stock are rocking,
And young green corn is merry alive,
With the shapes and shadows swimming by.
To the highest heights they fly,
Where Sir Urian sits on high—
Throughout and about,
With clamor and shout;
Drives the maddening rout,
Over stock, over stone;
Shriek, laughter, and moan,
Before them are blown.

JOHANN WOLFGANG VON GOETHE, 1749–1832
Faust (Anster's translation)

35

light a candle

Tonight create total darkness, then light a candle. To fully appreciate the experience and honor the act in the proper way, you might recite a very old chant:

Lord of fury, Lord of flame,
Smite the darkness with thy name.

Uta, Shamash, Baal, Rakashih, Ra, Mithra, Apollo, Lucifer... any one of a number of the Gods of light can be acknowledged. Murmur his name as you strike a match and, in one action, touch the flame to the candlewick.

Study the flame now as it sways to reveal your breath and the air currents in the room. It is easy to understand why the element of Fire was venerated by the ancients. You may know a feeling of curious contentment as you gaze steadily at the bright light before you.

Candles were used in religious rites as early as 3000 B.C. And they retained their sacred nature, for it was not until the Middle Ages that the wax candle came into general use as a means of illumination in the household.

In Witchcraft and ceremonial magic, lighting a candle is a usual prelude to the magic experience. The practical

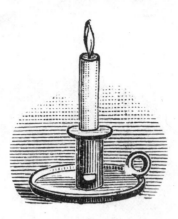

reason underlying the ritual is the need to concentrate psychic energy; the flame serves as a focal point. Beeswax candles formed by your own hand in any color you feel appropriate is the rule of witches. The ceremonial magician, however, follows a stricter path. The candles must be made by the practitioner from virgin wax (that taken from bees having made it for the first time), according to the *Key of Solomon*. The color of the wax is of vital importance and must correspond to the planet under whose aegis the rite will be performed.

Sun—Gold or Yellow
Moon—Silver or White
Mars—Red
Mercury—Mixed or Purple
Jupiter—Blue
Venus—Green
Saturn—Black

Some occult traditions required that the candle be anointed with oil, wrapped in parchment and buried in the earth (wick pointing to the north) for an interval of a Moon phase prior to the rite.

It is fortunate that beeswax candles cannot only burn best but are the easiest to make. The requirements are simple: a room at an 80° temperature, a sharp knife and a smooth board on which to roll and cut. Round wicks and the solid or honeycombed sheets of colored beeswax are easily available by mail from the candle supply houses listed on page 89.

Candle spells are many. A most effective means of summoning is recorded in Old English folklore. Thrust two common pins through a lighted candle's wick to form a "T" and slowly chant:

It's not this candle alone I stick,
but...'s heart I mean to prick.
Whether asleep or awaken be,
I summon his spirit to come to me.

When the flame has burned down to the crossed pins, the person desired will appear in person or in a dream.

Secrets entrusted to a few

The Unpublished Facts of Life

THERE are some things that can not be generally told—*things you ought to know*. Great truths are dangerous to some — but factors for *personal power* and *accomplishment* in the hands of those who understand them. Behind the tales of the miracles and mysteries of the ancients, lie centuries of their secret probing into nature's laws—their amazing discoveries of *the hidden processes of man's mind*, and *the mastery of life's problems*. Once shrouded in mystery to avoid their destruction by mass fear and ignorance, these facts remain a useful heritage for the thousands of men and women who privately use them in their homes today.

THIS FREE BOOK

The Rosicrucians (not a religious organization), an age-old brotherhood of learning, have preserved this secret wisdom in their archives for centuries. *They now invite you to share the practical helpfulness of their teachings.* Write today for a free copy of the book, "The Mastery of Life." Within its pages may lie a new life of opportunity for you. Address: Scribe H.P.K.

SEND THIS COUPON

Scribe H.P.K.
The ROSICRUCIANS (AMORC)
San Jose, California 95114
Please send me the *free* book, *The Mastery of Life*, which explains how I may learn to use my faculties and powers of mind.

Name_____

Address_____

City_____

State_____ Zip Code_____
Please Include Your Zip Code

The Rosicrucians

SAN JOSE   (AMORC)   CALIFORNIA 95114, U.S.A.

38

NOW, RIGHT AT HOME, YOU CAN LEARN HOW TO

BECOME A WITCH!

Unlock the secrets of the witches coven. Discover the ancient spells designed to give witches their tremendous powers…and make people obey them, fall in love with them, and bring them money. Learn the time-honored witches way to success in your chosen career and all your unfulfilled dreams and desires. Yes, ANY man or woman can learn how to become a genuine witch, thanks to this totally new kind of home study course. *Five easy-to-follow and inexpensive lessons is all it takes.*

The author of the course is Dr. Leo Louis Martello, scion of an ancient family of Italian-Sicilian witches, Elder of four different Witchcraft Traditions and High Priest of the Old Religion. Author of WITCHCRAFT: OLD RELIGION, Dr. Martello has packed over 25 years of experience as a practicing witch into this extraordinary course. He explains ALL . . . so clearly that *anyone* can start practicing *real* witchcraft from the very first day. There have been books on witchcraft before, but *never* before have there been at-home lessons on how to become a witch—*revealed by a genuine witch himself!*

You get all this in the first lesson alone! *How to make your own witches altar at home. *The tools to use in your magic rites and how to consecrate them. *The self-blessing ritual. "The power of the Pentagram. *A test of your own personal potential as a witch . . . *and much, much more!*

In the four lessons to follow, you'll discover how to make your own magic mirror, how to counteract a curse, how to invoke the Horned God, and salute the Mother Goddess, the witch words that give personal power . . . *everything,* in fact, that you need to know to become an effective practicing witch with all the powers that this implies. It's so *easy* when High Priest Martello *reveals all his secrets to you!*

To receive Lesson 1, mail the coupon today with just $4.95. Yes, that's all it costs to be led by the hand, step-by-step, into the great mysteries and powers of witchcraft. If you are not completely satisfied, simply return the first lesson for a full refund.

OCCULT CRAFTS LTD.
P.O. Box 72, Bronxville, N.Y. 10708

OCCULT CRAFTS LTD, Dept. WA6
P. O. BOX 72, BRONXVILLE, N. Y. 10708

YES I want to be a genuine witch. Send me Lesson 1 of "YOU Can Become a Witch," for which I enclose $4.95. If not satisfied, I may return Lesson 1 for a full refund. Otherwise send me the 4 succeeding Lessons in this complete course, automatically at the rate of about one lesson every two weeks, and bill me the same low price for each.

I enclose $4.95 for Lesson 1. Refundable if not satisfied.

Name_____

Address_____

City_____

State_____ Zip_____

39

THE HORSE

IN MYTH
AND
FOLKLORE

If you have a horse with four white legs,
Keep him not a day;
If you have a horse with three white legs,
Send him far away;
If you have a horse with two white legs,
Sell him to a friend;
If you have a horse with one white leg,
Keep him to his end.

This little Devonshire rhyme conveys one of the many folklore beliefs that have evolved over the centuries about one of nature's most splendid creatures. The place of the horse in myth and legend has long been assured.

Poseidon is credited with the creation of the first horse during a contest with Athena. Zeus had decreed that whichever deity created the most useful object to mankind should have the honor of naming the newly-founded city of Athens.

Athena dreamed up the olive tree and won the contest, but it has to be conceded that Poseidon's creation is more universal. Ancient paintings depict the sea god's chariot drawn by fabulous "sea horses" (hippocampi) whose rear quarters end in dolphin tails. The centaur is another curious hybrid—half man, half horse. Chiron is a famous mythological centaur, reputed to have tutored Asclepios, the god of medicine, in the healing arts.

Nearly all ancient nations have represented the ruler of the day as

> *"Fleetness is but one of the qualities admired in the horse — ancient people believe that the fastest mares were with foal from the winds."*

being drawn in his chariot by celestial horses across the sky, according to M. Oldfield Howey in his *Horse in Magic and Myth* (Wm. Rider & Sons, London, 1923). "Hence horses figure largely in solar rights and used to be lead in procession before the sun got shrines and in many countries were actually sacrifice to him."

The *ashvamedha* or horse sacrifice, a reflection of the earlier Scythian horse offerings to the Sun, was a distinctive Indian ceremony from 1000 to 50 B.C. and the horse often represented Surya, the Sun God. According to Norse myths it was Alsvith, the all-swift horse, that drew the chariot of the Moon. In Arab countries a white horse is still described as "moon-colored."

Fleetness is but one of the qualities admired in the horse — ancient people believed that the fastest mares were foal from the winds. Horses have also been symbols of pride, prophecy, and conquest. "Get on your high horse" is the colloquial term for pride. And some regions there has long been a superstition that a pure white horse confers on its rider the gift of great wisdom — provided he is riding the horse when consulted.

The horse is said to possess clairvoyance, often refusing to proceed or shying mysteriously when no visible obstacles are in view. They are believed especially susceptible to the evil eye and in Italy, are often adorned with brass amulets to avert the *jettatora*.

Horsehairs and horseshoes are thought to hold great magical potency, the latter regarded as representing the Moon and used as a talisman to seek her favor. An ancient Andalusian charm consisted of a staghorn attached to a cord made from the hair of a black mare's mane. According to legend, no horseman wearing such a charm could be thrown from his mount.

Love's MAGIC

By Martha St. Michael

The Pursuit of Cupid   Florence (1508).

If there's any doubt about the link between love and magic, consider for a moment the words used to describe an attractive woman. "Bewitching," "charming" and "enchanting" all reflect a time when sorcery and romance were one. Ever since the legendary Triston and Isolde shared a love potion, interest and intrigue in passion-arousing philters has flourished. For centuries, thwarted lovers have sought the magic brew which would enable them to win and secure the affection of a beloved.

The *Dictionary of Aphrodisiacs* (Citadel Press, New York, 1961) defines a love philter as "a magic potion usually intended to induce amorous effects on the drinker." But as you leaf through medieval recipes for love brews, the emphasis upon repulsive ingredients discloses the influence of an all-powerful celibate clergy whose aim may have been to discourage romance. Concoctions composed of excrement, frog bones, bitter roots, and unpalatable herbs would deter rather than promote desire. A successful love potion must be attractive to the eye, aromatic, and pleasing to the taste. It should be prepared with tenderness and presented with delicacy and grace. As you concoct your brew let the lines of the Roman philosopher Seneca run through your mind:

> *Love, my darling, and be loved*
> *in turn always,*
> *So that at no instant may our*
> *mutual love cease...*
> *From sunrise to sunset,*
> *And may the Evening Star gaze*
> *Upon our love*
> *And the Morning Star too.*

Venus is exalted during the sign of Pisces, making this time of year especially propitious for sharing a love philter.

Apricot Love Liqueur

Crumble to a powder one handful of the dried leaves of vervain or hemp. Dip seven dried apricots in honey and coat them with the powdered leaves. Steep the fruit in 1 cup of brandy for two weeks. Store in a glass jar with a tight lid and keep in a dark, cool, and secret place. Shake occasionally. Strain and serve in tiny liqueur glasses during the waxing moon.

Love-Apple Juice

Tomatoes were introduced into Europe from America during the sixteenth century. For more than one hundred years tomatoes were regarded with suspicion. But their original name, love apples, indicates an aphrodisiacal use.

To two cups of tomato juice add one perfect bay leaf and 1 teaspoon of dried basil, crumble through your fingers. Chill, strain, and serve in long-stemmed goblets.

Enchanting Cocoa

combine 3 tablespoons of cocoa (Hershey's is excellent) and three of sugar in a small saucepan. Add 3 tablespoons of Benedictine and a dash of vanilla extract to form a syrup. Stir and pour enough milk to make two cups of liquid. Heat over a low flame while stirring constantly. Just before the cocoa reaches the boiling point, remove from the heat and whipped to a froth with an eggbeater. Serve at once in handsome mugs.

LUNAR MOODS

How does the Moon affect all of us as it passes through the signs of the zodiac? Just as the Sun takes us through monthly changes, the Moon sets the general tone of day-to-day changes—some important, others less so. Paying attention to the Moon can pay off. Here are some bits of lunar information to help you get in tune with the Moon.

When the Moon is in:

ARIES, we want action. We tend to start projects although we may not finish them, feel physically restless, want things *now*. A headstrong, possibly selfish tendency—so remember to consider others when the Moon is in Aries.

TAURUS, enjoy: It can be a lazy or self-indulgent time, good for pleasant activities, artistic/sensual experiences. Continue trends rather than trying to "bull through." Charm melts stubbornness when the Moon is in Taurus.

GEMINI, relate: It's a busy, communicative, somewhat shattered time. Write letters, visit, pay attention to what's going on around you. Things skim along—double check details, avoid gossip if you can when the Gemini Moon is up.

CANCER, feel what's around you: Emotions are strong and energy is centered at home base. Concentrate on those closest to you, have at least one magnificent meal, and try not to be too touchy when the Moon is in ultra-sensitive Cancer.

LEO, express yourself: basic traits are emphasized, we tend to be more dramatic, and we may exaggerate. Praise really gets results now. Share treat, share some glory. Pride is a key word when the Moon is in Leo.

VIRGO, utilize skills: It's a good time to take care of business, organize, analyze, be of service, exchange and refine ideas. A mentally active time, not to be wasted. Take care of your own act, try not to be too picky when the Moon is in Virgo.

LIBRA, join forces: It's a sociable, easy Moon time when cooperation is a must. The pendulum swings both ways; you could get stuck in the middle. A creative time, but you may have a tendency to put things off. Pay attention to partners during a Líbra Moon.

SCORPIO, expect extremes: It's a time when desires are strong, opinions and energies intense. And either/or time, when actions have long-lasting results. Enjoy the volcano, but stay out of the lava when the Moon is in Scorpio.

SAGITTARIUS, explore: It's a time when interest focuses on far away things. A breezy, active period. Fun with friends is indicated. Expand, be different, but tone down the tendency to rationalize or ignore harsh reality when the Moon is in Sagittarius.

CAPRICORN, duty calls: Answer it. Setting and achieving goals are important now. Be aware of the "pecking order" even if it is silly. Drive, ambition, desire are strong. Do it! And soft-pedal a grumpy tendency when the Moon is in Capricorn.

AQUARIUS, sparks fly: It's an unpredictable time when the mundane and the bizarre mingle. We tend to be stubborn but changeable. Try to loosen up, and do at least one off-the-wall thing when the Moon is in flashing Aquarius.

PISCES, dream a little: It's a time to follow the flow, imagine, be a little "more." Idealism is high, but so is self-deception. The effects of illusion are emphasized. Try for results as well as reveries to get the best of the Pisces Moon.

When the Moon is in your Sun sign, you have a little added pizzazz. When the Moon is opposite your Sun sign, take it easy. A waxing Moon (new to full) is more forward-looking, better for starting new projects. A waning Moon (full to new) is better for maintaining the status quo and completing projects.

The Moon stays in the sign about two and a quarter days. On days when it changes signs, a mingling of influences is likely.

WARNING: Once you start studying our lady Moon, you may find it hard to stop. She is fascinating, varied, and close to home.

Illustrations by C. G. Leland (1891).

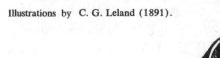

ᗰoon MAGIC

By Paul Huson

All hail, new moon, all hail to thee!
I prithee, good moon, reveal to me
This night who shall my true love be!

Charms such as this used to be whispered to the new moon to evoke dreams of a future lover. The wide use of such invocations in the past throughout Europe and North America indicates how universal was the belief in the Moon's supernatural powers. Today many of us may look at the Moon and see in our mind's eye only the desolate ball of rock revealed by the cameras of the Apollo spacecraft.

Maybe the ancients knew better. They noted how the moon's waxing and waning corresponded to the sea tides and the behavior patterns of people, animals, and plants; sages read in this an evident sign of the mysterious bond of communion in nature which they called Magic. To the classical pagans the Moon was the mistress of all magic, a symbol of the Goddess who ruled in the sky, on the earth, and beneath it in the land of spirits. Legendary Witches such as Medea addressed their prayers to this potent Goddess.

And not only legendary ones, it turns out. In 1886 Godfrey Leland, an eminent Gypsy lore researcher, obtained a handwritten manuscript of Tuscan spells from a Florentine fortuneteller named Maddalena. Most of its invocations were addressed to the Moon Goddess of the Romans, Diana, and to another goddess called Aradia. Leland recognized the book as evidence of the survival of the pre-Christian lunar witch cult and published the manuscript under the title *Aradia, or the Gospel*

46

of the Witches. According to the "Gospel," Aradia was born of the mating between night (Diana) and day (Lucifer) and sent earthward by her mother to teach the secret of witchcraft. Scholars today recognize Diana and Aradia as different aspects of the same Goddess. This deity was worshiped in Greece, where she was known as Hera, a name meaning "lady" or "mistress," and then honored in Italy as Jana, wife of Janus the oak God. The goddess ended up in classical mythology as two separate symbolic figures, Juno and Diana—although practicing pagans came to recognize her as an aspect of the Egyptian Isis. After the spread of Christianity had eliminated most overt paganism, worship of the goddess continued secretly in the Pyrenees, Italy, and Southeast Europe. In the area which is now Romania she was known as Irodiada, Queen of the Elves.

The Church preached against the goddess and her devotees in a variety of dogmatic tracts. The most famous of these, the *Canon Episcopi*, criticizes "certain" wicked women, who believe and profess that they ride out on beasts by night with Diana the Goddess of the Heathen or Herodiade, and a numberless multitude of women, and cover great distances in the silence of the night, and on particular nights are summoned to this service." Because of the similarity of names, the worthy churchmen confused Irodiada with the Biblical King Herod's wife, Herodias. A medieval legend of the period describes this down-graded Herodias as a "sad lady" to whom "one third of mankind is devoted." When she is now flying about in a whirlwind with her band of lost souls, Herodias may be found—rather significantly—robed in white and seated in old oak trees! The sadness of Herodias is attributed to her unrequited passion for John the Baptist. And this is another significant detail, for the Biblical story of course refers to Herodias daughter Salome as the lovelorn lass, not to the mother herself. Obviously the legend of Herodias' unrequited love is based on some other legend, and we have only to consult Leland's *Gospel of the Witches* to see which one.

The *Canon Espiscopi* also refers to Herodiade as Hulda, the name by which she was known in Germany. Her French devotees, on the other hand, called the Goddess Habondia or Bensozia—names derived from the Latin meaning "Lady of Abundance" and "Good Neighbor" respectively. The average godfearing peasant, however, accepted the Church's teaching about the Lady, and clung to the belief that she and her crew were thoroughly evil. The peasant would fire a gun into the storm clouds he imagined she was traveling in and shout the words:

Curse, curse Herodias,
Thy mother is a heathen
Damned of God and fettered
Through the Redeemer's blood!

According to Leland, the beneficent Aradia may still be invoked with the following potent spell uttered midnight in this way: One should perform it alone, on open ground with the moon visible. One should carry a horn cup filled with a mixture of wine and water, a red sachet of salt, and a talisman sacred to the goddess. The latter can be a sprig of rue or vervain, a stone with a hole naturally formed in it, or a lemon stuck full of pins with colored heads. (Classical witches such as Medea usually performed these spells barefoot to make contact with the earth, but this detail may have been overlooked by Maddalena's time.) The words should be recited slowly and intently, naming the favor one is imploring, with as many repetitions as one pleases. Drink a little of the water and wine, pour the rest on the bare earth.

Thus do I seek Aradia! Aradia! Aradia!

At midnight, at midnight, I go into a field

And with me I bear water, wine and salt,

I bear water, wine, and salt,

And my talisman, my talisman, my talisman

And a small red bag which I hold in my hand,

With salt in it, salt in it, salt in it.

With water and wine I bless myself,

I bless myself with devotion

To implore a favor from Aradia, Aradia!

48

earth religions supplies, inc.

THE WARLOCK SHOP division

send 50c for our mail-order catalog.
All Trains Boro Hall

300 HENRY ST. BROOKLYN, N.Y. 11201
212—625—9001

WITCHCRAFT SUPPLIES, BOOKS,
HERBS, EXOTIC OCCULT CURIOS Open 7 days a week noon till 10 P.M.

| VOLUME I | ISSUE I | 300 HENRY STREET, BROOKLYN, N.Y. 11201 | YULE 1973 |

Paganism?

*WHAT DO YOU KNOW ABOUT IT?

*WHAT WOULD YOU LIKE TO LEARN?

*WHAT AREAS INTEREST YOU?

SUBSCRIBE TO:

THE EARTH RELIGIONS NEWS
THE ONLY PAGAN TABLOID NEWSPAPER
DEDICATED TO THE PRACTICE AND STUDY OF PAGANISM

with

NEWS * EDITORIALS * BOOK REVIEWS
INTERESTING FEATURE ARTICLES ON WITCHCRAFT
MAGICK.....DIVINATION.....HERBS.....LEGENDS
MYTHOLOGY.....WORSHIP.....RITUALS ETC.

PLUS: THE TEEN AGE PAGAN PUBLICATION "MANDRAGORA"

CLASSIFIED ADVERTIZING AND DISPLAY ADS AN INDIVIDUAL AID FOR THE SERIOUS STUDENT
AS WELL AS THE INTERESTED ONLOOKER.

PRINTED ON THE EIGHT RITUAL OCCASIONS OF PAGANISM
SUBSCRIPTIONS: $6.00 FOR THE YEAR ($8.00 FOR FOREIGN SUBS.)

MAZES

Contemplate the maze; this most mysterious of primal symbols haunts us yet. Ancient Babylonian augers read the future in the bloody tangles of sheep entrails and recorded their predictions on clay tablets engraved with labyrinthine spirals, symbols of the infernal regions of the Underworld. Egyptian pharaohs of the Twelfth Dynasty built, on Lake Moeris, a monumental mortuary temple and administrative complex of three thousand rooms. Through its bewildering subterranean passages, only the souls of the entombed king-gods could safely make the all-important journey to the Land of the Dead.

It is said that this famous Egyptian maze served as a model for legendary Daedalus when he designed for King Minos of Crete the labyrinth beneath the palace at Cnossos to house the dreadful Minotaur. In the stinking depths of its abysmal lair, the Minotaur fed for generations on the tribute flesh of the brightest youth of the Greek world. The dreadful glut continued until young Prince Theseus of Athens,

The maze at Chartres Cathedral, 13th century.

16th century seal depicts the Minotaur as a centaur.

one of the great sacrificial heroes of mythology, submitted himself to trial with the monstrous unknown. With a borrowed sword of valor in his right hand and Ariadne's tremulous thread of love clutched in his left, he stalked the misbegotten beast to the bowels of the labyrinth. There, amid the litter of bones, Theseus killed the Minotaur and liberated Greece for its flowering. Out of this pithy legend came the classic labyrinth design so often found on coins and artifacts of the Mediterranean area.

By the twelfth century, the Pagan

symbol had insinuated itself into the cathedrals of Christianity. Exquisite variations of the design embellished the mosaic tile floor of many a holy nave in the Middle Ages. When medieval Witches danced widdershins under their Sabbath moons, spiraling leftwards faster and faster, invoking the power of sin the strategies by reversing the natural whirl of the universe, pious Christians shuffled on their knees around the mosaic cathedral mazes throughout Europe. These penitents, painfully inching their way along a symbolic *chemin de Jerusalem*, sought expiation for their sins in the Celestial City at the center.

But Time and its travelers change, and with the rebirth of faith in human nature the agony of the maze was transformed by a lighter approach to love and morality. In the seventeenth and eighteenth centuries, elaborate garden mazes were the fashion at the great estates of the European world. Then one might meander through

A prehistoric Scandinavian stone maze.

the charming confusion of, say, the Hampton Court Maze in England, where one was always assured of escape—or rescue—in time for tea; or play at hide and seek among the baroque hedgegrows of Louis XIV's "Labyrinth of Versailles," with statues of Aesop and Cupid (holding a ball of thread in his hand) stood their benign watch at the entrance.

Hints of the darker aspects of this ancient symbol remained in the strange turf mazes, cut by unknown hands in a lost time, that dotted the landscape of the British Isles for centuries. It was assumed that these mazes called Troy Towns had come to Britain with the Roman invaders. "Troy" is more likely derived from the Celtic root *tro*, meaning to turn or revolve and the maze patterns probably belong to the prehistoric era of the megalith builders. The Nordic stone mazes and the turf mazes of England were used in ritual dance but by the nineteenth century, only vague local customs could explain the symbolism. Villagers spoke of "playing May-eve games about them, under an indefinite persuasion of something unseen and unknown cooperating with them." Or they told how they "have often trodden (the maze) on a summer's evening and knelt at the centre to hear the fairies singing."

Most of the ancient mazes have gone under now, obliterated by the plow, the boot, and the bulldozer. There is however at least one modern professional labyrinthologist who, for about $10,000 (not including

Designs from *Concerning Mazes* by Stabius, Nürnburg (1510).

labor and materials), will plot for you a garden "wilderness" guaranteed to amaze your friends. Or if money is no object in one sense of ennui is oppressive, he has an idea for an arctic ice maze in which the "game" will be to find one's way out before dying of exposure. For more prudent games players, bookshops everywhere sell collections of increasingly difficult paper mazes designed to tease the eye and confuse the brain.

Modern-day counterparts of Theseus, enticed by the lure of the labyrinth, seek out the underground and underwater caves that honeycomb the globe. These spelunkers and scuba divers sometimes know, regrettably too well, the boneyards that lie waiting in the depths for foolhardy explorers who would reach beyond the limits of their lifelines. Always these adventurers must struggle to resist the urge to go just one more turning further, fascinated by the beckoning passage way that, who knows, might yet lead to the heart of the mysterious Earth. The urge and the fascination are ancient and instinctive.

The ultimate meeting of the labyrinthine emblem is elusive, like the goal of those surrealistic corridors we run in our restless dreams. Perhaps this archetypal pattern is after all the thumbprint of the unknown self. Among the swirls and blind alleys we seek our own center, holding fast on the timeless journey to our bit of Ariadne's thread.

"I Isis, am all that has been, that is, or shall be"

The Golden Ass of Apuleius
Translated by Robert Graves

Isis, detail from a wall painting, tomb of Seti I, XIX Dynasty.

The Glory of ISIS

By Barbara Stacy

The legacy of Isis, great prototype of all goddesses, shimmers down at us through the veil of the ages; exquisite, intriguing, unknowable. Yet even as we contemplate her infinite mystery, we sense the presence of Isis softly verging upon us—behind, beyond—as if we might turn suddenly and glimpse bare brown breasts and hear the rustle of white linen. The Isis cult developed into the most potent of all the Egyptian religions. Both Isis and her brother-husband Osiris

were born of the earth-god Geb and the Sky goddess Nut during the five strange days that fall between one Egyptian calendar year of 360 days and the next. The couple, betrothed since before their birth, symbolized the central religious belief of dynastic Egypt—that of death and resurrection.

The resurrection myth begins with their brother Set, jealous of Osiris's fame. Set carved a magnificent coffin and brought it to the palace during a feast, declaring that he who fitted perfectly could keep it. Jokingly, all the guests tried. When Osiris laid himself inside, Set nailed the lid, soldered it with hot lead, and threw the chest into the Nile.

Overwhelmed with grief, Isis cut off her hair, put on mourning, and searched up and down the Nile in vain. The coffin had been carried out to sea and washed ashore at Byblos, the royal city of Phoenicia. At the edge of the sea, the divine power within the chest caused a noble tamarind tree to grow. Its trunk enclosed the coffin and the tree gave off such glorious fragrance that the king and queen had it fashioned into a pillar for their palace. Isis, led to the site by sacred birds, rescued the coffin and, hid it in the marshes of the Nile delta. But the relentless Set found the chest, removed the body and hacked it into fourteen pieces, which he scattered widely.

Again the faithful Isis set forth on a search. Helped by her little son Horus, he who had the head of a hawk, she found thirteen of the pieces. The fourteenth, the genitals, had been cast into the Nile and devoured by fish—but Isis replaced this piece with a carved member of sycamore.

The grieving goddess wrapped the broken body of her beloved in strips of white linen for burial at Phylae. Over the body she performed the rites thereafter repeated at the ceremonial burial of all pharaohs. Isis then assumed the form of a sacred bird and · fanned the corpse with her wings. Osiris revived to become the ruler of the underworld, weighing the hearts of dead souls, and on the site at Phylae devotees built a temple of "unsurpassed magnificence."

The goddess has as many flashing facets as a diamond; her images shine, shift, and re-form. Isis was called *myrionymos*, "the one with ten thousand names." Her earliest aspect was that of earth goddess, especially corn mother; later she presented mankind with wheat and barley. As they cut the first stalks of a crop, early Egyptian reapers always atoned to Isis for the grain spirit slain under their sickles. She is called "Green Goddess," "Lady of Bread," "Lady of Abundance," and has been described as "she who has given birth to the fruits of the earth."

Isis reigned in the heavens as well; Sirius, the brightest star, was one of her chief symbols. On summer mornings, Sirius rises from the waves of the Mediterranean as a harbinger of good weather for mariners. Seamen worshipped Isis as "Stella Maris," the "Star of the Sea." She was as well the goddess of good fortune and magic, sometimes called "the Mighty in Magic."

Egyptians equally adored Isis in her domestic and maternal roles. She was the goddess of love, the early model of faithful wife and tender mother. Isis is frequently pictured suckling Horus. In this aspect she inspired devotion not unlike that paid to the Virgin Mary. Like the Virgin, Isis was surrounded by a halo of moral purity, of mysterious sanctity—a serene figure offering spiritual calm and the promise of eternal life. The goddess appealed greatly to all gentle spirits— and especially to women.

Isis, bas-relief in gold from the tomb of Amenophis II, XVIII Dynasty.

The power of Isis pervaded so much of all life, the mythology offered such richness, that she virtually became a one goddess pantheon. As the provider of corn she was identified with Demeter; as the goddess of love, with Aphrodite; as the goddess of magic, with Hecate. Isis has been perceived as Diana, goddess of the moon and the chase; Persephone, goddess of the underworld; and especially with Tyche (the Roman Fortuna), the goddess of good fortune.

The hieroglyph of Isis is a throne and the Isis cult blossomed into the official state religion. Egyptian queens were considered reincarnations of Isis and none took to this role with more delectability than Cleopatra. The beautiful queen appeared in the guise of Isis at all ceremonial functions and chose to be considered less royalty than divinity.

And so the early rustic goddess, adored by the simple, evolved into a highly sophisticated political force—for those who worshipped Isis acknowledged their loyalty to the reigning House of Ptolemy. The cult by no means limited itself to Egypt. Lovely shrines and temples dotted the seaports of Cyprus, Crete, and the coastal towns of Asia Minor. Athens built a marvelous temple to Isis, and in the jumble of religions that characterized late Rome, Isis worship was one of the most potent.

Pharaonic rule declined by about 200 B.C., and when the Roman Empire devoured Egypt, one would imagine that the Goddess of the Bright Star would have suffered eclipse. Rather, she shone

Greco-Roman version of Isis holding a sistrum.

ever more brightly. Freed of its political aspect, the religion took on yet another, deeper dimension—as a source of the Mysteries. We know little more about the rites of Isis than we do about Eleusis; adherents zealously guarded these secrets. But the story-teller Apuleius, himself an initiate, gives us a few intriguing clues in *The Golden Ass*. Lucius, its hero, is to be initiated. The consecration ceremonies are preceded by a ritual bath and ten days of abstention from wine, meat, and love. All that Apuleius says he can divulge of the ceremony is that "I approached the confines of death, trod the threshold of Proserpina, and returned born through

all the elements; at midnight I saw the sun gleaming with bright light; the gods below and the gods above I approached face to face and adored near by."

Priests of the Isis temples shaved their heads, wore luminous white linen, and lived as ascetics. Adherents worshipped the goddess at services twice daily. At dawn the priest flung open the temple doors and "waked up the deity." After praying, he made the rounds of the altars, performing at each the sacred ceremonial and pouring libations over each altar. At sunset, according to Martial, "the priest held up before the worshippers a vase of consecrated water, which they venerated as the first principle of all things."

The most important holiday, lsidis Navigium, occurred on March 5th and blessed and launched the first boat of the season. Apuleius describes its procession: "First came a line of masqueraders, strikingly costumed. At the head of the procession marched women clad in white, flowers in their hair and hands. These were followed by others who carried ivory combs which they employed in the pantomime of dressing the deity's hair, and others who sprinkled the streets with balsam and unguent. Next came a great number of men and women with waxen tapers, and then musicians with pipes and flutes. After these marched the train of mystics, men and women of all ages and conditions in pure white, the women with anointed hair covered with veils." These were followed by priests carrying symbols, including a palm tree with golden leaves, a golden lamp, and a golden vessel in the shape of a breast, from which the priest poured libations of milk on the ground. "After sending out the sacred ship, the mystics returned to the temple, deposited the holy symbols and after kissing the feet of the silver statue of the goddess went home, carrying branches of olives, flowers and herbs, and filled with joy."

The cult of Isis had an astoundingly long run. The lovely religion sprang into prominence along the Nile around 1700 B.C. and flourished well into the fourth century A.D. Along with the Mithraic cult, the followers of Isis were the bitterest antagonists of early Christianity. Only when the Coptic Christians finally triumphed in Egypt and strongly prohibited all the pagan religions did the worship of Isis cease. Her temples became churches and in their cool dimness the cross was carved over the ankh, the ancient Egyptian symbol of life.

How can we explain the vigor and glory of Isis? Perhaps the power radiated from the universal character of the goddess, who held within herself the virtues of all other goddesses. Perhaps it may be explained by the beauty of her ceremonies and the fascination of her Mysteries. To the faithful we know that · she offered absolutely everything— forgiveness, purification, regeneration, and immortality of the soul.

AN earth CHARM

By Selena Fox

NEARLY EVERY occult tradition views Earth in much the same way. Astrologers consider it the planet of stability, strength, and constancy—the elemental force governing the signs of Taurus, Virgo and Capricorn. A ceremonial magician conceives Earth as the basic physical plane: the site of manifestation. To a witch the Earth is the realm of secrets, treasures, buried potentials. In modern wiccan ritual, Earth is regarded as the Guardian of the North—abode of the Great Mother Goddess who offers healing, abundance and balance to those who attune to her creed.

Every human spirit needs the stabilizing influence of Earth. The ancients understood this basic requirement and drew upon its benefits. Amulets and charms charged by rite and thought were often the means they used.

Are you, or is someone you know, too easily swayed by the desires of others? If personal direction wavers in helpless fashion and energy is low, you can tap and store Earth's forces by making an old charm. A simple lemon prepared in the following way will restore inner stability to the one for whom it is intended.

Earth Pomander Charm
Assemble on the evening of the dark-of-the-moon:

> *1 fresh, unbruised, unflawed lemon*
> *2 ounces whole cloves*
> *1 ounce powdered orrisroot*
> *1 teaspoon each of powdered cinnamon, nutmeg, allspice, cloves, sandalwood, cardamom, and paprika*

Combine the powdered orrisroot and spices in a bowl. Pour the whole cloves into a second bowl. Place the lemon in a third bowl for ease in studding its skin. Orient a small table/altar to the compass points and place the three bowls upon it. Cast the circle in your customary manner, face north, and hold the lemon aloft in both hands while you dedicate the fruit to its purpose.

Close your eyes and visualize the person for whom you are preparing

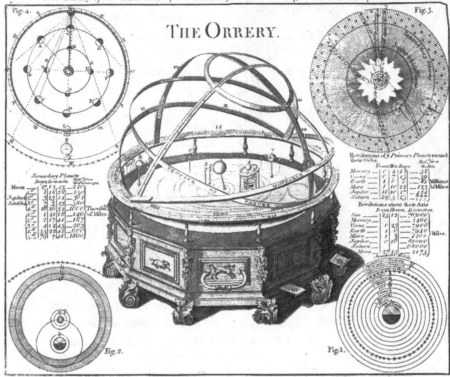

THE ORRERY.

Engrav'd for the Universal Magazine 1749 for J. Hinton at the King's Arms in St Pauls Church Yard London.

the charm. The lemon in its present state can be easily bruised just as its recipient is vulnerable. But by the time the charm is completed, the pomander ball will be as solid as the earth itself.

Pierce holes in the lemon skin with a bodkin (meat skewer or darning needle) and insert the whole cloves. As each clove punctures the lemon, imagine strength and energy entering the fruit. Continue until the lemon is completely covered with clove heads. The procedure will take time and patience, but perseverance is essential to the success of the charm.

Place the clove-studded lemon into the bowl of blended spices and carefully roll it back and forth until the entire sudace is thickly coated. Close down the circle and leave the pomander resting in the spice bowl in a private drawer or cabinet. No one else should see or touch the charm until the work is completed. Every evening for the two weeks of the waxing moon, roll the pomander in the spices while you concentrate on its purpose.

On the night of the full moon (as it rises) bind the charm with a red silk cord or ribbon. Blow the remaining powder to the four points of the compass. Let the pomander be hung in an appropriate place as a symbol of strength, protection, and directional guidance.

PUCK FAIR

One of the most notable festivals surviving from ancient times is the annual Puck Fair held at the tiny town of Killorglin in County Kerry, Ireland. Until recent years the fair was celebrated on the first three days of August—coinciding with the Celtic harvest festival of Lammas/Lughnassad—but is now held about one week later. Visitors come from all over Ireland for the fair and tourists turn up from other parts of the world as well.

Three days of celebrations center upon the crowning of King Puck, a male goat captured from the semi-wild herd that roams the nearby hills. King Puck is garlanded on Gathering Day, the first day of the fair. He. parades on a truck at the head of a procession and is crowned by a young virgin. Two days later, on Scattering Day, King Puck's brief days of glory end and again he is just a goat.

In legend the goat is a fertility symbol, said to represent the animal nature of man. The Puck Fair, celebrated at harvest time, might be presumed to have pre-Christian roots; certainly, the name is a clue. Puck, sometimes known as Robin Goodfellow, was a minor fertility god as well as hobgoblin. In the ancient Mummers' Play, he was portrayed as having horns and goatish feet

Puck was often helpful to man and much beloved in folklore, but he was a tricky creature. The mischievous little god loved playing jokes and could shift his identity and that of others also; in *A Midsummer Night's Dream* Shakespeare assures us that Puck turned simple Bottom into an ass.

Hobgoblins of similar humor are called pookas, said to be "extremely obscure and indefinite in representation." *Raphael's Familiar Astrologer*, published in London almost 150 years ago, explains that "the pooka appears as a black horse, an eagle or a bat and compels the man of whom it has got possession, incapable of making any resistance, to go through various adventures in a short time. He hurries with him over precipices, carries him up to the moon and down to the bottom of the sea."

Puck and his fellow pranksters delight in will-o'-the-wisp tricks to mislead travelers. "Pouk-ledden" is an old English term for going oddly astray, and locals still occasionally tell yarns about puck-leading. In *Harvey*, the hilarious play by Mary Coyle Chase, the protagonist is a huge invisible white rabbit said to be a pooka. Certainly Harvey leads his crony astray—into a good many bars.

So we'll drink to the Puck's Fair. There is no true record of when the fair began—King James I endorsed it with a charter in 1613—and the proclamation is rather banal in view of lively pooka theories. The official explanation for the fair was that during Cromwell's conquest of Ireland a stealthy English attack on the town was thwarted by the warning bleating of goats. Since then, says the fair's official brochure, the annual crowning of King Puck has commemorated the occasion. The story sounds like the kind of tale a staunchly Catholic-community would tell

as a rationale for a celebration that owes its origins to the heathens.

Puck, with various aliases, turns up all over the British Isles. But nowhere is the mischief-maker more evident than in Ireland. Several villages are called Puckstown. Pooka's Ford, on a river linking Limerick and Cork, marks a dangerous crossing place said to be haunted. In this locale the pooka is regarded as evil—surely a risk for any practical joker.

"The face of the country," wrote P. W. Joyce in *Irish Names Places,* "is a book which if deciphered correctly and read attentively will unfold more than ever did the cuneiform inscriptions of Persia or the hieroglyphics of Egypt." Joyce is puckish. And probably correct.

A BALLAD FOR
TROLLS

We are the trolls; we like the night.
We hate churchbells, gun powder, dynamite.
We fear sunlight.
Ymir, the first Frost Giant, was our father; we were his
      rampaging spore.
The Norse Gods cursed our chaos, murdered Ymir; set against us
      Thor and his clanging hammer.
They made Earth of Ymir's body, his briny blood the seas.
Mountains are his heaped bones; boulders are his teeth.
This dirt is our birthright, worth fighting for.
Even the gold in Ymir's teeth is ours; who steals it, buys grief.
We bear the tag of the devil; we are outcast Lilith's brood, without
      souls, the churchfolk say, and cannot love the Good.
Our eyesight is splintered; our logic's so askew, we think it fine to
      dine on cow cakes, drink our oxen's own home-brew.
Beltane fires enrage us; Balder's Balefires built at crossroads
      make us run.
The rood and the mistletoe spoil our fun.
Speak our names and we are stunned.
We turn to stone if we look at the Sun.
We hate fishermen, billy goats, boys.
We hate noise.
We are ugly; best left alone.
Once we were blundering giants, one-eyed, defiant.
We're closer now to moles, with knotty tails, frowsy heads, noses
      like poles; living in holes.
Our offspring are mere muppets, silly and droll.
We never die; we go on growing very old, sitting in holes
      lit by goldlight, silvershine, diamond glitter, copper glow—
Earth rooted treasure, still ours; guarding it is our sullen goal.
Make no mistake; we still collect our toll.
We have no wits, so cannot win; but without souls,
      how can we sin?
Who covets Earth is our kin.
We are Trolls.

                                     –BARBARA LEHMAN

RAVENS

By Barbara Lehman

Once upon a midnight dreary, while I pondered, weak and weary, over many a quaint and curious volume of forgotten lore, it occurred to me that in our search for true illumination we humans have a habit of discrediting our faithful torchbearers along the way, as if they were so many burnt . out candles. Take the raven, for example. Wherever they told stories of the raven he always started out as a beautiful white bird, pure as a dove, the trusted confidant of the gods and heroes of the Light.

A white raven was the oracular bird sacred to Apollo. When Apollo fell in love with a mortal woman, Coronis, he set the raven to watch over her, for she was rumored to be unfaithful. The bird dutifully reported back to the god that his beloved was philandering with another mortal. Apollo was so enraged at this news that he turned the raven black and called him a corrupt and presumptuous informer. Was that fair?

The raven had no better luck with Noah. Out of all the birds in the Ark, Noah picked the shining white raven to be the first to search for dry land. He found none, for it was too soon. He flew around and around patiently waiting for the waters to recede, as he did not wish to return to the weary survivors of the Flood bearing bad news. We all know what happened then. As for the raven, he was declared absent without leave for failing to return on schedule and was sentenced to be forever black, to eat carrion, to be called unclean. Nevertheless, he was honored by such great prophets and saints as Elijah and St. Anthony for having fed them and kept them alive during their sojourns in the desert. But who remembers that?

The raven was treated with more respect in Celtic and Norse mythology where he was a magnificent battlefield bird. In heraldry the raven is a symbol of one who inherited little from his ancestors but made his fortune by his own strength and cleverness. The

early Danes fought under a raven banner which was described by their enemies as being pure white until the heat of battle, at which time a raven would appear upon the banner, with drooping wings if the Danes were to be defeated, or with wings in full spread if they were to win. The god Odin (Woden) had two ravens, Hugin (Thought) and Munin (Memory), who set out at first light each morning to scout the worlds of the living and the dead and returned to Valhalla before breakfast, to perch upon Odin's shoulders and report the news of the day. It was they who whispered into his ear the secret hiding place of the magic cauldron Odhroerir in which dead warriors could be restored to life. During the Wild Hunt—those stormy nights when ghost riders thundered across the skies reliving past glories- the two ravens always accompanied the phantom flight. Odin himself sometimes led the hunt in the form of a raven.

The fighting Celts worshipped a triad of war goddesses, Ana-Badb-Macha (collectively the Morrigan), whom they invoked in times of distress upon the battlefield by blowing trumpets that imitated the call of the raven. The goddesses would appear upon the field in the shape of ravens. The name Macha was an ancient word for raven. In modern Irish the raven is called "bran." Bran the Blessed, one of the great Welsh heroes, had a raven as a constant companion. When Bran gave his life to save his people his head was cut off and buried in London facing the sea, where it continued to warn the

people against invasions. Legend has it that the safety of the kingdom depends on keeping Bran's head in London and for that reason, they say, tame ravens are kept in the Tower of London to this day. The thread continues in the Bayeux tapestries where William the Conqueror is pictured fighting the Battle of Hastings under a raven banner. Among Cornish folk a tradition that King Arthur lives on in the shape of a raven makes them reluctant to kill those birds.

For the Indians of the Northwest Pacific Coast, the raven was a powerful totemic figure, a triumvirate creator-transformer-trickster. Though he was honored with the title Raven who Sets-Things-Right, he met with the usual human ingratitude. It was a pure white raven who transformed the earth from a wasteland into a paradise for the first humans. For love of them, and at their pleading, he stole from the Old One (a rich miser who lived at the end of the world) food, fresh water, and fire. Dropping some of each on his return flights, he created mountains, forests, rivers and streams, and filled them with animals and fishes so the people would never again go hungry. Because he pitied men for their lives of dreary darkness, he stole the Old One's bag of stars and

the Moon bag and flung them into the sky. Finally he stole the great bag of the Sun. During one of his forays the raven got stuck in the smoke hole of the Old One's tent where he hung helpless until his beautiful white feathers were coated a sooty, perpetual black. Though mankind accepted his gifts, they called him thief, glutton and unclean! It has been the raven's fate, as it is with all true seers, to be reviled. He is universally an omen of death and pestilence. Though the records show that he has served mankind faithfully and intelligently, he is considered a tricky devil whose appearance means trouble. And about this matter of color, even today in the Ozark Mountains you might find old-timers who will swear that baby ravens are white until they leave the nest. Full-fledged ravens area lustrous black, with a high purple sheen to their plumage which is full and ruffled at the throat. Princely looking creatures, but there is something ominous about them, like the mythic images in Hitchcock's movie The Birds.

And one thinks of that solitary bird perched above Poe's chamber door, muttering "Nevermore." Was it only lost Lenore, or did he ponder something else, some dark justice to tie the score?

The Phoenix

By Barbara Stacy

MOST CREATURES spring from other creatures. But there is only one phoenix ranging the sky, and this rarest of birds clones itself everlastingly from the burned bones of its own body.

When it has divided the air for five hundred years and its wings falter, the phoenix builds itself a nest atop an Arabian date palm. In this tree it collects cinnamon, spikenard, and myrrh, and of these splendid materials builds a heap on which to enact its fiery, perfumed death.

The nest of leaves and bark becomes both sepulcher and cradle.

Here the bird flutters its wings so rapidly that sparks glitter among feathers, and in this way flames begin snapping from beak to claw. The dying bird sings so melodiously, so gloriously that a host of other birds gathers to listen, and the phoenix expires singing its incomparable dirge in a sphere of spicy sweetness.

A worm humps its way out of the ashes. From this smallness and smoothness, a young phoenix emerges nine days later. Some ancient peoples tell us that the bird was crimson and gold and resembled an eagle; other ancient peoples tell us that it was purple and resembled a heron; all tell us that it was a creature of unsurpassed beauty.

Its first act is to pat together a little egg of its own charred remains mixed with myrrh. With the egg in its beak the phoenix flies to Heliopolis, the City of the Sun along the banks of the Nile. It is accompanied by throngs of birds; more join the flock in flight. And in Egypt, every five hundred years, the phoenix was indeed welcomed by high ritual in the Temple of the Sun; we know of one such celebration during the reign of Ptolemy III. The bird deposits its father-self egg on the altar and swoops out to begin its cycle anew.

Such is the legend of the phoenix. We might have guessed its Arabic origin from the sensuousness and poetry of the story, but the legend persisted in Egypt, ancient Greece and Rome, and throughout Europe well past the Middle Ages.

Alchemists chose the phoenix as their symbol and early chemists were located by the sign of the phoenix swinging above the door. The Old Testament mentions the phoenix (Job XXIX, 18), and Christian monks who wrote the medieval Book of Beasts took the phoenix as a point of departure for a scolding: "If the Phoenix has the power to die and rise again, why, silly man, are you scandalized at the word of God..."

Beginning with the Renaissance and early scientific observation, the phoenix vanished from bestiaries. But the bird has never migrated from poetry. Since antiquity the phoenix has burned brightly in the hearts of poets, both as immortality symbol and as exotic legend. None wrote more beautifully about the bird than John Dryden:

So when the new-born Phoenix first is seen

Her feathered subjects all adore their queen,

And while she makes her progress through the East,

From every grove her numerous train's increased;

Each poet of the air her glory sings,

And round him the pleased audience clap their wings.

Firegazing

The divinatory art of pyromancy or firegazing has been practiced since ancient times. Reading the message of the flames was often the duty of a religious priesthood or of professional augurs but as the method was simple, many individuals performed the ritual for themselves. Anyone wanting a fiery omen to foretell the outcome of a proposed venture could proceed in the following manner:

Build a fire and pay homage to its warmth and beauty. Gaze deep into the heart of the blaze and concentrate on a question that may be answered by a positive or negative response. When the fire is reduced to glowing embers, cast upon it a handful of pounded dried peas. If the peas catch fire quickly and burn silently, the omen is good. Should the flames leap high and burn brightly,

forming an upright triangle, success is assured. Failure to burn, heavy smoke, crackling, and erratic flames bending from side to side are all ill omens. And if the fire blazes swiftly and suddenly goes out, it is a warning that danger surrounds your question.

When your question concerns love, substitute a dried branch of vervain or bay laurel for the peas. Vervain is traditionally used to dismiss love, and bay laurel is said to invite it.

If you have no specific query in mind but merely want some kind of portent, poke a dying fire and count the flames that blaze anew to this rhyme:

A gift, a ghost, a friend, a foe,
A letter to come, a journey to go.

Another kind of firegazing offers a deeper and less obvious source of revelation. This exercise of presage took the form of a game in colonial America. When a family gathered before the fire of an evening and one member of the group seemed withdrawn and silent, the cheerful question, "What do you see in the fire m'dear, what do you see in the

fire?" would be asked. The answer had to be three fire images, quickly found and announced without second thoughts: for instance, a "ship at sea, a marigold, a knight who threatens me." All the family would comment, offer interpretations or guess what the visions foretold. As each family member in turn was challenged to seek his or her own pictures in the fire, the atmosphere took on a warm glow, and laughter and good spirits often restored the troubled member.

But the game of firegazing wasn't restricted to family activity. Shy lovers often employed the language of fire symbols to express their regard. And the old custom could serve the local witch as well.

If a nervous visitor found it awkward to confide a problem, and the witch failed to divine it by psychic means, the familiar question could serve to lessen the tension. The forthcoming answer chosen from the haphazard patterns of a hearth fire provided a source of conversation and revealed hints of the nature of the difficulty. Soon the whole story would tumble out.

But even if you never use a fire as an oracle nor visit a witch, finding images and omens in the flames or in the glowing embers of a dying fire, is a strangely refreshing pastime. The stimulation of imagination can be its own reward.

LUCKY
13
THIRTEEN

Any of this sound familiar? It is Friday the 13th. A candle flickers, dripping wax on an ancient volume while thunder rumbles and rain lashes the French windows. (As we all know, the sun never shines on Friday the 13th.) There is a pounding at the door and unexpected guests arrive, seeking shelter from the storm. Twelve people fill the room and gather around the hearth. A later pounding at the door announces the presence of another guest, *the thirteenth*. Consternation. Everyone knows that thirteen is an unlucky number- a theme familiar to lovers of Gothic novels, whodunits, and horror films.

Witches have the opposite perspective on thirteen. For followers of the Old Ways, numbers often have meanings different from those ascribed by other systems.

Since the earliest written records, every number has been assigned certain significance. Ceremonial magicians place great importance on precise numbers and tables of numbers, while New Agers calculate the vibrations of numbers. But the tradition of Witchcraft is largely oral and rarely committed to written records. Nor did it need to be, for all wisdom was already contained in Nature to be read by "those who have eyes to see," in numbers relating to the changing face of the moon, the fingers of the hand, the petals of a flower, the cycles of the seasons; numbers could unlock cosmic secrets.

The main reason for the Witches' veneration of thirteen is potent: the year contains thirteen lunar months, and so the number is sacred to the Moon Goddess of Witchcraft. For this reason, too, thirteen is the ideal number of Witches in a coven; and thirteen Witches in a circle represent the Thirteen Moons of the Wheel of the Year. Thirteen also figures in two other numbers especially lucky for Witches—thirtynine, which is three times thirteen, and one hundred sixty-nine, which is thirteen times thirteen.

One of the earliest recorded stories concerning the number thirteen is a Norse myth. It relates of a great feast

Sleeping Beauty   Arthur Rackham

held at Valhalla, attended by twelve gods who probably represent the signs of the zodiac. Balder, beautiful and beloved, was among them. Jealous Loki, offended at not being invited, arrived anyway, swore vengeance, and killed Balder. The theme presages the story of the Last Supper, in which Jesus and eleven apostles share ritual bread and wine. The thirteenth guest is, of course, the betrayer Judas.

Another retelling of misfortune from the thirteenth guest is the lovely fairy tale "Sleeping Beauty." Twelve Witches are invited to celebrate the birth of the beautiful princess. Each arrives with a gift: beauty, wisdom, humor, and so on. The twelfth Witch, the wisest, senses danger and withholds her benefit. Enter the uninvited and offended guest, the thirteenth Witch.

In her anger, the last Witch wishes for the princess on her sixteenth birthday to prick her finger on a spindle—another symbol of the Moon

Goddess—and die. Now the twelfth Witch amends the curse from death to long sleep. To prevent the fulfillment of the evil wish, the king banishes spinning wheels and spindles from the kingdom. But on her sixteenth birthday, the princess finds a spinning wheel; curious about the strange device, she tries to use it. The princess pricks her finger and falls into a long sleep.

There is no surprise ending here. Everyone knows that years later a prince is magically drawn to the castle, now overgrown with briars. When he beholds the beautiful face of the apparently dead princess, the prince is overwhelmed with love and kisses her. The kiss of true love resurrects the princess, and she and Prince Charming live happily—well, you know how long.

To Witches, such simple fairy tales "for the children" are fraught with profound symbolism. The elements of this tale, familiar to many myths the world over, deal with the maiden or virgin. The Celtic goddess Bride (Brigid) perhaps, or her Mediterranean sister Persephone, whose birth contains the factor of youthful death, are examples. As she reaches maturity, like the ripening grain, the maiden experiences death and is eventually resurrected by the kiss of her consort, the Sun God or Spirit Father. Actually the thirteenth Witch, the Moon Goddess in her aspect as the Crone, gave Sleeping Beauty the greatest gift of all, the gift of immortality. For without death, there can be no resurrection.

The number thirteen has also oddly played an important role in American history. It is not by coincidence that the original colonies were thirteen in number. Our first official flag, affectionately known now as the Betsy Ross, featured a circle of thirteen white stars (pentacles) on a blue field and thirteen red-and-white stripes. These stripes were actually strips of cloth, like the traditional red-and-white streamers which entwined the May Pole and which may have had their origins in the resurrection cult of Cybele and Attis. I am not suggesting that those delegates from the thirteen original colonies—sitting in that stuffy room in Philadelphia on those hot July days in 1776 drafting the Declaration of Independence and the Bill of Rights—were actually a coven of Witches. I am suggesting however that the Old Gods move in mysterious ways to protect their hidden children.

As the number thirteen seems unlucky to the uninitiated, Friday the 13th seems even more so. But keep in mind that Friday is named for the Goddess Freya, the Norse deity of love, beauty, and fertility. And perhaps the combination of the goddess' name day with her sacred number seems to be more than those who do not know the light of her love can endure. So should you ever find yourself in a room with twelve other people and it happens to be Friday the 13th, fear no evil. Thank the gods of the Old Religion and await the magic.

—PAULINE CAMPANELLI

72

A Thessalian Moon Charm

Thessaly is a pastoral region in northeastern Greece long famed as the haunt of witches. Mt. Olympus, abode of the ancient Greek deities, is in Thessaly. So is the site of the inspiring Pierian Spring of the Nine Muses, goddesses of the arts and sciences. Yet Thessaly is primarily renowned for its witches. Their sorcery to draw down the moon has captured the imagination of writers for centuries.

Sophocles and Aristophanes wrote of the Thessalian witches in the 5th century BC. Plato writes of them a century later. Horace, Virgil, Ovid, and Lucan hail the moon-drawing charm at the turn of the Christian era. John Dryden in 17th-century England described a heroine whose "eyes have power beyond Thessalian charms to draw the moon from heaven."

Today the phrase calls to mind a ceremony performed by contemporary English witches in which the High Priestess becomes the Moon Goddess incarnate. A tape recording of this ritual inspired Margot Adler's study of NeoPagans in America and gave her its title: *Drawing Down the Moon*

But there is another ceremony less well known and similar in theme. We believe this personal and simple rite is probably closer to the original sorcery. Its purpose is to renew psychic energy and increase divinatory perception.

To Draw Down the Moon

At the time of the Full Moon closest to summer solstice and when the Moon is high, go to an open space carrying a small bowl of fresh spring water. Position yourself so as to capture the Moon's reflection in the bowl. Hold it as steadily as you can in both hands for a slow and silent count to nine. Close your eyes and while holding the image of the Moon in your mind, drink the water to the last drop.

THOTH TIME

The Western world's first historical magus is undoubtedly Thoth, ancient Egypt's god of wisdom and magic. His symbolic ibis-headed figure appears on the earliest monuments of the Old Kingdom, and it is speculated that the concept of Thoth as a deity was established before 4000 BC.

From that remote date to the turn of the Christian era, Thoth retained his essential character as patron of learning and keeper of arcane lore. Magical texts, the celebrated Emerald Tablet among them, compiled during the 1st century AD were often attributed to Hermes Trismegistus, a designation honoring Thoth as three times greater than his Greek equivalent. Greeks and Romans were in awe of the spiritual achievements and occult disciplines preserved by the far older Egyptian culture. The 18th century philologist, Court de Gébelin, believed the Tarot cards comprised a sacred and secret doctrine known to the ancient Egyptians. He called the deck "The Book of Thoth."

Thoth is the Greek name for Egypt's Divine Scribe. He is identified in hieroglyphics as *Tehuti*, a Moon-god" He who dispels darkness with his light." The baboon, a highly intelligent and social animal, was his creature. Thoth represented knowledge, good order, invention, and something more—a quality subtle and compelling—the sense of magic. A hint of this theme is recorded in the Pyramid Texts of the Sixth Dynasty (2625–2475 BC):

"Thoth who gives to thee thy heart (understanding); that thou mayest remember what thou hadst forgotten."

A thousand years later in the reign of Ramses II, a wise man would address Thoth:

"O thou sweet Well for the thirsty in the desert! It is closed up for him who speaks, but it is open for him who keeps silence. When he who keeps silence comes, lo he finds the Well."

Perhaps it was in the spirit of Thoth, who was also known as the Measurer of Time, that the Egyptians devised the earliest known calendar dated 4241 BC. This arbitrary scheme of 12 months and 365 days, with variations, has been in continual use ever since. When the Dog Star rises in the east before dawn and the Nile overflows its banks, the Egyptian New Year is born. The first month is named for Thoth, a traditional time for divination and magical work. Translated to our current Gregorian system, the first day of Thoth begins at dawn on August 29. Certain days of this month are more appropriate for ritual than others. A papyrus in the British Museum's vast collection (this one is No. 10,474) lists the favorable days of the Thoth.

August 29 and 30; September 2, 6, 7, 14, 15, 16, 21, 22, 24, 25, 26, and 27.

※ Capella

※ Pollux

※ Aldebaran

※ Procyon   ※ Betelgeuse

※ Rigel

※ Sirius

THE WINTER CIRCLE

On a clear night in early February between seven and nine PM, look to the southeast for one of the heavens' most memorable sights - the Winter Circle. Seven stars of the first magnitude coil in and around the constellation of Orion.

The three stars in a row that form the Hunter's belt point directly to Sirius, the brightest star in our sky. The ring goes clockwise to Procyon, due north to Pollux, Capella is at 12 o'clock high, Aldebaran at 3, Rigel at 5, and spirals in to end with Betelgeuse, the left shoulder of Orion.

SIRIUS - The Latin name comes from the Greek word meaning "scorcher," but is commonly known as the Dog Star from its place in *Canis Major*, Big Dog. This is the Star of Isis known as Sothis to the ancient Egyptians. It is brilliant, bluish, and the first star you'll see after nightfalL

PROCYON - A yellow-white star of *Canis Minor*, Little Dog, is named from the Greek phrase "before the dog" because it rises just before Sirius.

POLLUX - Castor and Pollux are the legendary twins of Gemini. Pollux, the brighter of the two, is yellow.

CAPELLA - "The kid" or "little goat" in Latin is the bright yellow eye of Auriga, the Charioteer.

ALDEBARAN - The orange-red eye of Taurus, the Bull. Its Arabic name means "the follower" and refers to the star's relation to the cluster of starlets known as the Pleiades, which forms the Bull's hump.

RIGEL - The brightest star in Orion is blue-white and represents the Hunter's right foot. Rigel means "foot" in Arabic.

BETELGEUSE - "Shoulder of the giant" in Arabic and the red star delineating the left shoulder of Orion, the Hunter. Betelgeuse is the second brightest star in the constellation often called "Winter's Centerpiece."

O Trivia, Goddess, leave these low abodes,

And traverse o'er the wide ethereal roads,

Celestial Queen, put on thy robes of light,

Now Cynthia named, fair regent of the night.

At sight of thee the villain sheaths his sword

Nor scales the wall, to steal the wealthy hoard.

0 may thy silver lamp from heaven's high bower

Direct my footsteps in the midnight hour!

-JOHN GAY
From *Trivia, or the Art of Walking the
Streets of London*, Book Ill. (1716)

BAST
GODDESS OF CATS

In the fantastic pantheon of Egyptian animal gods that so dismayed the Greeks, obsessed with human perfection, none held a more revered place than the cat goddess Bast. The ibis—bird, the bull, the crocodile, the hawk-all had their own strange cults. But the Egyptians especially revered the feline spirit and worshiped two cat goddesses, both Bast (or Bastet) and her lion-headed sister Sekhmet.

The sister goddesses personified the fascinating dual nature of the cat. Sekhmet represented the power of the earth's supreme hunter—cunning, swift, and lethal, the animal red in tooth and claw. While the Sekhmet cult predated that of Bast, it sprang from worship even more ancient. Man the hunter believed that he could control nature by propitiating what threatened, and numerous wild cat cults existed from earliest time, especially that of the lion and leopard in Africa and that of the jaguar in South and Central America.

Early man also believed that by ritual he could partake of the qualities of particular animals; and the wild cat's hunting skill, courage, and strength were man's own survival mechanisms. In later cultures, the power of the strong cat evolved as largely symbolic; often lions, leopards, or jaguars were carved on city gates as protective forces.

While Sekhmet inspired awe, Bast inspired love and devotion. The Egyptians were the first to domesticate the cat, doubtless breeding the smaller ones to rid the granaries of mice—no insignificant task. Egypt was an agrarian culture, thanks to the rich Nile delta, and keeping grain storehouses wholesome had life-and-death implications. Even the symbols of Egyptian royalty delived from agriculture—the crook (or sickle) and the flail , used to winnow wheat from chaff.

But we can't doubt that the Egyptians tamed the cat for another obvious reason—because the beautiful creature is simply a delight to be around. Sleek, elegant, subtle, we still encounter in affectionate pets the wilder feline spirit. The cat that spends the afternoon snoozing in a sunny doorway becomes transformed at night. We catch glimpses of her in the moonlit grass with eyes like mirrors: stalking, motionless as stone, bounding with a dazzling burst of speed, pouncing. And another mouse or snake is vanquished. At such times, we can imagine ourselves viewing a feline on the African veldt as if through a mystical peephole to the dawn of time.

Bast has attributes of both the Sun and the Moon, but essentially Bast is nocturnal, a goddess of darkness and keeper of lunar secrets. In the intricate web of Egyptian-Greek-Roman mythology, Bast is linked with Diana, goddess of the moon, and with Diana's other entity, Artemis, the virgin huntress. According to one legend, Diana disguised herself as a white cat in order to seduce Lucifer, god of darkness and light. The result of this peculiar union was Aradia, destined to teach the art of witchcraft to mortals blessed with gifts. In this aspect, Bast and cats in general have abilities to ward off evil spirits.

Egyptians also believed that Bast and her fierce sister were daughters of Ra, the Sun god. Linked with the Sun, Bast was worshiped as the Lady of Life, an expression of the ancient feminine principles of fertility and maternity. She is one of the all-seeing eyes of Ra. The Egyptian name for the cat is *mau*, which sounds like cat language and also means "to see."

Bast worship centered in the sacred city Bubastis, now in ruins and marked on contemporary maps as Tell Bast. According to the Greek historian Herodotus—who visited Egypt in 445 BC when the temple was already 2,000 years old—this was the most glorious of all Egyptian sacred sites. An impressively wide avenue led to the structure on an island surrounded

by Nile-fed canals. A grove of tall trees circled the central shrine, built of red granite and enclosing the altar with the cult image. Inside the temple, superb murals and hieroglyphic inscriptions honored the goddess.

The Egyptians celebrated numerous Bast holidays during the year at Bubastis, and in the spring thousands of devotees from all over the country gathered for the most important festival of the year. They traveled along the Nile, singing, dancing, and drinking wine until they reached Bubastis. At the site, the celebrants drank more wine and offered sacrifices. Then the cult statue of Bast was removed to a barge and made its way with splendid ritual down the Nile.

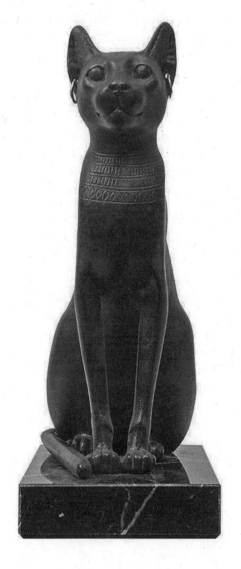

Bast was also worshiped at the domestic hearth, for every cat was considered an embodiment of the goddess; killing a cat was punishable by death. Pets were adorned with gold earrings, jeweled collars, and silver chains. Artists especially loved Bast. Her exquisite statuary is visible today in museums the world over. Sometimes as all cat, sometimes as a cat-headed woman, her many forms are a reflection of the age old belief in the animal's transformational ability.

The Egyptian cat cult seemed to have nine lives, lasting with enormous devotion through the Greek and Roman eras all the way down to Christian times. Bast vanished only in 392 AD, when the Christian emperor Theodosius outlawed all forms of paganism.

But Bast still lingers in vestigial form: she has crept into our hearts on little cat feet. Human beings will always adore the cat for enriching our lives with her beauty and unique character. There is no creature on earth remotely like a cat except a cat. We gaze into the creature's magical eyes, which reflect an elusive, enigmatic reality that human beings may glimpse but never penetrate.

—BARBARA STACY

MIDSUMMER MAGIC

Between 11 and 12 on John's day, the unbetrothed girls gather nine sorts of flowers; they are twined into a wreath, of which the twiner must have spun the thread in the same hour. Before the fateful hour is past, she throws the wreath backwards into a tree; as often as it is thrown without staying on, so many years will it be before she is married. All this must be done in silence.

Among the notes in *Teutonic Mythology* by Jacob Grimm, English translation, 4th edition, 1882.

Summer solstice was once a high holiday celebrated all across Europe and the British Isles. The early Christian Church adopted the festival dedicating the longest day of the year to St. John the Baptist. Despite the change of name and strong opposition, the old ways persisted. The thrill of Midsummer-fires when the people "rub the sacred flame, run through the glowing embers, throw flowers into the fire, and join hands in the circular dance" was too pleasurable to be abandoned. Jacob Grimm viewed the event as the survival of a once dominant religion which sought to awaken latent psychic powers and perceptions by means of traditional rituals.

Flowering sweet herbs were a most vital part of the ceremonies and Shakespeare was clearly fascinated by the lore. The plot of *A Midsummer Night's Dream* centers around a plant shot by Puck's arrow.

It fell upon a little Western flower,
Before milk-white, now purple with love's wound,
And maidens call it love-in-idleness.

The flower is the *Viola tricolor*, our popular garden heartsease, wild pansy, or Johnny-jump-up so called because of its delightful habit of self-sowing. Shakespeare's Oberon, king of the fairies, describes its properties:

The juice of it on sleeping eyelids laid
Will make a man or woman madly dote
Upon the next live creature it sees.

St. John's wort, the bright golden wildling, takes its name from the holiday and along with daisies, clover, feverfew, rue, vervain, meadowsweet, orpine (Midsummer Men), and lavender make up the "nine sorts" of flowers; the traditional bouquet and an essential part of the Midsummer festival of our ancestors.

And while we have the art of Shakespeare, Ingmar Bergman, and Woody Allen to remind us of the glory of June enchantment, every year the same flowers gathered ages ago bloom in our gardens or forgotten meadows perpetuating the magic of Midsummer.

MOON GARDENING

BY PHASE

Sow, transplant, bud and graft   *Plow, cultivate, weed and reap*

NEW	First Quarter	FULL	Last Quarter	NEW
Plant above-ground crops with outside seeds, flowering annuals.	Plant above-ground crops with inside seeds.	Plant root crops, bulbs, biennials, perennials.		Do not plant.

BY PLACE IN THE ZODIAC

Fruitful Signs

Cancer — Most favorable planting time for all leafy crops bearing fruit above ground. Prune to encourage growth in Cancer.

Scorpio — Second only to Cancer, a Scorpion Moon promises good germination and swift growth. In Scorpio, prune for bud development.

Pisces — Planting in the last of the Watery Triad is especially effective for root growth.

Taurus — The best time to plant root crops is when the Moon is in the sign of the Bull.

Capricorn — The Earthy Goat Moon promotes the growth of rhizomes, bulbs, roots, tubers and stalks. Prune now to strengthen branches.

Libra — Airy Libra may be the least beneficial of the Fruitful Signs, but is excellent for planting flowers and vines.

Barren Signs

Leo — Foremost of the Barren Signs, the Lion Moon is the best time to effectively destroy weeds and pests. Cultivate and till the soil.

Gemini — Harvest in the Airy Twins; gather herbs and roots. Reap when the Moon is in a sign of Air or Fire to assure best storage.

Virgo — Plow, cultivate, and control weeds and pests when the moon is in Virgo.

Sagittarius — Plow and cultivate the soil or harvest under the Archer Moon. Prune now to discourage growth.

Aquarius — This dry sign of Air is perfect for ground cultivation, reaping crops, gathering roots and herbs. It is a good time to destroy weeds and pests.

Aries — Cultivate, weed, and prune to lessen growth. Gather herbs and roots for storage.

Consult our Moon Calendar pages for phase and place in the zodiac circle. The Moon remains in a sign for about two-and-a-half days. Match your gardening activity to the day that follows the Moon's entry into that zodiac sign.

SPRING RESOLUTION

There's a certain fine edge of determination we all need to win through in difficult tests of will power. Whether you are trying to eradicate a bad habit, lose that last five pounds of unwanted weight, overcome lassitude, or achieve some other personal goal requiring flinty discipline—this is the time of year to firm up the will to win .

Rituals gain strength with repetition. The Seven-Day Rite of Spring performed from the first night of the New Moon following the vernal equinox to its completion a week later, supplies a source of power you can draw on in time of need. The first New Moon of springtime this year falls on March 23. There are decisions to make and quests to fulfill before that date.

The single most important element of the ceremony is the incense you will choose to sanctify the work. Incense is a strong stimulant to the psyche and sensual memory is particularly significant to the success of the operation. You might plan to use an unfamiliar scent in order to make the experience unique. Elemi, a fragrant resin, is recommended by many in the craft as an additive to the customary cone or powdered incense products. Should elemi prove difficult to obtain, you'll not go wrong by burning pure frankincense on a charcoal block.

The Seven-Day Rite of Spring

When the sun returns to our climes and day is longer than night again, secure for yourself one half hour of privacy on the night of the first New Moon of spring. Place a small amount of incense on a glowing coal and watch its smoke rise. As you inhale the fragrance, hold out your hands before you with palms down. Grasp your left thumb with the four fingers of your right hand. Press your right thumb into the center of your left palm and hold it there with the four fingers of your left hand. (If you are left handed, reverse the procedure.) Let your clasped hands rest comfortably in your lap and close your eyes. When, after a few minutes, you become aware of the throb of your pulse—concentrate on your intention. Consider the means by which you intend to succeed in your project and link these with the smell of the incense and the beat you feel in your hands. Some choose to intensify the experience with the addition of music. Continue until the incense has burned away and you feel the work is done.

Repeat the ceremony for seven nights in a row at approximately the same time and in the same place.

CLASSICAL MOONS

Artemis. Greek goddess of wild nature, associated with the Moon as her twin brother, Apollo, is with the Sun.

Cynthia. A name for the Moon derived from Mt. Cynthus on the Greek island of Delos where Leto gave birth to Artemis and Apollo.

Diana. An Italian wood deity who became identified with the Greek Artemis and, like her, symbolized the Moon.

Hecate. A primitive Greek goddess of three realms—heaven, earth, and sea. The Moon before rising, after setting, and for the three nights when it is lost from sight belong to Hecate.

Luna. A Roman epithet for the Moon goddess depicted as winged and driving a chariot drawn by two white horses.

Phoebe. When a bright Moon shines high in the sky, Artemis is called Phoebe as her twin Apollo becomes Phoebus in bright aspect.

Selene. The Moon goddess in the Greek legend who fell in love with the sleeping shepherd boy Endymion.

Trivia. The triple form of Hecate and the Moon made the point where three roads met sacred—*tri*, three and *via*, road. The Romans knew Hecate as Trivia, goddess of witchcraft.

APPLE PIE ORDER

The apple is a mythic emblem of love, immortality, and magic. Norse myths tell of gods who kept themselves eternally young by partaking of the golden apples of Iduna, goddess of youth and spring. Welsh legend links apples and immortality, for kings and heroes were said to go after earthly death to Avalon, the island paradise of apple trees. An ancient law from the *Triads of Ireland* demands the death penalty for felling an apple tree, signifying its sacred nature. As a symbol of love and beauty, a golden apple was the prize won by the goddess Aphrodite, judged by Paris as the most desirable in the Greek myth. Although commonly accepted as the "forbidden fruit," no mention of the apple is to be found in the Bible story of Eve's temptation. "The tree of the knowledge of good and evil" growing in the Garden of Eden bore a different fruit.

Beyond its magical virtues, the apple is as delicious as it is beautiful. Apples were so popular a dessert in ancient Rome that they gave rise to the expression: *ab ovo usque ad mala*, from the egg to the apple meaning from start to finish—in Victorian parlance, soup to nuts. The Emperor Claudius praised an apple pie made with honey and spices that he enjoyed in 46 A.D.

The phrase of our title is of uncertain origin, but suggests perfection. And sweetened and spiced tart apples baked in a crusty nest is a perfect dessert.

HONEY APPLE PIE

2 9-inch pie shells (frozen)
5 cups of tart apples, sliced
1 teaspoon flour
½ teaspoon cinnamon
¼ teaspoon nutmeg
1 tablespoon lemon juice
1 teaspoon grated lemon rind
2 tablespoons butter
⅔ cup honey
Confectioners' sugar

Defrost pie shells. Peel, core, and slice about half a dozen tart apples to make 5 cups. Preheat the oven to 450 degrees. Fill the bottom crust with the sliced apples and sprinkle over them the flour mixed with cinnamon and nutmeg, lemon juice, and rind. Dot the surface with butter. Cover with a latticework of pastry strips cut from the second pie shell and bake in the hot oven for 10 minutes. Reduce temperature to 350 degrees, and bake for another 30 minutes, or until the crust is golden and the apples tender. Remove the pie from the oven and pour the honey through the openings in the top crust. Let the pie stand for at least one half hour and serve dusted with confectioners' sugar.

Albrecht Durer (1493).

CELESTIAL GEMS

By consulting a wide spectrum of sources—ancient, classical, medieval renaissance and modern—we've assembled a list of the jewels most consistently linked with a particular heavenly body down through the centuries of Western occult tradition.

Agate - Mercury
Alexandrite - Mercury
Amber- Moon
Amethyst - Jupiter
Aquamarine - Venus
Beryl - Venus
Bloodstone - Mars
Carbuncle - Venus
Carnelian - Sun
Cat's Eye- Sun
Chalcedony - Saturn
Chrysoprase - Venus
Crystal - Moon
Diamond - Sun
Emerald - Venus
Garnet- Sun
Jacinth - Jupiter

Jade - Venus
Jasper - Mercury
Jet- Saturn
Lapis-lazuli - Jupiter
Malachite - Venus
Moonstone - Moon
Onyx - Saturn
Opal - Mercury
Pearl - Moon
Peridot - Venus
Quartz - Moon
Ruby- Mars
Sapphire - Jupiter
Sardonyx - Mercury
Topaz- Sun
Tourmaline - Mercury
Turquoise - Venus

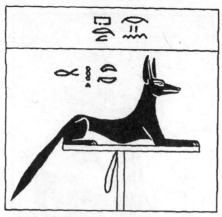

Detail from the Month-Table, Ramesseum, 13th century B.C.

NIGHT OF THE JACKAL

Winter, the night of the year, belonged to the Egyptian god Anubis. Symbolized as a jackal—a nocturnal animal and wild member of the dog family—his primary function in Egyptian myths was as protector and faithful guardian.

One of the oldest gods of a culture which existed continuously for over 3.000 years, Anubis played many roles. He was Lord of the Nether World, god of embalming, and judge of the dead, for it was Anubis who held the scales of truth to determine the virtue of the deceased. By the time the Osirian mortuary ritual was established, Anubis was portrayed with a human body. Only his jackal-head identified his character.

Among the treasures from Tutankhamen's tomb (c. 1350 B.C.) is a life-sized statue of a jackal. There he is, black and lean, recumbent yet alert; an ideal representation of a guardian being. Few peoples captured the quality of animals with such skill and fidelity as did the ancient Egyptians.

The constellation the Egyptians identified with Anubis is the one we call the Little Dipper. The Romans knew it as Ursa Minor, the Little Bear, but also named it Cynosura, the dog's tail. This pattern of stars contains the single most important celestial body in the night sky—the North or Pole Star. As a constant guide to due north, it has served humans well. So, in the form of a constellation (possibly the original concept), Anubis is steadfast, dependable, and always visible.

Many of us across America share our home with a fine black dog. Many more successfully use the image of Anubis as a visualization focus when casting spells of protection. And if the winter seems especially long and your peace of mind feels threatened, take time to walk out on a clear Moonless night. Look to the north and count out the seven stars of his constellation while you say:

Anubis, the good oxherd, bring in the light to me.
For thou shalt give protection to me here tonight!

The prayer comes from the Leyden Papyrus, an Egyptian document of practical magic that dates from the 3rd century A.D.

86

TO THE EVENING STAR

THOU fair-hair'd angel of the evening,
Now, whilst the sun rests on the mountains, light
Thy bright torch of love; thy radiant crown
Put on, and smile upon our evening bed!
Smile on our loves, and, while thou drawest the
Blue curtains of the sky, scatter thy silver dew
On every flower that shuts its sweet eyes
In timely sleep. Let thy west wind sleep on
The lake; speak silence with thy glimmering eyes,
And wash the dusk with silver. Soon, full soon,
Dost thou withdraw; then the wolf rages wide,
And the lion glares thro' the dun forest:
The fleeces of our flocks are cover' d with
Thy sacred dew: protect them with thine influence.

William Blake

The White Doe

Shape shifting is a familiar theme in witch legends. One of the oldest English tales with this motif concerns Lady Sybil of Bemshaw Tower in Lancashire. She was beautiful, wealthy, "intellectual beyond most of her sex," and irresistibly drawn to the practice of Witchcraft for which she showed remarkable talent. Lady Sybil loved wild nature with all of her heart and enjoyed nothing so much as to ramble through the deep ravines of Cliviger Gorge in the form of a milk-white doe. One May Eve while in this guise, she was captured by Lord William of Towneley Castle with the magical help of another Lancashire witch, the famous Mother Helston.

It all began in early spring a long, long time ago. Lord William had nearly despaired of ever winning the lovely heiress of Bernshaw Tower as his bride. She was indifferent to his courting and repeatedly spurned his advances. But Mother Helston prepared a powerful spell woven into a long silken cord and loaned Lord William her own familiar, a fierce black hound. With these the nobleman won his heart's desire for at cock's crow the captive doe became Lady Sybil now docile and subject to his will. But Lord William made a fatal mistake when he offended Mother Helston by failing to thank her for her efforts on his behalf.

Within one passage of the moon the spell was lifted and Lady Sybil sought her freedom. Lord William was forced to hold her prisoner under the constant guard of his manservant Robin. One night while Robin dozed a splendid white cat tried to slip by him. Robin woke with a roar and with his dagger, struck off the cat's paw. When he stooped to pick it up, there instead was the severed hand of Lady Sybil, easily identified by an· elaborate diamond ring she wore on her forefinger. The hand was returned to its owner and magically restored to Lady Sybil's arm although a faint red line remained. Lord William tried his best to make amends, but it was too late. The lady's health declined after this episode and she soon died.

According to her wishes, Lady Sybil was buried in Cliviger Gorge close by Eagle Crag where as the white doe she had been run to ground by Mother Helston's hound. And when darkness falls on May Eve, so the legend tells, doe and hound and ardent hunter return to haunt the night .

A Bevy of Swans

Many of England's earliest printed books dealt with the subject of hunting. It became customary to include in these volumes a listing of the proper terms designating groups of animals. The lists were called Nouns of Venery (an Old French word for the art of hunting Nouns of Assemblage. *The Book of St. Albans*, published in 1486, contained 164 such terms. The following selection is drawn from that and other early sources.

Antelopes: a herd.
Apes: a shrewdness.
Asses: a pace.
Badgers: a cete.
Bears: a sloth.
Bees: a swarm.
Birds: a flock.
Boars: a sounder.
Bucks: a brace.
Cats: a clowder.
Cattle: a drove.
Chickens: a brood.
Cranes: a sedge.
Crows: a murder.
Cubs: a litter.
Deer: a herd.
Elks: a gang.
Ferrets: a fesnyng.

Fishes: a shoal.
Flies: a swarm.
Foxes: a skulk.
Goats: a trip.
Goldfinches: a charm.
Hares: a down.
Hawks: a cast.
Horses: a harras.
Hounds: a pack.
Kangeroos: a troop.
Kittens: a kindle.
Larks: an exaltation.
Leopards: a leap.
Lions: a pride.
Mares: a stud.
Moles: a labor.
Monkeys: a troop.
Mules: a barren.

Nightingales: a watch.
Owls: a parliament.
Peacocks: a muster.
Ponies: a string.
Porpoises: a school.
Pups: a litter.
Ravens: an unkindness.
Seals: a pod.
Sheep: a flock.
Squirrels: a dray.
Starlings: a murmuration.
Swallows: a flight.
Swans: a bevy.
Toads: a knot.
Turtles: a bale.
Whales: a gam.
Wolves: a route.
Woodpeckers: a descent.

♄

SATURNALIA

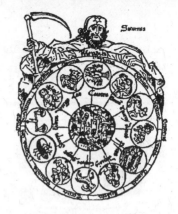

Saturn, dark and brooding, holds a scythe as he governs the affairs of Earth within the zodiac circle. The cardinal points of the compass match the cardinal signs indicating winter solstice is at hand. Late December is the time of year when Saturn comes to power. He wears the sixpointed star known as Solomon's seal, a mystic symbol of the union of body and soul. The unknown European artist who made this 16th-century woodcut based his conception of Saturn on traditions reaching back in time to the days of the Roman Empire.

The character of Saturn wasn't always gloomy. As an early Roman god of seed-sowing and harvest, his nature was robust and rustic. It was only when he became equated with the Greek god Kronos that aspects of cold cruelty and self-serving ruthlessness appeared. And no wonder.

In Greek mythology, Kronos was the most powerful of the Titans, elder gods who ruled the world many ages ago. To foil a prophesy that one of his own children would dethrone him, Kronos devoured them at birth. Zeus, his sixth child, was spirited away to safety by his mother who then deceived Kronos by presenting him instead with a stone wrapped in swaddling clothes. This, too, he apparently swallowed without ill effect. But Zeus, grown to manhood, forced his father to disgorge the family and with the help of his brothers Poseidon and Hades, deposed Kronos who fled to Italy in exile. Hidden in the myth is a Greek theme that Kronos personifies Time

and Time cannot successfully consume the Heavens of Zeus, the Seas of Poseidon, or the Underworld of Hades. And then the Romans added a sequel to the story.

Kronos, it seems, upon arrival in Italy to join his identity with Saturn, ushered in a veritable Golden Age of freedom, peace, and prosperity. It was one of those rare eras in human history when no class distinctions existed. All people were equal. It is this happy interval that came to be celebrated in later Roman times by the midwinter festival of Saturnalia.

The Romans considered festivals as elements of good government and social order. The darkest days of the year were enlivened by Saturnalia which began on December 17 with sacrifices and an open-air banquet attended by all. The wealthy made gifts to the poor, schools had a holiday, the law courts closed, all work was stopped, no criminals were punished for six days, slaves were free and waited on by their masters, and people gambled for nuts (symbols of fruitfulness)—not quite the licentious picture painted by later historians. It was a time of merrymaking and thoughtfulness. Wax candles and little clay dolls were traditional gifts. For one glorious week of good will, Rome commemorated the Time when the spirit of ancient Greece ennobled Roman vitality with the greeting—*io Saturnalia.*

MORGAN ∨ LE FAY

One of the most fascinating aspects of mythology is tracing the twists and turns of stories through the mists of time. Mythological beings that spring into legend as benevolent creatures often devolve into creatures of evil, especially so if they are seductively beautiful. Sometimes, like the Arthurian fairy Morgan le Fay, they almost vanish from lore.

Morgan is too interesting to lose. She was King Arthur's half-sister, the daughter of his mother Igraine, and her English name derives from the French *Morgain La Fee* or "fairy." Her father ruled the enchanted island of Avalon, an orchard-dotted kingdom with roots in Celtic mythology. 12th-century Breton minstrels, racially akin to the Welsh, sang of her charms in Arthurian lays. But earlier historians claim that the Morgan of legend derived from an ancient pagan deity, a river goddess. Her watery origins echo her Italian guise, Fata Morgana (*fata* is Italian for fairy), as does the term's other meaning—a mirage or glamorous illusion sometimes viewed in the sea by sailors.

Morgan le Fay learned magic and healing powers at Merlin's knee. He taught her the secrets of the stars, to fly as a raven, and to hide herself in spider's guise. All the subtle arts were hers, and she was bewitchingly beautiful.

Whatever her origins, Morgan was essentially a "good fairy" in her earliest aspects. At Arthur's birth, she bestowed on him gifts of strength, dominion, and long life. When Arthur was mortally injured in battle, he fled by boat to Avalon and Morgan tenderly healed the king as he lay recovering on her golden bed.

Morgan le Fay's powers included restoring youth to the old She attended the christening of a baby born to the King of Denmark, became enamored of the beautiful infant, and promised him that he would achieve eternal life as her paramour. Prince Ogier became a soldier famous for valor, and in his old age she had him survive a shipwreck near Avalon. Morgan's spell brightened Ogier's eyes, straightened his bent back, and the Dane again became a handsome youth. The amorous fairy crowned him with myrtle, the herb of Venus and forgetfulness; Ogier lost all memory of his mortality and remained blissful happy in the sensual paradise of Avalon.

But as Christianity gained

Morgan and Urien   Will Bradley (1902).

ascendance, we encounter the flip side of the Morgan myth. Seductive women, particularly those with roots in pagan sexuality, were considered "unclean" and malevolent tales arose around them. Now stories evolved of an enchanted Valley of No Return on Avalon, lush with greenery and flowers watered by a spring that sparkled like diamonds. Morgan lured knights into the valley, where they abode in hedonistic bliss, all thoughts of fighting forgotten—living death for a knight.

Morgan was sometimes sited in Camelot, living as a courtier with her husband Urien and secretly jealous of Arthur's power. She relished seducing the young knights sworn to purity and was careful to keep her debauches a secret. But as time passed the passionate fairy became heedless or too arrogant to care about discretion, and her jealous lovers grew quarrelsome. Finally Queen Guinevere, long before her own seduction of Sir Lancelot, discovered Morgan with a lover and recounted the adultery to the king. Protective of Urien's honor and desiring to avoid a scandal, Arthur let

Morgan off with a stern warning.

Expressing regret but enraged at the humiliation, Morgan plotted revenge. One summer afternoon, Arthur was hunting deer and in the hills beyond Camelot became separated from his men. From a riverbank he saw anchored a glimmering crystal boat with silken sails that floated toward him. Arthur stepped aboard. All afternoon and night the floating jewel moved downriver, sails fluttering with breezes from another world. Arthur slept. When he awoke, he was in a foul prison.

The prisoner would only be freed, he was told, by winning a duel. Arthur agreed, and from a messenger secretly sent by Morgan received a sword fashioned to look like Excalibur, his own magical weapon that could defeat any foe, and his shield with healing powers.

The king's sword felt strangely heavy and lifeless, but the knight's sword flashed with fire, cutting through Arthur's mail. Covered with blood, Arthur fought on, receiving cut after cut and wielding his useless sword as a club until his foe staggered dizzily. Two hours passed and the fight raged, both combatants near death, neither yielding.

Suddenly the battle was interrupted by a tall, pale woman of fairy origin. In a "high voice as chill as the waters of a mountain lake" she cried that the knight had Excalibur and the king had a blunt forged sword. Magically, Excalibur and the shield were restored to the rightful hands. With the shield Arthur's wounds were healed and with the sword he immediately overcame his adversary. The knight confessed that Morgan le Fay had given him Excalibur, and Arthur spared the brave man's life.

More tricks followed, each more diabolical that the last, but none that could prevail over Arthur, even more powerful than his sister and equally clever. Finally, one winter afternoon, when snow lay thick over Camelot and the howling of wolves echoed in the forest, a messenger arrived from Morgana—a comely young woman, so shy her voice could scarcely be heard.

"Your sister sends greetings, lord," she whispered "She desires that you take this gift, and she promises that in whatever way she has offended you, she will make amends in what fashion you demand."

"Does she so?" said the High King. "Let us see the gift of peace."

The gift was a cloak of creamy wool with decorative border of silver and gold, exquisitely crafted, lightweight and warm. The woman said softly that Morgan had woven it

Arthur reached for the cloak and then paused.

"Maiden," he said, "I wish first to see it upon your shoulders." The rosy flush left the maiden's cheeks and she backed slowly away. "Lord, it is not seemly that I wear a king's garment."

"Nevertheless, wear it now," the king commanded.

Slowly the messenger swung the cloak around her shoulders and gave one cry only, a cry lost in an explosion of flames. Her hair rose in crackling threads, her face blackened and peeled, and the cloak's fire devoured her body until only a cluster of cinders showed where she had stood.

And the fiery finale is the last we hear of Morgan le Fay, who faded into retreat far from the haunts of men and almost forgotten by tellers of old tales and singers of old songs.

BARBARA STACY

Arthur Rackham

THREE SPINNERS

Greek and Norse mythology portray fate in precisely the same way—as three wise women spinning the thread of life.

The Greek conception is as clear and bright as sunshine. The Three Fates are robed in white: Clotho holds the spindle, Lachesis measures the distribution of chance, and Atropos, "she who cannot be avoided," carries the shears with which she cuts life's thread when death comes. The Fates, *Moirae* in Greek, *Parcae* in Latin, are the spirits of birth, who, according to Hesiod, give us evil and good to have. As daughters of Night and Erebus (son of Chaos and a personification of darkness), the Three Fates represent a triumph of light, reason, and order. To call upon the Fates in time of trouble was to desire a possible thing by the will of a sound mind.

In Germanic and Scandinavian traditions the Fates are called the Norns, a far more complex and mysterious trio. As in Arthur Rackham's illustration for Wagner's *Der Ring des Nibelungen*, shown above, they sit at the foot of the sacred ash-tree known as Yggdrasil whose roots, trunk, and branches bind together the universe. The Icelandic *Elder Edda* names the Three Norns as Urda, the Past; Verandi, the Pres-

CLOTHO.   LACHESIS.   ATROPOS.

MŒRÆ, OR THE FATES.

ent; and Skuld, the Future. They guard Urda's wondrous spring of white water from which they nourish the roots of the Tree of Life. As weavers of fate and mistresses of life and death, they assign to us our good or ill fortune. The Norse myths define the darker aspects of life on Earth, for the World Tree is constantly threatened by an evil serpent that gnaws on the tree's roots. In this perilous situation there is no security, only a delicate balance to be maintained with courage, hope, patience, and chance.

As England became Christianized, the new God's greatest rival was Wyrd, the Anglo-Saxon pagan goddess of destiny. Her disciples, the "field-spinners," were chiefly concerned with divination and giving counsel. The thread of life they held was called *cleowen*, Anglo-Saxon for ball of yarn, from which is derived our English word "clue" or "that which guides in any doubtful or intricate matter."

Modern Witches are the true spiritual descendants of these legendary spinners of long ago, for we can successfully shift a negative pattern, boldly add a ray of hope, and with a light heart, capture good luck as it flies over the web of time.

THE SISTRUM

Egyptian priestesses shook the sistra in religious rites and processions from earliest times. The musical instrument, oval like the lunar orbit, must have been considered magical in and of itself, for the Egyptians made tiny replicas to serve as amulets. Always associated with women, the sistrum became an integral element in the worship of Isis, but never her primary symbol.

A change occurred when the cult of Isis was transplanted to Greece and Rome. There the goddess was always portrayed carrying the sistrum in her right hand, and the sacred instrument assumed a deeper significance. Plutarch, the Greek essayist, writing around the turn of the Christian era described its power:

"The sistrum shows that whatever exists ought to be shaken and never cease from movement, but should be aroused and agitated as if it were asleep and its life quenched. For they say that by the sistrum they drove Typhon away; by this they set forth that destruction binds and halts, but by means of movement generation frees nature."

His reference to Typhon, the monster of Greek myth, alludes to warfare and explosive behavior. Volcanic eruptions which from time to time rocked the region possibly shaped the fearsome character of Typhon. And his nature was not only related to volcanic activity and hot winds, but also to bad dreams, rape, and brutal inclinations.

Early in this century, Elizabeth E. Goldsmith, in her study *Life Symbols*, (G.P. Putnam's Sons, 1924), observed:

"Isis the immortal, the goddess of life, the eternal feminine has many symbols, but only one weapon, one instrument to play upon when she wants to change conditions, to startle us into consciousness, to make us see the meaning of our habitual acceptances, and that's the sistrum- an instrument that now as ever is a particularly valuable feminine adjunct."

While gentle distraction or unexpected action may often ward off violence, it is the decision to no longer tolerate outrageous conduct that is the true message of the sistrum.

Greco-Roman priestess of Isis

EGYPTIAN JUDGMENT

The Pyramid Texts, discovered just over a century ago, form the oldest body of literature to survive from the ancient world. Some fragments date from before 3400 B.C. Variants of the earliest writings transcribed in later centuries have come to be known collectively as the Book of the Dead. Over the passage of thousands of years, one theme remained constant—of all virtues none ranks higher than truth.

The ancient Egyptians enjoyed life and aspired to repeat the experience after death. Sacred texts were guidebooks for the soul's journey from death to renewal. Their cheerful title for the mortuary manuals was the *Book of Coming Forth by Day*.

Perhaps the most characteristic ceremony described in the Book of the Dead, is the weighing of the heart, symbol of the conscience. The drawing above is a detail from the Papyrus of Ani, a scribe who lived about 1350 B.C. The scene takes place in the Hall of Maat, goddess of Truth, whose emblem is the ostrich feather.

The deceased Ani stands expectantly at the far left as his heart is weighed against Truth, in the form of Maat's feather. Two goddesses identified as Meskhenet and Renenet stand between Ani and his soul, the man-headed bird called the Ba. The goddesses are witness to Ani's goodness, for they have watched over him. The figure closest to the scale is the god Shai, whose name means Destiny. Shai, according to Egyptologist E. A. Wallis Budge, is more "likely to be Ani's guardian spirit, perhaps even the spirit of his father, whose presence testifies to the gods that Ani is supported by his counsellor and protector of his family in spirit-land". Budge cannot say exactly what the box with the human head shown above Shai represents, but suggests that it may depict the deceased in an embryonic state.

The jackal-headed Anubis kneels on the other side of the scale as he supervises its balance. Behind him stands Thoth, the ibis-headed god of wisdom, ready to record the result. The baboon perched on top of the standard, an associate of Thoth, makes sure that all is correct.

As we can see, the trial goes well for Ani, because his heart is determined to be as light as a feather.

Circle of Fire

Have you ever been momentarily overwhelmed by a feeling of hopelessness? Heed the warning and look to your enemies. A strong possibility exists that you have been ill-wished, "overlooked" as the elders would say. Witches are commonly blamed for casting evil spells, but in truth very few indeed care to risk a Three-Fold Return. This conviction that a curse sent forth will return thrice to haunt you is a doctrine bred in the bone and one as old as the craft itself.

Keep in mind that psychic attack is often the work of an amateur with latent power enlivened by envy or rage. Hate is a strong motivation and a sharp weapon. However, a malevolent thrust from the mind of a novice is over in a flash. An untrained will cannot sustain the proper degree of concentration needed to do real harm. Nonetheless, it is only wise to identify the perpetrator and protect yourself from further negativity.

Visit the ocean (or any free-flowing body of water) to fortify confidence with an ancient Irish pagan prayer.

I bind to myself this day
The swiftness of the wind,
The power of the sea,
The hardness of rocks,
The endurance of the earth.

Cense the air of your home to purify the space and comfort the spirit under siege. Frankincense and myrrh are incenses notable for driving away the forces of evil intent.

Of all the earth's herbal gifts, none affords more effective protection than rue, the "herb of grace." Hang a fresh bunch over your doorway and carry a dried sprig to shield against harm from the ill-wisher.

One of the simplest means to defeat psychic attack is the Circle of Fire.

In privacy and complete darkness, light a candle. Take a deep breath and stand as tall as you can. Face east and raise the candle high above your head for a moment. Bring the flame down to eye-level and hold it there while you turn slowly in a right-hand circle three times. Concentrate your full attention on the blue of the flame as you rotate in place. Raising the candle high again, salute the east as you complete the final circle. This erects a barrier through which no evil thought can pass.

❋❋❋❋❋❋❋❋❋❋❋❋❋
FOLK PROVERBS

Birds of prey do not sing.

-GERMAN

Live with wolves and you will learn how to howl.

-SPANISH

A fox should not be of the jury at a goose's trial.

-ENGLISH

No one ever saw a goat dead of hunger.

-FRENCH

When a dove begins to associate with crows its feathers remain white but its heart grows black.

GERMAN

Speak of the wolf, and you will see his tail.

-FRENCH

It is a sorry bird that fouls its own nest.

-GERMAN

Fine words do not feed cats.

-ITALIAN

Eagles fly alone; sheep flock together.

-SPANISH

We are all living upon a frog's back, and some day the frog will jump.

-JAPANESE

Going to the law is losing a cow for the sake of a cat.

-CHINESE

It is better to live one day as a lion than a hundred years as a sheep.

-ITALIAN

Contempt penetrates even the shell of the tortoise.

-PERSIAN

It's a bold mouse that nestles in the cat's ear.

-ENGLISH

Death rides a fast camel.

ARABIC

THE CELTIC TREE CALENDAR

Beth (Birch)   December 24 to January 20

Luis (Rowan)   January 21 to February 17

Nion (Ash)   February 18 to March 17

Fearn (Alder)   March 18 to April 14

Saille (Willow) April 15 to May 12

Uath (Hawthorn) May 13 to June 9

Duir (Oak)   June 10 to July 7

Tinne (Holly) July 8 to August 4

Coll (Hazel)   August 5 to September 1

Muin (Vine)   September 2 to September 29

Gort (Ivy)   September 30 to October 27

Ngetal (Reed)   October 28 to November 24

Ruis (Elder)   November 25 to December 22

December 23 is not ruled by any tree for it is the "day" of the proverbial "year and day" in the earliest courts of law.

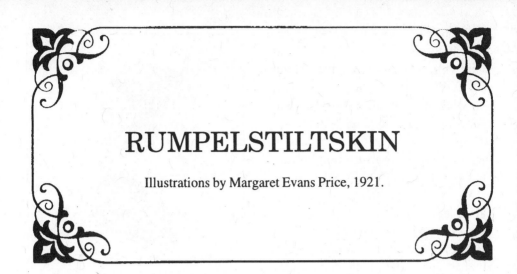

RUMPELSTILTSKIN

Illustrations by Margaret Evans Price, 1921.

THERE was once upon a time a poor miller who had a beautiful daughter. Now it happened one day that he had an audience with the King, and in order to make himself seem important, he said, "I have a daughter who can spin straw into gold."

The King said to the miller, "That's an art that interests me. If your daughter is as skilled as you say, bring her to my castle tomorrow, and I'll put her to the test."

When the girl was brought to him, the King conducted her to a chamber full of straw, gave her a spinning wheel and spindle, and said, "Now set to work. You have the night, and if by tomorrow at dawn you have not spun this straw into gold, you must die." With that, he locked the door of the chamber, and left her alone inside.

There sat the poor miller's daughter, and didn't know what in the world she was to do. She had not the least idea how to spin straw into gold, and she became more and more distressed until at last she began to weep. Then all at once the door sprang open, and in stepped a little man who said, "Good evening, miller's daughter, why are you crying so hard?" "Oh," answered the girl, "I'm supposed to spin straw into gold, and I don't know how to do it." The little man said, "What will you give me if I spin it for you?" "My necklace," said the girl.

The little man took the necklace, sat down before the spinning wheel, and whir, whir, whir, in a trice the bobbin was full. Then he put on another, and whir, whir, whir, the wheel went round three times, and the second was full. And so it went on till morning, when all the straw was spun and all the bobbins were full of gold.

As soon as the sun rose the King came, and when he saw all the gold he was astonished and delighted, but his heart lusted all the more after gold. He had the miller's daughter taken to another room full of straw, much bigger than the first, and bade her to spin that too, in one night, if she valued her life. The girl didn't know what to do, and she was weeping when the door opened as before and the little man appeared and asked, "What will you give me if spin the straw into gold for you?" "The ring on my finger," answered the girl. The little man took the ring, began to whir again at the wheel, and by dawn he had spun all the straw into glittering gold.

The King was overjoyed at the sight, but his greed for gold was still not satisfied. So he had the miller's daughter taken to an even larger chamber full of straw and said, "You still have to spin all of this tonight; but if you succeed you shall become my wife." "She's only a miller's daughter, it's true," he thought, "but I'd never find a richer woman if I were to search the whole world over."

When the girl was alone the little man came for the third time and said, "What will you give me if spin the straw for you this time?" "I've

nothing more to give," answered the girl. "Then promise me your first child if you become Queen."

"Who knows what might happen?" thought the miller's daughter, and, besides, she did not see any other way out of her difficulty. She promised the little man what he demanded, and in return he spun the straw into gold once more. When the King came in the morning and found that everything had gone as he desired, he married her, and the miller's beautiful daughter became a Queen.

When a year had passed a fine son was born to her, but the Queen had forgotten all about the little man when he suddenly entered her chamber and said, "Now give me what you promised." The Queen was terrified and offered the little man all the riches of the kingdom if he would let her keep her child. But the little man said, "No, I would rather have a living creature than all the treasures of the world."

Then the Queen began to moan and weep to such an extent that the little man was sorry for her. "I will give you three days," said he, "and if within that time you can guess my name you may keep the child."

Now the Queen pondered all night long over all the names she had ever heard, and sent a messenger all over the country to inquire far and wide what other names there were. When the little man arrived the following day, she began with Casper, Melchior, and Balthazar, and all the names she knew, one after another. But after each one, the little man said, "That's not my name." The second day she had inquiries made all round the neighborhood for the names of people living there, and suggested to the little man all the most unusual and strange names—Cowribs, Spindleshanks, Bootlacebut his answer was always: "That's not my name."

On the third day the messenger returned and announced, "I've not found any new names, but as I was passing the corner of a wood near a high hill, where the fox says good night to the hare, I saw a little house, and in the front of the house burned a fire, and round the fire an odd little man was hopping about on one leg and singing:

Tomorrow I brew, today I bake,
And then the child away I'll take;
For little deems my royal dame
That Rumpelstiltskin is my name!

You can imagine the Queen's delight at hearing the name, and when the little man arrived shortly afterwards and asked, "Now, my lady Queen, what is my name?" She asked first: "Is your name Conrad?" "No." "Is your name Hal?" "No." "Is your name, perhaps, Rumpelstiltskin?"

"The fairies told you that, the fairies told you that!" shrieked the little man, and in his rage he stamped his right foot into the ground so hard that it sank up to his waist; then in a passion he seized his left leg with both hands and tore himself in two.

–THE BROTHERS GRIMM, 1812.

The Moon and the Weather

Pale Moon doth rain,
Red Moon doth blow,
White Moon doth neither
Rain nor snow.

Clear Moon, frost soon.

A dark mist over the Moon
is a promise of rain.

The heaviest rains fall
following the New and the
Full Moons.

The Full Moon eats the
clouds away.

A New Moon and a windy night
Sweep the cobwebs out of sight.

A Red Moon is a sure sign of
high winds.

And should the Moon wear a halo
of red, a tempest is nigh.

Many rings around the Moon
signal a series of severe
blasts.

A single ring around the
Moon that quickly vanishes
heralds fine weather.

When the New Moon holds
the Old Moon in its arms
(ring around the New Moon)
disasters at sea occur.

Sharp horns on the Sickle
Moon indicate strong winds.

When the moon's horns point up,
the weather will be dry.

When the Moon's horns point
down, rain spills forth.

Blunt horns on a Crescent
Moon presage a long spell
of fair weather.

GOAT SONG

Since the dawn of time, the goat has held divine significance in many cultures. The sacred robes of Babylonian priests were made of goatskins. The zodiacal Capricorn with head and body of a goat and a fish's tail, was established as early as the 15th century B.C.; the Sea Goat appears engraved on gems dated to the height of Chaldean rule in Babylon. A cuneiform inscription calls the goat "sacred and exalted,"- and at that time this sign was designated as the "Father of Light." Despite the glory the goat enjoyed among the ancients, its present reputation as a symbol of lust and evil is due to the devil-lore devised by medieval churchmen.

Perhaps the goat's character as loathsome and unclean began when the early Hebrews chose it as the animal to carry away the sins of the community in an annual rite of atonement. The hapless scapegoat was driven into the wilderness to perish bearing all the blame for crimes committed by others.

How wildly different is the ancient Greek symbolism regarding the same animal. Associated with the gods Dionysus and Pan, the goat represented the pure, spontaneous joy of being alive. The great god Zeus was nurtured by the she-goat Amalthea. Her name is given to the mythical Horn of Plenty, the cornucopia promising its possessor an abundance of all things desired.

We owe the art of drama to the music and dance celebrations honoring Dionysus. The goat and the god were one-the essence of high spirits and joyful abandon. The chorus and dancers wore goatskins and the rites were performed in an orderly manner until a singer named Thespis broke the rules and began a dispute with the choral leader. His action established dialogue and ever after the religious rituals were plays, for the unexpected is in the very nature of the god himself. Thespian became another word for actor. The highest form of drama, the tragedy, means goat song in Greek.

In northern Europe, the goat was revered for its playful nature, a nature firmly ruled by discipline. The love goddess of Germanic tribes rode a goat to the May Eve revels. She held an apple to her lips, a hound and a hare ran beside her and a raven flew overhead. Thor, the red-headed Norse god of thunder, drove a chariot drawn by two fierce goats. Both god and goddess were in complete control of their animals.

The Greeks warn us that when we deny the wildness in human nature, we court disaster. The message from the North is just as wise: we should acknowledge the wildness, use it to advantage, and learn to temper its force with strength and understanding.

THE ROWAN TREE

So potent is the flower or berry or wood of the rowan or witchwood or quicken or whicken-tree or mountain ash against the wiles of the elf-folk, that dairymaids use it for cream-stirrers and cowherds for a switch.

WALTER DE LA MARE

The bright red berries of the mountain ash give this tree its Scottish name "rowan" from the Gaelic *rudha-an*, the red one. An older and more romantic name is *luisliu*, flame or delight of the eye. The scarlet berries also account for its growing high on mountains along with the birch, for birds feast on the berries and drop seeds in crevices at altitudes as high as 3000 feet where the tree springs up and flourishes. Although the most common name for the rowan is mountain ash, it has no botanical relation to the true ash save for a resemblance in its smooth grey bark and graceful ascending branches. Other names for the rowan are whitebeam, quicken and witch-wood, the later possibly deriving from the Anglo-Saxon root *wic*, meaning pliable.

Scandinavian myths assign the rowan to Thor, god of thunder. All across northern Europe it was the custom to plant rowan trees near farm buildings to gain the favor of Thor and insure safety for stored crops and animals from storm damage. A necklace of rowan beads enlivened

Daleschamps   Lyons, 1586.

the wearer and twigs were carried as protective charms.

Rowan figures prominently in Scottish folklore as a sure means to counteract evil intent. It was believed that a christened person need only touch a suspected witch with rowan wood in order to break a spell as the poet Allan Ramsay wrote:

Rowan tree and red thread,
Will put witches to their speed.

Yet, a century earlier, in the case of Margaret Barclay, such a charm was damning evidence. Brought to trial for witchcraft in the town of Irvine, Ayrshire, Scotland in 1618, her conviction was assured when a piece of rowan tied with red yarn was found in her possession.

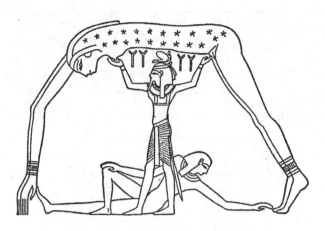

EARTH, WIND AND SKY

The ancient Egyptian conception of the world is illustrated above. The goddess of the heavens, her body decorated with stars, spans the sky vault supported by four pillars and the god of air. The earth god is prone below. Egyptian cosmogony differed from that of most other cultures in perceiving the earth as male. The Egyptologist, E.A. Wallis Budge, described the qualities of the deities in Egyptian Religion (London, 1899):

SHU, son of Ra and Hathor, was the personification of sunlight, air, and wind. He it was who made his way between the gods Seb and Nut and raised up the latter to form the sky, and this belief is commemorated by the figures of this god in which he is represented as a god raising himself up from the earth with the sun's disk on his shoulders. As a power of nature he typified the light, and, standing on the top of a staircase, he raised up the sky and held it up during each day. To assist him in this work he placed a pillar at each of the cardinal points, and the "supports of Shu" are thus the props of the sky.

SEB was the son of Shu, and the "father of the gods," these being Osiris, Isis, Set, and Nephthys. He was originally the god of the earth, but later he became a god of the dead as representing the earth wherein the deceased was laid. One legend identifies him with the goose, the bird which in later times was sacred to him, and he is often called the "Great Cackler," in allusion to the idea that he made the primeval egg from which the world came into being.

NUT was the wife of Seb and the mother of Osiris, Isis, Set, and Nephthys. Originally she was the personification of the sky, and represented the feminine principle which was active at the creation of the universe. According to the old view, Seb and Nut existed in the primeval watery abyss…and later Seb became the earth and Nut the sky. These deities were supposed to unite every evening, and to remain embraced until the morning, when the god Shu separated them, and set the goddess of the sky upon his four pillars until the evening. Nut was, naturally, regarded as the mother of the gods and of all things living.

The Unicorn and the Maiden

Unicornis the Unicorn, which is also called Rhinoceros by the Greeks, is of the following nature. He is a very small animal like a kid, excessively swift, with one horn in the middle of his forehead, and no hunter can catch him. But he can be trapped by the following stratagem.

A virgin girl is led to where he lurks, and there she is sent off by herself into the wood. He soon leaps into her lap when he sees her, and embraces her, and hence he gets caught.

From A Latin *Bestiary*, 12Th Century.

Diana and the Date Palm Tree

In ancient days when the Amazons, a mythic race of women warriors, ruled in Asia Minor, a meteorite fell from outer space and struck a date palm tree. The tree became an object of worship, for the Amazons believed the spirit of their goddess had come to reside there.

After the Greeks had defeated the Amazons, occupied their territory, and founded the city of Ephesus, somehow the site of the date palm retained its sacred nature. There the Greeks built a shrine to honor the goddess, for they identified the Amazonian deity with their own Artemis, virgin goddess of the hunt. Centuries passed and the simple shrine evolved into a mighty temple considered the most impressive of the Seven Wonders of the World. Under Roman rule, Ephesus became one of the largest cities of the ancient world and Artemis, its patron goddess, came to be known by her Roman name, Diana.

As the Christian sect arose, St. Paul's missionary efforts were thwarted in Ephesus and the New Testament records his encounter with the local silversmiths. The apostle's preaching threatened their livelihood—making silver replicas of Diana's statue for sale to the thousands of pilgrims who came to honor her. Paul was soundly defeated on this occasion and forced to flee the city. Future historians would take cruel revenge.

The graceful figure of a "huntress, chaste and fair," protectress of youth and wild creatures, was and is to the present day denounced as an erotic monster, a demon fertility goddess of Asiatic origin. St. Jerome (c. 340–420) may have been the first of many to declare Diana was *multimammia*, having many breasts. He was mistaken. Compare the date palm tree with the statue of Diana. It is clear that the "breasts" are a decoration of fruit—a memory, if you will, of the original tree that inspired the sculptor's figure.

The Dancing Deaths.   Nuremburg, 1493.

DANSE MACABRE

Zig, ziz, zig, death in grim cadence
Strikes with bony heel upon the tomb.
Death at midnight hour plays a dance.
Zig, ziz, zig upon his violin.
The winter winds blow, the night is dark,
Moans are heard through the linden trees.
Through the gloom the white skeletons run,
Leaping and dancing in their shrouds.
Zig, ziz, zig, each one is gay.
Their bones are cracking in rhythmic time,
Then suddenly they cease the dance.
The cock has crowed! The dawn has come.

-HENRI CAZALIS (1840-1909)

The poem recounts an old medieval legend of the dance of the skeletons, and inspired French composer Camille Saint-Saëns to write his symphonic poem, *Danse Macabre.* Twelve strokes of the harp announce midnight. Death tunes his fiddle. The dance begins with the rattling of skeleton's bones, provided by the xylophone to the eerie accompaniment of violins. A waltz version of the *Dies Irae* , or old Latin Hymn for the Dead, becomes increasingly wilder until the cock crows, in the voice of the oboe, heralding dawn. The ghostly revelers must return to their tombs.

APOLLO

Of Apollo we sing, the Brilliant One, god of sunlight, god of music.

And more glittering powers, as complex and multiple as any deity commanded on Mt. Olympus. He was the god of poetry and dance, painting and sculpture, science and philosophy, the protector of cities and colonies, herds and flocks. The god of youth, Apollo was depicted with golden curls and ravishing androgynous beauty, usually with a lyre and often with arrows as patron of hunters.

And perhaps most important, the god of prophecy. His most celebrated shrine, one of the mightiest Greek sanctuaries, was at Delphi, sited in a deep cavern from which "emanated prophetic vapors," according to one source.

Accounts of the sanctuary echo down the ages, notable in both myth and history. The most bizarre myth—that the center of this was the *axis mundi*, the center of the world. At this site rested a large circular netlike relic, the "naval stone" or *omphalos*, flanked by two golden eagles. The birds alluded to the belief that Zeus had marked the midpoint by releasing the eagles from opposite ends of the earth and signifying where beak met beak.

The relic was guarded by Pytho, a monstrous serpent terrorizing the countryside. Apollo slew Pytho—a

Greek version of the universal hero/dragon myth—and purified himself from the kill by nine years of exile. Upon his return, Apollo established the site as his own sanctuary and installed a prophetic high priestess, the ambiguous Delphic oracle.

That's one story. Another claims that Apollo took over the Delphic cult and its priestesses, the Sybils, from his grandmother Phoebe, the Shining One, third in succession of the female deities to have oracles at the cavern. Feminists focus on this version, according as it does with the historical argument that a patriarchal culture engulfed an earlier goddess-centered religion, now lost.

The Delphic high-priestess, known as the Pythia, sat on a tall three legged stool and answered visitors' questions. Predictions flew from her mouth in a frenzy of ravings the Greeks believed were divinely inspired prophesies, although often not readily understood. The location was further memorialized by the Pythiads in Apollo's honor, great athletic games held every four years.

Such a magnificent god implies magnificent lineage, and indeed he had. Mighty Zeus himself was Apollo's father, his mother the Titaness Leto. He was born on the island of Delos, twin to the revered Artemis, goddess of the hunt and as associated with the Moon as Apollo was with the Sun. High magic attended at their very birth, for moments after Artemis emerged from the womb she helped her mother give birth to Apollo. The twins remained close companions, often hunting together with their enchanted golden bows and attended by nymphs required to be virgins.

Apollo's lyre was also golden, and from its strings emerged ravishing harmonies. On occasion his musicianship was challenged, and he exacted horrendous penalties for such hubris. When the satyr Marsyas dared to suggest a musical contest, flute against lyre, Apollo handily won—and flayed Marsyas alive for his presumption. The god also engaged in a similar contest with Pan, pipes against lute, and again Apollo won. King Midas, who witnessed the event, dissented and declared that Pan's rustic airs were more

lovely. Apollo, appalled by such depraved taste, caused Midas to grow asses' ears.

The god had many loves, both male and female, but despite his radiance all affairs of the heart seemed to range from luckless to disastrous. Daphne was his first love, evoked by the malice of Cupid. When Apollo saw the son of Venus playing with arrows, he rebuked the child for playing with warlike weapons. Cupid responded by drawing from his quiver two arrows, a gold one to excite love, a lead one to repel it. With the gold arrow he shot Apollo through the heart; with the other, he shot the nymph Daphne.

Apollo pleaded for her love, but she took flight—and even as she fled, she charmed him. "The wind blew her garments, and her unbound hair streamed loose behind her," the mythologist Bullfinch assures us. "So flew the god and the virgin, he on the wings of love, and she on those of fear." In a panic, Daphne called upon her father, a river god, to save her. "Scarcely

had she spoken when a stiffness seized all her limbs; her bosom began to be enclosed in a tender bark; her hair became leaves; her arms became branches; her foot stuck fast in the ground, as a root; her face became a tree-top." The nymph had been changed into a laurel tree, and Apollo, amazed, kissed the bark tenderly. He declared that forever the laurel would be sacred, honored as his crown and as a wreath for heroes. The story inspired a festival, the Daphnephoria or "bringing the laurel," featuring sprigs of the tree in initiation rites for young men "dressed as Apollo"—that is, nude.

As for male lovers, Apollo was most passionate about Hyacinthus. The two were inseparable, and for the beautiful youth Apollo neglected his arrows and his lyre. One day they played quoits, and Apollo heaved the discus high and far. Hyacinthus, excited with the sport, ran forward to seize it, eager to make his own throw. The discus struck him on the forehead and he fell. Apollo struggled to staunch the flow of blood, but the wounded youth's life flickered away, even beyond the skill of the god of healing. Apollo was devastated and swore that Hyacinthus would remain alive in story and song. "My lyre shall celebrate thee, my song shall tell thy fate, and thou shalt become a flower." When Apollo spoke, the blood on the ground beneath the youth's head ceased to be blood, but flowers that return every spring to remind us of Apollo's beloved.

The cult of Apollo at Delphi had an amazingly long run. Historians believe that it was established by the 8th century B.C., but may have been much older. Prophesies flowed from the site until 394 A.D., when the Roman Christian emperor Theodosius the Great shut it down.

Today an ancient replica of the original improbable naval stone rests in a museum at Delphi, a wrinkled reminder of over a thousand years of Apollonian sacrament and eerie glory.

—BARBARA STACY

At Delphi in 1893, French archaeologists unearthed two large marble tablets. A hymn to Apollo, composed in 278 B.C., was engraved on them:

> *I will sing in praise of thee,*
> *glorious son of Zeus!*
> *Who dwellest on the snowy peak of the hill,*
> *where in sacred oracles to mortal men*
> *Thou dost proclaim tidings prophetic,*
> *from the divine tripodic seat.*
> *Thou hast driven forth from his place*
> *the dragon who watched over the shrine,*
> *And, with thy darts, hast forced him to hide*
> *far in the dark underwood.*
>
> *Muses come from deeply wooded Helicon,*
> *Beautiful fair-armed daughters of the*
> *loud-singing god, dwelling there;*
> *Praising their noble kinsman, even Phoebus,*
> *with golden hair,*
> *To the lyre they sing their songs.*
> *He hovers o'er the twin-headed peak of*
> *Parnasse, and he haunts the rocky places,*
> *Round about famous Delphi and Castalia's*
> *plentiful springs, full of waters deep and clear,*
> *And presides o'er Delphi with its oracle*
> *true in prophecy.*

The Wind　　　　　Philip Hagreen, 1921

WIND SONG

Wind and Witchcraft are akin. Witch lore records the tale of a medieval Finnish Witch who sold wind to becalmed sailors bound up in three knots of rope. The first knot unloosed a gentle breeze; the second brought forth a gale; the third, a tempest. Estonian Witches were said to thrust a knife into a block of wood from the direction they wished a wind to blow.

In Scotland the Witch, with proper ceremony, could raise the wind by dipping a rag in a fast-moving brook and then beating it three times on a square stone while chanting:

Upon this stone I knock a rag
To raise the wind in the Lady's name,
It shall not lie or cease or die
Until I please again.

English Witches could whistle up the wind. In the first light of dawn, facing the point of the compass from which they wished the wind to come, they would summon it with three long, clear whistles blown between the first and fourth fingers of the right hand.

There's a magic moment when Witches first realize—know beyond a shadow of a doubt—that they belong to the Craft. Many say their calling came as a voice in the wind.

Among Aradia's gifts of power to the Witch, as recounted in Charles G. Leland's translation of the *Vangelo della-Streghe*, or *Gospel of the Witches*, is the ability to understand the voice of the wind. The symbolic meaning is clear. The motion of human affairs—thoughts, opinions, values— are like the winds: they rise, shift, fall, back and veer; they prevail for a while, freshen into gales only to die again. Change alone endures, and change is the essence of Witchcraft.

Casting a spell or making a wish initiates change. When ritual is matched to nature in the form of the winds, the chances of success are markedly increased. There's a wind for every purpose under the sun.

The EAST WIND belongs to new ventures and blesses ambition with energy. Call upon it for courage, patience, and clarity.

The SOUTH WIND favors love, imagination and fulfillment. Use it in love enchantments and to achieve harmony in close relationships.

The WEST WIND erases doubt, guilt, fear, envy and hate. It will renew confidence and restore hope.

The NORTH WIND brings with it wisdom. It transcends the other winds as a source of spiritual strength. It protects and increases intuition and divinatory power.

Hel, Goddess of Death   Johannes Gehrts, 1883

Daughter of Darkness

The Scandinavian goddess Hel made her home beneath the first root of Yggdrasil, the giant ash tree that held the world together. Guarded by her faithful dog, Garmr, Hel ruled the icycold underworld of Nifelheim. In early Norse myths all dead souls either spent their afterlife in burial mounds watched over by attendants or joined Hel in her murky domain. Later legends rewarded heroes slain in battle with new life in the glorious halls of Valhalla.

Like the Greek god of the underworld, Hades, whose name and home were the same words, Hel gives us our English word "hell" from an Old Norse root meaning "covered" or "concealed." Hel's world was gloomy, but not a place of torment as penalty for earthly sins. Occasional visits occurred from the fierce wolf, Fenrir, and the serpent, Jormungard, for they were Hel's kin. All three were fathered by Loki, the handsome, sly, and dangerous god whose actions would, an oracle declared, eventually bring the downfall of the gods and victory of chaos as the world ends.

JANUS

January was named for Janus, the porter or janitor of heaven. He was the guardian deity of gateways, depicted as having two opposite faces, because every door looks two ways. Janus was a concept unknown to the Greeks, but from earliest times one held in high esteem by the Romans, who placed him on almost equal footing with Jupiter. The aid of both gods was invoked prior to every undertaking. To Janus the Romans ascribed the origin of all things: the change of seasons, the ups and downs of fortune, and the civilization of the human race by means of agriculture, arts, and religion. The heads of Janus are crowned with a crescent Moon, the form of the waxing and waning Moons. He holds a key in his left hand to show it is within his power to unlock the future as well as lock away the past. The scepter in his right hand symbolizes his control of the progress of all undertakings. The public worship of Janus was introduced into Rome during the time of Numa Polllpilius (715-672 B. C.), but it seems likely that his conception as a deity is as old as the Rome of Romulus.

Rapunzel   H. J. Ford, 1889

RAPUNZEL

Once upon a time there lived a man and his wife who for a long time had wished in vain for a child, and at last the woman had reason to believe that heaven would grant her wish. There was a little window at the back of their house, which overlooked a splendid garden full of all manner of beautiful flowers and vegetables. It was, however, surrounded by a high wall, and no one dared to enter it, for it belonged to a sorceress of great power who was feared by everybody.

One day the woman, standing at her window and looking down into the garden, saw there a bed planted with the most beautiful rampion. They looked so fresh and green that she longed to eat them. The desire increased day by day, and because she knew that she could not have any, she pined away and became quite pale and miserable. Then her husband grew alarmed and said, "What ails you, dear wife?"

"Oh," she said, "if I don't get some rampion to eat from the garden behind our house, I shall die." Her husband, who loved her dearly, thought to himself, before you let your wife die you must fetch her some of that rampion, cost what it may. So at twilight he climbed over the wall into the forbidden garden, hastily gathered some rampion leaves and returned with them to his wife. She immediately prepared a salad and ate it with great relish. It tasted so good that the next day her longing for it increased three-fold. If she were to know any peace of mind, there was nothing for it but that her husband should climb over the garden wall again and fetch her some more. So at dusk he returned, but as he climbed over the wall he was terrified to see the witch standing before him. "How dare you," she said as she angrily glared, "climb into my garden and steal my rampion like a thief? You shall suffer the consequences."

"Alas!" he answered, "temper justice with mercy. I am only here by necessity. My wife sees your rampion from our window, and she has such a longing for it that she will die without it." The anger of Mother Gothel, for that was the name by which she was known, cooled a little and she said to him, "If it is as you say, you may take as much rampion as you like, but on one condition only—that you give me the child that your wife is about to bring into this world. All will be well with it, and I will give it a mother's care." The man in his terror agreed to everything she asked. And when the child was born, the enchantress appeared, named the baby Rapunzel, which is the German word for rampion, and took the child away with her.

Rapunzel was the most beautiful child under the sun. When she was twelve years old, the witch shut her up in a tower which stood in a forest. It had neither stairs nor doors, but only high up at the very top a small window. When the witch wanted to get in she stood below and called:

"Rapunzel, Rapunzel,
Let down your hair. "

Rapunzel had splendid long hair, as fine as spun gold. When she heard Mother Gothel's voice, she would undo her braids and wind them around a window hook. Then her hair would drop about twenty yards to the ground, and the witch would climb up by it.

After several years it happened that the king's son was riding through the forest and passed by the tower. As he drew near it he heard someone singing so sweetly that he stopped to listen. It was Rapunzel, who in her loneliness passed the time singing to herself. The king's son longed to see the singer, and he sought for the door of the tower but there was none to find. He rode home,

but the song haunted his memory so much that he returned every day to the forest to listen. One day, when he was standing behind a tree, he saw the sorceress coming and heard her call:

"Rapunzel, Rapunzel,
Let down your hair. "

Then Rapunzel let down her braids, and the witch climbed up to her. If that is the ladder by which one ascends, he thought, I'll try my luck. And the following day, as darkness fell, he went to the tower and called:

"Rapunzel, Rapunzel,
Let down your hair. "

Right away the hair fell down and the prince climbed up it.

At first Rapunzel was terrified, for she had never set eyes on a man before. But the prince spoke to her so kindly, and told her that her song had touched his heart so deeply that he could find no peace of mind till he had seen her. Then Rapunzel

Rampion

lost her fear, and when the prince asked her to marry him she consented at once. She thought, he is young and handsome, and I'll certainly be happier with him than with my old godmother. So she put her hand in his and said, "Yes, I will gladly go with you, only how am I to get down from this tower? Each time you come, bring a skein of silk with you and I will twist it into a ladder, and when it is long enough I will descend by it, and you will take me away on your horse."

They arranged that he should come and see her every evening, for the old enchantress only came in the daytime. The old witch suspected nothing till one day Rapunzel said unthinkingly, "How is it, Mother Gothel, that you are so much harder to pull up than the young prince? He is always with me in a moment."

"Oh, you wicked child," cried the witch. "What are you saying? I thought I had shut you safely away from the whole world, and yet you have deceived me." In her rage she seized Rapunzel's beautiful hair, twisted it twice around her left hand, snatched up a pair of scissors with her right, and snip, snap, cut it off. The beautiful braids lay on the floor. And, worse than this, she was so heartless that she took Rapunzel to a wilderness, and there left her to live in great grief and misery.

In the evening of the day on which she had driven Rapunzel away, the sorceress fastened the braids to the window hook, and when the prince came and called out:

"Rapunzel, Rapunzel,
Let down your hair. "

She lowered the hair. The king's son climbed up as usual, but instead of finding his beloved Rapunzel, he found the witch, who glared at him with angry, glittering eyes.

"Aha," she cried mockingly, "you have come to fetch your lady love, but the pretty bird has flown . She sings no more, for the cat has seized her and will scratch your eyes out too. Rapunzel is lost to you. You will never see her again."

The prince was beside himself with grief, and in his despair he leaped from the tower. He escaped with his life, but his eyes were scratched out by the thorns among which he fell. He wandered, blind and miserable, through the forest, eating nothing but roots and berries, and weeping and lamenting over the loss of his lovely bride. So he wandered for several years in misery and happened at last upon the desert place where Rapunzel had been living in great poverty with the twins she had borne—a boy and a girl. He heard a voice which seemed strangely familiar to him and he went toward it, and when he approached, Rapunzel recognized him at once and fell on his neck and wept. Two of her tears fell upon his eyes, and they became quite clear again, and he saw as well as he had ever done. The prince took her to his kingdom, and they lived happily ever after.

A CATALOG

A collection of hard-to-find, quality items sure to be of interest to the serious practitioner. To obtain your copy of this full-color catalog, send $2 along with your name and address to:

Witchery
Post Office Box 4067
Middletown, Rhode Island, 02842

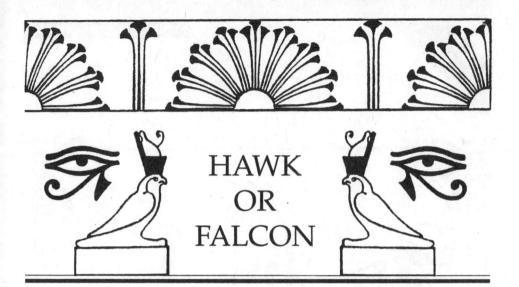

HAWK OR FALCON

THE SOARING flight of a hawk is one of nature's most thrilling sights. Early Egyptians, observing the bird's dominion of the airy realm, referred to the bird as "God of the Sky." They named the hawk Horus and worshipped him before the dynasties began, believing that this bird's quality defined a vision of all that was worthy of respect and devotion. His right eye represented the Sun; his left, the Moon; and the stars shone in his speckled plumage. Temple priests must have tamed and tended the wild birds, for they were depicted in ancient art perched on a block without tether, free to fly as they chose.

As the culture progressed, the sun god Ra evolved into the supreme

KHENSU, *the Moon*

HORUS, *the Sky*

RA, *the Sun*

Horus presents life and stability to Osiris

originated in China around 2000 B.C., spreading westward to India, Arabia, and Persia over a long passage of time. The returning Crusaders introduced the hunting tradition to Europe and the British Isles, where it found great favor within the royal courts.

The words "falcon" and "hawk" are used interchangeably, but in the sport of falconry sharper distinction is drawn. The hawk is short winged with bright yellow eyes; the falcon long winged with dark eyes. The bird favored by hunters is the female peregrine falcon. She is larger and more powerful than the male, as is the case with all the birds of this particular species.

deity. But the image of the hawk persisted in Ra's symbolic figure as a hawk-headed human wearing a sun disk on his head. The sky god Horus retained prestige by a mystical identification with royal power, and later artists added a pharaoh's crown to the hawk image.

Centuries passed and new legends bequeathed Horus to Isis and Osiris as their son, and over time the myth extended to portray the hawk god as the heroic avenger of his father. In Egypt, the hawk remained a spiritual presence in the sacred precincts of the temple, too revered a creature to be used for sport. The 5th-century B.C. Greek historian Herodotus visited Egypt and noted: "For killing a hawk, whether deliberately or not, the punishment is inevitably death." The hawk was the primary symbol of honor, dignity, and supremacy for over the three thousand years of ancient Egyptian culture.

Hunting with birds of prey

But it isn't necessarily the hunter going forth with a hooded bird on his gauntleted wrist who experiences the richest pleasure of falconry. That must belong to those who tame and train the noble birds. One can imagine a spiritual kinship existing between the temple priests of ancient Egypt and their medieval counterparts preparing the birds for the field. Even today, the art is practiced in isolated

123

Royal Hawking Party

Paris, 1493

regions where vast open countryside exists. Great patience, determination, and an intuitive gift are required to gain the trust and affection of wild creatures. This especially applies to hawks and falcons, by nature restless, moody birds. Long hours in darkened rooms, often late into the night, feeding and stroking the bird with a feather is the centuries old method of taming. Feather-stroking is essential; oil from human skin can disturb the bird's plumage by removing a natural protective coating. A quiet meditative state, slow movement and soft words calm the bird during the process. And the reward far outweighs the effort, for the quality of an established rapport between human and bird is intensely satisfying—more than that, inspiring. A hawk inspired an English poet when he sought a creature to match the character of his beloved.

Merry Margaret,
As midsummer flower,
Gentle as falcon
Or hawk of the tower.

-JOHN SKELTON
c. 1460-1529

The Pied Piper of Hameln

The Pied Piper of Hameln did actually exist. Although his visit to the little town in northwest Germany happened centuries ago, details are a little vague. Essentially, the tale is of a town that hired a flute-playing ratcatcher to rid the place of vermin and then declined to pay his fee. In revenge, the legend goes, the Piper returned to lure away the local childen with his siren song.

The Brothers Grimm, Goethe and Robert Browning have all immortalized the story which is depicted in a series of frescoes on the walls of a 16th-century house in Hameln. Every Sunday between mid-May and mid-September the legend is re-enacted on the outdoor terrace of the Hochzeithaus, a 380-year-old festival hall, with locals garbed in historical costumes playing the parts of councillors, citizens, children and rats.

Hameln was founded on the banks of the River Weser near the site of a 9th-century Benedictine abbey and was an important market town by the time the Pied Piper was hired to get rid of the rats which plagued the numerous grain mills. On the Piper's fatal return trip he supposedly enchanted 130 children with his playing, leading them to a hill south of town into which they disappeared forever.

The tale, known throughout the world, has been translated into dozens of languages and is even taught in the curriculum of some schools. According to legend, on the Piper's return wearing "a wondrous red hat," he sounded his pipe when most people were in church and all the children ran out to follow him. Only two children survived: one who was blind, the other a little boy who ran back to fetch his coat and was left behind.

Many theories have arisen to explain the story, some suggesting that the childen were caught up in some ecstatic dance: some regions at that period of history were afflicted by a kind of medieval "disco fever" although this idea is given less credence than the theory that the children of Hameln were young people who left town at the behest of agents seeking colonists for Transylvania. The Exodus of the Children of Hameln was first documented by a local ecclesiastic in 1384—but he didn't mention any ratcatcher. That apparently attached itself to the legend later.

At any rate, residents trade heavily on the tale today. A Pied Piper greets visitors with music and poetry, conducting them through the ancient streets. An enchanting carillon, a chime of bells with moving clockwork figures, marks the passing hours as it retells the story that brought fame to the tiny German town.

THE GREEN MAN

An intimate involvement with nature is central to the life of the Witch. Mother Nature is a familiar symbol personifying the Goddess in her role as Earth Spirit. Scientists have expressed the same idea in the Gaia hypothesis suggesting that our planet is a single living organism. Recently there has been a reawakening of Mother Nature's male counterpart—the Green Man, a potent figure illustrating a unity between humanity and the plant world.

The origins of the Green Man are ancient. We first meet him over 5000 years ago in the Neolithic art of central Europe. His is a very masculine face thrusting forth from a wreath of foliage, the vegetation curling to become his hair and beard. Green Man images in Celtic art predate Rome's conquest of Gaul. Masks of the Green Man appear in Roman sculpture and architectural detail during the 1st century A.D. In Romanesque, Gothic, and Renaissance art the Green Man appears again and again. He gazes from the extraordinary carvings and paintings in great cathedrals and decorates the pages of illuminated manuscripts. In a later and lighter vein, many 18th-century English inns were named for him and their hanging signs portrayed him.

Evidence is not only visual. Euripides presents an ancestor of the Green Man as a form of Dionysus in *The Bacchae*. Ovid, in *Metamorphosess*, introduces a plant spirit inhabiting a man's body as Vertumnus, god of autumn fruits. In the Arthurian legends we meet him in the tale of Sir Gawain and the Green Knight. Folk hero Robin Hood, Shakespeare's Herne the Hunter in *The Merry Wives of Windsor*, Tolkein's ents, the talking trees of Oz all echo the Green Man theme. Composers too, have invoked his spirit. He comes to us in the music of Wagner, the Pastorale Symphony of Vaughan Williams, and in a wealth of folk songs.

Welcome the Green Man as an emblem of our unity with nature.

—DIKKI-JO MULLEN

MYTHIC SWANS

Zeus, sky god of the Greeks, chose the guise of a swan in order to seduce Leda, queen of twilight. Their coupling produced two eggs. From the first came Castor and Pollux, the heavenly twins, and the second held Clytemnestra and the ill-omened Helen of Troy. Some scholars say Leda' s spouse Tyndareus fathered one set of twins, but authorities differ over which egg was which. The famous myth inspired a host of painters, especially during the Italian Renaissance, and most major museums display a version of Leda and the Swan. The poet Yeats was moved to write a superb account of the seduction: "A sudden blow: the great wings beating still above the staggering girl ... "

The swans of northern Europe differ from the carnal nature of the Mediterranean myth. These are ethereal, mystical creatures, as in the tragic Celtic tale The Children of Lir, or the swans that assume human form like those immortalized by Tchaikovsky's brilliant score for the ballet Swan Lake. All the myths appear to share the theme of transformation.

But the most intriguing swan myth concerns transition and is found in Finland's ancient epic poem, the Kalevala. Sibelius, the great Finnish composer, reflects the atmosphere of that runic legend in his hauntingly beautiful tone poem, Swan of Tuonela. Tuonela, the land of death, is a dark underground kingdom ringed by a black river upon which glides a majestic swan singing a plaintive melody. The swan is the spirit guide as the soul passes from one place to another. Whoever hears this sad song must leave the reality of this world and venture into a strange, unknown land.

Aubrey Beardsley

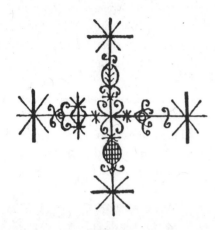

VOODOO MESSENGER

The *vèvè* (vev-vay) is a sacred element always present in a Voodoo ritual, a magical design representing astral forces. The drawing would be incised on a carefully swept earthen floor, the lines filled in with cornmeal. The design is made to summon a particular god or goddess, known collectively as *loas*, and serves as the prelude to a spiritual ceremony.

The symbol above belongs to the quicksilver god Simbi, a *loa* of many forms. He has been called the Voodoo Mercury, the quickening force of the great god Legba, who symbolizes the Sun and is the essential center of the Haitian belief system. Simbi is the Sun's messenger, with the power to confer the ability needed to successfully accomplish a difficult task. Milo Rigaud, author of the definitive *Secrets of Voodoo*, equates Simbi with the archetypal Thoth-Hermes-Mercury as the

one "who leads the dead in all directions bordered by the four magic orients of the cross." In the vaster and more flexible world of the spirit, Simbi guides us from the visible to the invisible. The journey begins at the crossroads.

> *Spirit in the wood make the*
> *blood run fast,*
> *Spirit in the wood make*
> *the beauty last,*
> *Keep the hope alive while the*
> *youth go past,*
> *Aye, Simbi l'eau. Aye, Simbi l'eau.*

The chant is actually the lyric of a song popularized here by an Afro-Cuban band in the late thirties. The melody and words, accompanied only by an insistent drum beat, were unique and captured the imagination. It may well have been based on a genuine prayer to the fiery young god who wrought miracles.

Horse and Rider   Yoruba, Nigeria

THE IRISH TRIADS

NINTH-CENTURY Irish monks fleeing the Viking terror found sanctuary in continental monasteries, but undoubtedly felt the pain of exile. Evidence that a longing for home occasionally seized the priests is preserved in their beautifully rendered Latin manuscripts, now Church treasures. Often in the margins of the vellum masterworks are found fragments of Old-Irish thought jotted down in Gaelic, clearly remnants from an earlier oral tradition.

Kuno Meyer, German scholar and philologist, collected and translated the marginal notes and presented The Triads in a 1906 lecture series to the Royal Irish Academy.

Three signs of ill-breeding: a long visit, staring, constant questioning.

Three candles that illume every darkness: truth, nature, knowledge.

The three great ends of knowledge: duty, utility, decorum.

Three things that corrupt the world: pride, superfluity, indolence.

Three things that come unbidden: fear, jealousy, love.

Three keys that unlock thoughts: drunkenness, trustfulness, love.

Three sisters of youth: desire, beauty, generosity.

Three sparks that kindle love: a face, demeanor, speech.

Three laughing-stocks of the world: an angry man, a jealous man, a niggard.

Three excellences of dress: elegance, comfort, lastingness.

Three signs of a rogue: bitterness, hatred, cowardice.

Nine Sacred Herbs

Anglo-Saxons believed disease was spread by toxins blowing in the winds. Songs, salt, water, and herbs were trusted means of protection from the flying venom. The Lacnunga, a 10th-century herbal, names nine sacred plants and a chant in their praise.

These nine attack against nine venoms.
A worm came creeping and tore asunder a man.
Then took Woden nine magic twigs and smote the serpent
That he in nine pieces dispersed.
Now these nine herbs have power
Against nine magic outcasts,
Against nine venoms, against nine flying things,
Against the loathed things that over land rove.

MUGWORT

MUGWORT. *Artemisia vulgaris*—guards against the unseen power of evil. The dried leaves stuffed in a pillow bring sweet dreams, lend vigor when steeped in bath water, and prevent fatigue on a long journey.

PLANTAIN. *Plantago major*—is the Saxon *way* broad in old herbals, for it thrives beside roadways. Fresh leaves draw out infections, halt bleeding in minor wounds, and ease discomfort from burns and stings.

WATERCRESS. *Nasturtium officinalis*—supplies a generous amount of vitamin C. Its juice added to water is a tonic to erase listlessness.

PLANTAIN

WATERCRESS

NETTLE

CAMOMILE

BETONY. *Stachys betonica*—appears as the fourth herb in later versions of the Nine Herbs Charm. *Atterlothe* of the original listing defies translation. Betony, however, serves well as a substitute, for it was anciently regarded as a cure for all ills of the body and the soul.

CAMOMILE. *Anthemis nobilis*—never fails to lift the spirits with its sweet scent. *Maythen*, as it was known to the Saxons, is the "plants' physician," as it revives ailing plants when set near them. Humans enjoy its benefits as well.

NETTLE. *Urtica dioica*—serves many useful purposes. The leaves staunch bleeding and soothe burns. Its seeds stimulate appetite. Nettle juice is an excellent hair lotion.

CRAB APPLE. *Pyrus malus*—has long been associated with health and renewal. The original wild apple from which all varieties derive is said to promote deep sleep and increase energy.

CHERVIL. *Anthriscus cerefolium*—may possess a powerful brain stimulant. It was once the sovereign remedy to restore the will to live. THYME, *Thymus serpyllum*, occurs in other lists of the Nine Sacred Herbs, and is said to cheer melancholy natures.

FENNEL. *Foeniculum vulgare*—conveys longevity, gives strength and courage while its pleasant aroma discourages evil spirits. Fennel in the diet promotes good eyesight and fights obesity.

THYME

CRAB APPLE

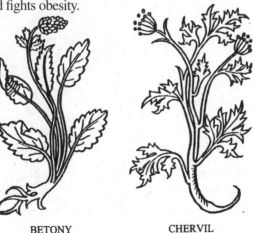

BETONY   CHERVIL   FENNEL

INSTANT RECALL

When an ancient Greek scratched his head and tried to recall something elusive, he invoked Mnemosyne, the Goddess of Memory. She was a Titaness, one of the large results of a union between Heaven (Uranus) and Earth (Gaia). Mnemosyne herself was a notable mother. When she lay nine nights with the ever-amorous Zeus, she gave birth to the Nine Muses—the lovely sisters that inspire arts and science.

Sometimes the goddess is fickle and refuses to yield the memory we seek. In order to outwit her, a number of devices have evolved called, in her honor, "mnemonics."

Some are generally familiar. When it's time to reset clocks, we remember the ever-popular spring forward, fall back. For spelling, it's I before E except after C, or when sounded as "ay" as in "neighbor" and "weigh." ROY G. BIV is the man who helps you remember the spectrum order—red, orange, yellow, green, blue, indigo, violet. And every do-it-yourselfer knows that tool usage calls for righty tighty, lefty loosey.

Music students are familiar with Every Good Boy Deserves Fruit, the EGBDF that signifies the lines of the musical staff. FACE tells you the spaces. Guitar players remember the tuning with Eat All Dead Gophers Before Easter, signifying the order of strings.

To remember the order of the planets from the Sun outward—Mercury, Venus, Earth, Mars, Jupiter, Saturn, Uranus, Neptune, Pluto—keep in mind that My Very Educated Mother Just Served Us Nice Pickles. Never Eat Soggy Waffles provides the compass points, but if you can't remember the four you probably shouldn't be running around loose outdoors anyway.

Science students use long-cherished memory aids of all kinds. For the sympathetic nervous system: fight or flight. The parasympathetic: rest and digest. Toronto Girls Can Flirt And Only Quit To Chase Dwarves tracks the hardness scale for minerals from talc to diamond. I like the blitheness of the medical treatment, "If the face is red, raise the head. If the face is pale, raise the tail."

Many children's rhyming games are disguised mnemonics. From my own days as a champ jump roper, particularly adept at Double Dutch, I suddenly remember one surely intended for learning numerical sequence: One, two, buckle my shoe/three, four, shut the door five, six, pick up sticks seven, eight, lay them straight nine, ten, big red hen.

—BARBARA STACY

Ars Memorandi   Paris, 1470

THE WISE FOOL

The Fool, from the Rider pack created by A.E. Waite and drawn by Pamela Coleman Smith in 1910.

At first glance the Fool seems to be a symbol of our power-lessness over fate. But bearing in mind his ancient geneaol-ogy, beneath the Fool's apparent weakness we know he hides a secret strength: his fool's luck. He will bob up again. He will return to life. He will win at last. Moreover, the Fool has exchanged outward contrivance for inner power. He has turned his glance inwards and come to terms with the Night side of Nature within himself.

—PAUL HUSON
The Witches' Almanac, 1976

ORION

He wheels across the heavens, Orion the Hunter, almost but never quite catching up to Taurus the Bull. Like the soldier, it is the hunter's destiny to slay, whether animal or mortal. And according to Greek mythology, so Orion fulfilled his fate before being dispatched skyward.

His story is interesting from birth. Two legends of his nativity come down to us, although one astonishing tale intrigues us by its very lack of details—he was born, according to some ancients, when three gods urinated on a bull hide buried deep in the earth. Otherwise Orion is simply known as the son of Poseidon. Like the other sea deity's children, the Hunter is gigantic and handsome. At birth, the father bestowed upon Orion the ability to walk on water, a gift of godly beauty.

Orion lived on the island of Chios, and a fire kindled in his heart for the exquisite Merope, daughter of the king. He was spellbound by her flowing locks, her smooth cheeks, the redness of her lips, and he burned to possess her. But Merope, unmoved by his splendor, avoided him. Nonetheless, Orion begged King Oenopion for his daughter's hand.

Oenopion was the son of Dionysos and had inherited the god's tricky character. The king agreed to the marriage, harboring a plan to dupe Orion. "We can have the wedding," he told the hunter, "only if you rid my kingdom of wild beasts."

Orion wielded his club and set to work—boars, panthers, lions, small furry squeakers, no creature was spared in his nuptial frenzy. The carcasses were laid in tribute at the silver-shod feet of Merope, who gazed at the gifts in horror. The more inert animals Orion piled up, the more she loathed him.

When the only creatures surviving were farm animals and tame deer, pets of the islanders, Orion approached the king and asked to set the wedding date. "Soon, soon," Oenopion assured him. Months passed and still the king remained vague. At last Orion realized that he had been deceived, and that "soon, soon" was the royal equivalent of never, never. He approached Merope and reminded her that he had labored mightily to rid the realm of wild animals and that the king had promised her hand in marriage. Again the handsome hunter sought Merope's love and pleaded with her to become his bride.

"Marry a savage like you? I would just as soon marry a wild bull," she told him icily.

Maddened by her scorn and her father's cunning, Orion took by force what he had hoped so long to be conferred. When Oenopion learned that his daughter had teen ravished, his rage was boundless. He beseeched his godly father to punish the giant. Dionysos made Orion drunk, put out his eyes, and cast him out on the beach.

Blind Orion wandered alone and desolate until he heard the clanging of a hammer. Following the sound, he discovered the forge of Hephaestus. The smithy-god took pity on Orion's plight and gave him an apprentice, Kedalion, as a guide. Riding on the giant's shoulder, the youth led him on the long journey east to the abode of the sun god Helios, who restored Orion's eyesight with a beam.

With renewed vision, Orion's exploits with women continued and several stories account for his launch skyward. He became the companion of the archer-goddess Artemis, and together they spent long dappled days at chase in the forest. Their affinity inspired jealousy in her twin, Apollo, concerned for his sister's chastity. One day while Orion was striding underwater far from shore with just his bobbing head visible, Apollo pointed out the black speck on the horizon and maintained that Artemis couldn't shoot that far. The goddess drew her bow and knocked him dead with one fatal shot. When Orion's body rolled back to shore, Artemis bewailed him with many tears, although deities seldom cry. She atoned by placing him in the sky with a club, sword, lion's skin and belt of stars.

Another story maintains that Orion raped one of the chaste followers of Artemis, and the goddess avenged her huntress by sending a monstrous scorpion to sting the giant. And as Artemis placed Orion among the stars, she also thrust the scorpion into the sky. When the constellation Scorpio is just rising, still chasing Orion, the Hunter is just starting to disappear behind the western horizon.

But you may prefer the Pleiades account, the most fanciful tale. These were the seven daughters of Atlas, virgin companions of Artemis. Orion vigorously pursued them all, and the terrified sisters prayed for rescue from the lecherous giant. Zeus responded by changing them into doves and then into stars, where they still flee before Orion in the constellation Taurus. Six are pale, although visible, and Electra, the seventh, is said to hide her face so she might not behold the ruin of Troy, founded by her son. The poet Tennyson obviously miscounted the number of Pleiades, but in fine lines: "Many a night I saw the Pleiades, rising through the mellow shade,/Glitter like a swarm of fireflies tangled in a silver braid."

And so go the lovely Greek stories of the huge galactic chase, Scorpio pursuing Orion, relentless Orion still pursuing the shy Pleiades.

—BARBARA STACY

The Evil Eye

For only last night, as they whispered, I brought
My own eyes to bear on her so, that I thought
Could I keep them one half minute fixed, she would fall
Shrivelled; she fell not; yet this does it all!

-ROBERT BROWNING

Renaissance Italy is the scene of Browning's poem. It tells of a young woman rejected by her lover who visits an alchemist to procure poison to kill her rival. Denied the power of the Evil Eye, she must resort to other means.

The Evil Eye is an age-old concept. The glittering, penetrating glance that can wreak havoc has ever been a source of fear, and protection from its force a universal concern. Innumerable incantations, talismans, and charms have been devised to avert the Evil Eye. And how ancient and widespread is the belief that certain individuals possess the ability to inflict harm with a baleful stare is clearly revealed in many languages.

Arabia: *'ain al-hasad, 'ain·al-Jamal*
Armenia: *paterak*
China: *ok ngan, ok, sihi*
Corsica: *innocchiatura*
Denmark: *et ondt oje*
Egypt: *iri-t ban-t, sihu*
England: *evil eye*
Ethiopia: *ayenat*
France: *mauvais oeil, mauvais regard*
Germany: *übel ougen, bose Blick*
Greece: *baskanos*
Holland: *booze blik*

Hungary: *szemveres*
India: *ghoram caksuh*
Ireland: *droch-shuil, bad eye, ill eye*
Italy: *jettatura, oculi maligni, mal' occhio, fascinatio*
Norway: *skjoertunge*
Persia: *aghashi*
Poland: *zte oko*
Scotland: *ill Ee*
Sardinia: *ogu malu*
Spain: *mal de ojo*
Syria: *'aina bishâ*

THE AMAZONS

A nation of famous women who lived near the river Thermodon in Cappadocia (modern Turkey). All their life was employed in wars and manly exercises. They never had any commerce with the other sex; but, only for the sake of propagation, they visited the inhabitants of the neighbouring country for a few days, and the male children which they brought forth were given to the fathers. The females were carefully educated with their mothers. They founded an extensive empire in Asia Minor, along the shores of the Euxine (Black Sea). They were defeated in a battle near the Thermodon by the Greeks; and some of them migrated beyond the Tanais (the river Don), and extended their territories as far as the Caspian sea.

Themyscyra was the most capital of their towns; and Smyrna, Magnesia, Thyatira, and Ephesus, according to some authors, were built by them. Diodorus says that Penthesileia, one of their queens, came to the Trojan war on the side of Priam, and that she was killed by Achilles, and from that time the glory and character of the Amazons gradually decayed, and was totally forgotten. Diodorus mentions a nation of Amazons in Africa more ancient than those of Asia who flourished long before the Trojan war, and many of their actions have been attributed to those of Asia. It is said, that after they had subdued almost all Asia, they invaded Attica, and were conquered by Theseus. Their most famous actions were their expeditions against Priam, and afterwards the assistance they gave him during the Trojan war; and their invasion of Attica, to punish Theseus, who carried away Antiope, one of their queens. They were also conquered by Bellerophon and Hercules. Among their queens, Hippolyte, Antiope, Lampeto, Marpesia, are famous. Curti us (1st century biographer of Alexander the Great) says that Thalestris, one of their queens, came to Alexander, whilst he was pursuing his conquests in Asia, for the sake of raising children from a man of such military reputation; and that, after she remained 13 days with him, she retired into her country. The Amazons were such expert archers, that, to denote the goodness of bow and quiver, it was usual to call it Amazonian.

—A CLASSICAL DICTIONARY
J. LEMRIERE 1911

HIGH JOHN
de Conquer

High John was a mythic hero during the years of African slavery in the Americas. Signifying a spirit of hope against all odds, High John brought courage and comfort to the beleaguered people. Zora Neale Hurston called him "our hope-bringer—the power and soul of our laughter and song," (*The Book of Negro Folklore*, Langston Hughes and Arna Bontemps, Dodd, Mead & Co., N.Y. 1958.)

Hurston writes: "High John de Conquer came to be a man, and a mighty man at that. But he was not a natural man in the beginning. First off, he was a whisper, a will to hope, a wish to find something worthy of laughter and song. Then the whisper put on flesh. His footsteps sounded across the world in a low but musical rhythm as if the world he walked on was a singing drum." The old tales say High John returned to Africa when slavery ended, "but he left his power here," Hurston tells us, "and placed his American dwelling in the root, of a certain plant. Only possess that root. and he can be summoned at any time."

The true root that bears his name is more than likely the sweet potato, a staple crop of the West Indies and our Southern states. It is the original potato, *Ipomoea batatus*, producing an edible root rich in starch and sugar. The plant's twining high-climbing vine adorned with violet or pale pink trumpet flowers attests to the virtue and quality of the godlike figure. The legendary root should not be confused with a Mexican medicinal root called "jalap," but marketed under the name of High John the Conqueror root. This odd case of mistaken identity would surely bring a chuckle from High John.

Today, those who practice conjure magic, and there are many, rely on High John's root as a last resort when all else fails to produce a successful outcome. Zora Neale Hurston remarked, "Thousands upon thousands...do John reverence by getting the root of the plant in which he has taken up his secret dwelling, and 'dressing' it with perfume, and keeping it on their person, or in their houses in a secret place."

As an amulet, a sliver of High John the Conqueror root holds a subtle power to change bad luck to good and dismiss melancholy. Its virtue brings success in any situation, encourages clear thinking, and renews hope and courage.

Rock painting from Tsibab ravine, South West Africa

FOUR WINDS

When the wind sets from the east
The spirit of the wave is stirred.
It longs to rush past us westward
To the land over which the sun sets,
To the green sea, rough and wild.

When the wind sets from the north,
It urges the dark fierce waves,
Surging in strife against the wide sky,
Listening to the witching song.

When the wind sets from the west,
Over the salt sea of swift currents,
It longs to go past us eastward
To capture the Sun-Tree
In the wide, far-distant sea.

When the wind sets from the south,
Over the land of the Saxons of stout shields
And the wave strikes the isle of Scit,
It surges up to the top of Calad Net
With a leafy, grey-green cloak.

–From *Celtic Tree Magic*

Griffins

From *Magical Creatures*

THE GRIFFIN is a rarity, doubly royal. The creature has the head and wings of an eagle, king of birds, and the body of a lion, king of beasts; it is symbolically potent for dominion over earth and sky. Griffins are notable for their strength and intelligence, and an old text assures us that they are the size of eight lions and have the strength of one hundred eagles. A griffin can "bear to his nest flying a horse and a man upon his back or two oxen yoked together as they go at plow." The concept of mighty eagle-lions arose in the Middle East, and they often turn up in the art of the ancient Babylonians, Assyrians and Persians.

As befits royalty, griffins love anything that glitters, especially gold. They have the ability to sense buried treasure, and atop the trove they build nests of gold and lay eggs of agate. Many a missing jewel might have been found in the cache of a griffin high in a mountain aerie. They defend their riches against all possible plunderers, and griffins became notable as ferocious guardians of precious things, both their own and those of emperors and gods. The ancient Greeks believed that griffins, the duality both sun creatures, drew the golden chariot of the sun god Apollo across the sky each day. Alexander the Great yearned for his own griffin to fly him to the edge of the sky. Nemesis, goddess of retribution, held griffins sacred and sometimes called upon their services to enact revenge. But in its most noble portrayal, valiant and forbidding, the griffin emerged during the Middle Ages as a key figure in heraldry. It arises rampant on the coats of arms and banners of kings, generals, aristocrats—in "wakeful custody," balanced on one or two lion paws, ready to strike with talons. Fierce images of griffins often loom from Gothic churches as gargoyles, in earlier versions created to scare demons or avert evil, in later architecture mainly ornamental.

Griffins had no particular enmity for people, but they dispatched dragons, snakes and horses, although they sometimes mated with mares. Their progeny were hippogriffs, an odd assemblage of feathered flying horses.

The most famous griffin, superstar of the species, bumbles its delightful way through the pages of Lewis Carroll's *Alice in Wonderland*. A surrealistic punster, the Gryphon informs Alice that he studied with a classical master and learned Laughing and Grief.

"And how many hours a day did you do lessons?" asked Alice.

"Ten hours the first day; nine the next; and so on."

"What a curious plan!" exclaimed Alice.

"That's the reason they're called lessons," the Gryphon remarked, "because they lessen from day to day."

Gryphon fast asleep   **Sir John Tenniel, 1865**

The Shepherd's Ring in England's Northamptonshire was damaged during World War I. No trace of it remains

THE LABYRINTH

Having begun a journey, turn not back, for the furies will be your attendants.

-PYTHAGOREAN MAXIM

A labyrinth is a winding path resembling a maze, but free of trickery. Here you encounter no confusion, disorientation or dead ends—a single route leads to a center and you simply retrace the only way out. It is an archetype, a divine imprint. Once begun, the path must be completed.

Labyrinths have been created by cultures around the world for the past five or six thousand years, some formations so old dating is difficult. Many such designs turn up on ancient coins and vases. In Egypt the funeral temple of Amenemhet III, now in ruins, was a famous early labyrinth. Herodotus recorded three hundred rooms in this lost labyrinth, just in the area aboveground, said to surpass even the pyramids in splendor and wonder.

The word "labyrinth" itself derives from *labrus*, referring to the double-headed ax carried by members of the bull cult in Crete. The source points to Daedalus, the hero who constructed the complex pathway that contained the savage mythological bull, the Minotaur.

Currently the labyrinth is being rediscovered as an aid to spiritual growth and awareness, an almost forgotten mystical tradition struggling for rebirth in our time.

What is the secret of the labyrinth's attraction? The patterns, ranging from simple to complex, are magical tools that help to encourage the solving of problems and empower our creativity. The act of walking the path inspires focus, clears the mind and may give insight into the spiritual journey.

The walk is in three stages, and the practitioner of magic will recognize the honoring of past, present and future reflected in the sequence of the design. Entering and following the mysterious winding path leading to the center point, cares and concerns fall away and we experience a quieting of the mind, a cleansing. We release trivia and illumination may occur as the seeker nears the center. At the center, stay for awhile, pause to reflect and meditate. What is meant to be received from higher consciousness and the divine ones will come through. Union happens on the way out. Healing forces and higher energies magically merge, adding to our health and power. Positive changes may soon make their appearances.

The labyrinth is a form of mandala. It facilitates transformations of the heart, and those who work with these mysterious patterns become adepts of survival and courage. The influences increase each time the labyrinth is walked.

THE LABYRINTHIAN PATH

Clear the mind by concentrating on the breath. Feel the pace the body wants to move and begin the walk. The first step involves allowing the mind to become quiet. Simply following the winding path is calming. Even those who have difficulty concentrating on a regular meditation will experience a natural rhythm and harmony while proceeding through the labyrinth. There are five choices to consider for those entering the labyrinth.

The Path of Image—Allow the quiet mind to explore dream fragments. Talk to the characters in the dream. Those with active imaginations respond well to this.

The Path of Silence—Strive to be as completely quiet and empty as possible. Reflect on the words of Thomas Carlyle, "Silence is the element in which great things fashion themselves together."

The Path of Prayer—Begin to pray for needs to be fulfilled. Whether it is for courage, perseverance, guidance or release, the labyrinth experience seems to expedite the answer to prayers.

Escape and Release—The walk heals. Escape from old hurts, mistakes and resentments occurs. The relief forgiveness brings is the goal here.

Find an Answer—When truly puzzled, asking for the answer to a dilemma while walking the labyrinth can bring a miraculous revelation.

At the onset of the 21st century, some communities are creating labyrinths as a way to cope with the challenges of modern life. Travelers to Europe and the Mediterranean can rediscover traditional labyrinth sites, among the most famous that located in Chartres cathedral. The Woodlawn Chartres labyrinth, illustrated below, has been recreated in Orlando, Florida. If you have no access to a labyrinth, you can get a subtle sense of the practice by tracing the illustration with a pencil, following the step-by-step guidelines for the actual walk. The labyrinth is an ancient device for spiritual progress, and even the miniature armchair version may provide some magical experiences.

—DIKKI-JO MULLEN

Addenda. Mazes, near relatives to

The labyrinth at Chartres is 40 feet across and formed by blue and white stones

labyrinths, are springing up in corn fields throughout the U.S. The puzzling walks through the stalks are local commercial entertainments that help prop up dwindling farm profits. The first maze designed by Brett Herbst of Pleasant Grove, Utah, brought in 18,000 people in three weeks. Herbst then formed his company, The Maize. Now he makes a living forming the zigzag foot paths for other hard-pressed farmers—yet another chapter in an ancient historic observance.

Khnemu forms a king on his potter's wheel

SACRED RAM

On a steep cliff wall in Algeria where the Sahara Desert meets the Atlas Mountains is a remarkable engraving made over seven thousand years ago. An enormous ram towers over a man whose arms are raised as if in awe. The ram wears a decorative neck band and is crowned with a large disk from which rays emanate. This area was once fertile land where herds of wild sheep grazed and the ram commanded interest and respect.

The image portends the sanctity the ram would eventually hold farther east in the Nile Valley. In ancient Egypt's predynastic times Khnemu, a god associated with creation, was portrayed as a ram or a ram-headed man crowned with the solar disk. The great god Amon, whose worship combined with the power of the Sun god, Ra, claimed the ram as his symbolic creature. The massive complex of ruins at Karnak includes a magnificent avenue of ram headed sphinxes leading to the Great Temple of Amon-Ra. God of gods, Amon-Ra signified a mysterious hidden force that created and sustained the universe. Greek and Roman visitors would equate Amon-Ra with their chief god Zeus/Jupiter.

The Roman astrologer and poet Manilius credits the Egyptian priesthood with the development and refinement of astrology. And it may be due to the prestige of Amon-Ra that Aries the Ram is the first sign of the zodiac. "Resplendent in his golden fleece the Ram leads the way," wrote Manilius around the turn of the Common Era. The "golden fleece" refers to the ram of Greek myth that saves two children from death and is then sacrificed to the gods, his fleece later becoming the prize sought by Jason and the Argonaut expedition. The astrological personality assigned to the Ram in the West is bold and audacious.

Amon-Ra wears a tall feathered crown, but is also depicted as a ram or a goose

THE LION

The King of Beasts' likeness is probably the most widely used animal symbol. Lions appear on dozens of flags throughout the world and are used in the logos of innumerable and diverse businesses ranging from makers of mineral water to a movie studio. That so many desire an association with such an animal is understandable given all the traits we humans assign this noble creature: courage, fidelity, compassion, and leadership.

The lion has an ancient association with gods and royalty. The Egyptian goddess Sekhmet is portrayed as lion headed; she is the fierce, warlike twin to the more mild cat goddess Bast. The sun god Mithras is linked to the lion and is sometimes portrayed as having a lion's head, with the mane being the rays of the sun. Both Buddha and Christ are associated with the lion. Christ was referred to as the Lion of Judah, and Buddha's throne is represented as a Lion's Throne. The flag of Tibet, in fact, features the snow lion.

Traditionally, the sun and lion are linked. Joseph Campbell refers to the lion as the solar beast, "At the sound of its roar, the grazing herds of the plain take flight, as do the stars of the sky at sunrise." Kings often choose the sun-lion as an emblem. The link between the two is not reserved for royalty alone. Each of us feels the power of the midsummer sun most fully at the time when the sun passes through the constellation Leo.

The territorial nature of this magnificent animal is legendary. Its fierceness and loyalty make the lion the ideal guardian. Palaces and temples have been guarded by lions, either living or carved from stone, since antiquity. Perhaps the fact that a lion seems to sleep with its eyes open gives him an unequalled air of vigilance. There are many tales of the protective compassion and friendship lions have shown to man, most notably in the story of "Daniel in the Lion's Den" and "Androcles and the Lion." Modem children have a kind and heroic lion figure to love in "The Lion King."

Chinese New Year celebrations always incorporate the Lion Dance, in which two performers, one as the head and one as the body and tail, dance to scare away bad luck and bring good luck and happiness for the new year.

The earthly king of beasts has a counterpart in the sky—the eagle, another solar creature. The two are combined to form the mythological creature the gryphon (or griffin), who has the eagle's head and wings, and the body and tail of the mighty lion.

—JEAN MARIE WALSH

Queen of Shades

The sign of Virgo may be named for a mysterious dark goddess who rules the underground kingdom of death. Persephone, daughter of the grain goddess Demeter, was called Kore (maiden or virgin) in the dialect of Attica, the form in which most classical Greek literature is written. Even when she became a queen Kore was still the name the goddess bore, possibly due to the fame of a Homeric Hymn.

It tells of a maiden abducted in her youth by Hades, god of the underworld, and destined by the gods to be his bride. She was partially ransomed by the grief of her mother, for Demeter withheld her fruitfulness and forced a compromise. The gods agreed that Persephone would spend two-thirds of the year aboveground and the other third, the four months of winter, in the world below with her grim consort. The myth, an allegory of the changing seasons, gives promise of rebirth. The seed planted in autumn will sprout forth in springtime. Because Persephone ate pomegranate seeds while in the house of the dead she had to return, abiding by an archaic law. The Sun leaves the constellation of Virgo at the autumnal equinox, coinciding with the time when Persephone joins her consort below.

We glimpse the mature Queen Persephone only through the mists of myth and poetry. Zeus was said to have called her 'the noblest of my daughters." Homer titled her "the awesome one" and "giver of wisdom." Her character is portrayed as gracious and compassionate. Ovid tells us that she is faithful to Hades, but has no children by him and prefers the company of Hecate, goddess of witchcraft, to his. Yet another source records Persephone's jealous rage when Hades finds other women attractive. In two instances her revenge transformed them before dalliance with her spouse became a serious matter- one into a mint plant and the other, a white poplar tree. Evidently Hades took this in stride, for romance was not in his nature.

Centuries passed before the queen of the underworld again caught the imagination of poets and painters. In Victorian England, the Pre-Raphaelites restored Persephone to vivid life on canvas. Swinburne honored her in verse.

Pale, beyond porch and portal,
Crowned with calm leaves, she stands,
Who gathers all things mortal
With cold immortal hands;
Her languid lips are sweeter
Than love's who fear to greet her
To men that mix and meet her
From many times and lands.

-From The Garden of Proserpine

Aesop's Fables　　　　　　　　　　　　　　　　　　　　Ulm, 1476

The Fir and the Bramble

A TALL FIR was boasting to a lowly Bramble, and said, "You pathetic creature, you are of no use whatsoever. Now look at me! I am first in the forest for beauty and rank. I am useful for all sorts of things, especially when men build houses. They cannot do without me then." But the Bramble replied, "Ah, that is all very well, but wait till the woodsmen come with their axes and saws to cut you down. Then you will wish you were a Bramble and not a Fir."

MORAL: Better to be poor and carefree than rich and worried.

THE BLACK DOG

British folklore is rich with tales of a ghostly black dog that appears out of nowhere to guide and protect a traveler passing through a dark wood or other dangerous terrain. When the journey ends and safety is assured, the guardian dog vanishes into thin air. One such tale appeared in English travel writer Augustus Hare's *Memorials of a Quiet Life,* 1872. A young man named Johnnie Greenwood, responding to an emergency, was required to cross a mile of dense forest to reach his destination.

"At the entrance of the wood a large black dog joined him, and pattered along by his side. He could not make out where it came from, but it never left him, and when the wood grew so dark that he could not see it, he still heard it pattering beside him. When he emerged from the wood, the dog had disappeared, and he could not tell where it had gone to. Well, Johnnie fulfilled his obligation, and set out to return the same way. At the entrance of the wood, the dog joined him, and pattered along beside him as before; but it never touched him, and he never spoke to it, and again, as he emerged from the wood, it ceased to be there.

"Years after, two condemned prisoners in York Jail told the chaplain that they had intended to rob and murder Johnnie that night in the wood, but that he had a large dog with him, and when they saw that, they felt that Johnnie and the dog together would be too much for them."

MEDUSA

Three appalling sisters "not to be approached and not to be described" inhabited a murky cavern at the mouth of the underworld, according to ancient Greek mythology. Eurale, known as "the Far Springer," Sthenno, "the Mighty," and Medusa, "The Queen," were Gorgons, daughters of ancient sea gods. The sisters defied description because they were lethally grotesque, for any creature that saw them was turned into stone. The Gorgons were notable for glares like wild beasts and tresses of living, hissing serpents"—over their terrible heads a great Dread quivers," according to Hesiod.

But a parallel myth relates that Medusa, unlike her sisters, had been born a mortal of consummate beauty. Weary of the dreary cave, Medusa begged Athena for a new life in a sunny climate. When Athena denied the plea, Medusa reviled the goddess. "Once mortals see me," Medusa boasted, "they will no longer consider you the most beautiful." Athena disdained to take offense, but the insult that followed provoked her fury.

Sea gods adore mortal beauty, none more so than Poseidon. The erotic green god learned of the exquisite Medusa, found her agleam in the dark cavern, and spirited her to the temple of Athena. There she lay with him, the desecration of Athena's shrine adding to her pleasure. In revenge for the sacrilege, Athena transformed Medusa into that most terrifying of creatures, a Gorgon like her serpent-embellished sisters. And like her sisters, all who perceived Medusa turned into stone.

Such evil power would seem to render Medusa invulnerable, but never underestimate the ingenuity of a Greek hero. Perseus, the son of Zeus and Danaë, lived on the island of Seriphus and its king had tricked the youth into a quest for Medusa's head. Perseus persuaded the Graiae, sisters of the Gorgons, to divulge the location of the cave. The Graiae, "Gray Ones," as weird as their siblings, had only one eye and one tooth between them, passing the rudimentary treasures to share. Athena and Hermes advised Perseus to steal the eye and return it only for the information. The ruse worked, and the deities further aided Perseus by providing him with winged sandals for flying, a helmet for invisibility, a curved sword and a brightly shining shield. Perseus flew to the cave and guided by the reflection in the shield, cut off Medusa's head as she slept. Athena laid claim to the severed head, the design of which formed the protective ornament of her shield.

From the blood of the deed sprang Medusa's son by Poseidon, the winged horse Pegasus. He flies the night sky as a constellation, the heavenly progeny of an outlandish union in a sacred site.

—BARBARA STACY

THE LANGUAGE

Herbs are one of Nature's finest gifts. They flavor our food, heal our ailments, offer protection in the form of amulets, please us with their fragrance, and delight our eyes with the subtle beauty of their blossoms. Once you have studied herbal blooms and appreciated the intricate quality of their forms, showy tame flowers of the garden often lose their appeal. A tradition of awarding flowers with sentimental significance flourished during Victoria's reign in England. Herbs were not forgotten, for their virtues had been established long before pleasure gardens existed. The following list has been compiled from numerous sources, including old herbals and gardening books of the 19th century.

Amaranth—unfading
Angelica—inspiration
Balm—sympathy
Basil—hatred, love
Betony—surprise
Borage—courage
Bugloss, Viper's—falsehood
Burnet—merry heart
Chamomile—patience, humility
Chicory—frugality
Coltsfoot—maternal care
Coriander—hidden merit
Cumin—fidelity, avarice
Dandelion—oracle
Elder—compassion
Fennel—flattery
Flax—appreciation
Forget-me-not—true love
Foxglove—sincerity, adulation

OF HERBS

Fumitory—hatred
Heliotrope—eternal love
Henbane—defect, flaw
Hollyhock—ambition
Horehound—health
Houseleek—vivacity
Hyssop—sacrifice
Larkspur—fickleness
Laurel, Bay—glory
Lavender—purity
Lily—glory
Marigold—disappointment
Marjoram—happiness
Mint—wisdom
Mugwort—refreshment
Nettle—cruelty
Pansy—sadness
Parsley—festivity
Pimpernel—assignation

Poppy—oblivion
Rose—love, grace
Rosemary—remembrance
Rue—purification
Saffron—mirth
Sage—immortality
St. John's wort—protection
Sorrel—affection
Southernwood- constancy
Speedwell—fidelity
Stonecrop—tranquility
Sunflower—fool's gold
Tansy—hostility
Thistle—austerity
Thyme—bravery
Valerian—readiness
Vervain—soul healer
Violet—loyalty
Wormwood—displeasure

OLD IRISH CHARMS

Today I gird myself with the strength of heaven,
The light of the sun, the brilliance of the moon,
The glory of fire, the impetuousity of lightning,
The speed of the wind, the profundity of the sea,
The stability of earth, the hardness of rock.

> *I call on the seven daughters of the sea,*
> *who shape the threads of long life:*
> *Three deaths be taken from me,*
> *Three lives given to me,*
> *Seven waves of plenty poured for me.*

May my seven candles not be quenched.
I am an invincible fortress, I am an unshakable cliff,
I am a precious stone, I am the symbol of seven riches,
I summon my good fortune to me.

From *Celtic Tree Magic*

FRANKINCENSE

The name alone evokes an image of Three Wise Men crossing a vast desert as they follow a star. Frankincense, one of the gifts they carried, had been scenting Egyptian temples for thousands of years before the birth of Christ. The ancients perceived that the smoke rising from the glowing aromatic substance had an elevating and soothing effect on the mind and emotions. Such rare quality caused frankincense to be reserved for religious rites. And a tradition born in antiquity has lived on to perfume many contemporary church services.

The English name comes from Old French *franc encens: franc*, pure, and *encens*, incense. The fragrant gum resin is extracted from small trees that chiefly flourish in Somalia—the land Egyptians called Punt. Herodotus, writing in the 5th century B.C., mentions the lively trade taking place throughout the Middle East, "...the Chaldaeans alone offer something like two and a half tons of frankincense every year at the festival of Bel." Such a treasure was destined eventually to escape sacred precincts and find its way into the secular world.

Frankincense resin burned on a charcoal block remains the traditional way to fume an atmosphere. Luckily, aromatherapy's rise in popularity has made the scent widely available in the form of essential oil. Robert B. Tisserand's *The Art of Aromatherapy*, a standard reference guide, recommends the smell of frankincense to alleviate depression, melancholy, confusion, indecision and the dwelling on unpleasant past events. Essential oil is too strong to apply directly to the skin, but may be enjoyed in a variety of ways. A tiny amount achieves an exquisite result: half a teaspoon to a cup of sweet almond oil for a scented massage and a scattering of seven drops to perfume a warm bath. Sprinkle a few drops in a small bowl of hot water to inhale or pour a similar mixture into a plant mister to diffuse the air.

The strange elusive odor of frankincense engages the mind in a subtle manner; it erases doubts that cloud the present and gives hope for the future.

THE SACRED WAY

As with the Egyptians, ancient Greeks were also provided with guide-books to the afterlife. Texts derived from the Orphic mysteries were often engraved on leaf shaped sheets of beaten gold and placed in tombs.

"Now you will find to the left of the halls of Hades a spring, and beside it a white cypress standing. Do not approach this spring. You will find on the other side a spring with guards before it. Say to them:

I am a child of Earth and Sky,
Of heavenly race, you know it well:
But I am parched with thirst, I perish.
Give me, quickly, the cool water
From the Lake of Recollection.

And they shall give you to drink from the holy spring, and you will continue on the long, sacred way which other mystai gloriously walk."

ROCK OF THE SUN

The great Calendar Stone of the Aztecs was thrown into the marshes surrounding Mexico City by Cortez and the Spanish invaders in 1521. Discovered there three centuries later, the treasure was restored and now rests in the National Museum. The intricately engraved stone was completed and dedicated in 1481 during the reign of Axayactl. The ornamentation, based on a calendar system inherited by the Aztecs from earlier high cultures of the region, is more accurate than European versions. Unaware of its value, the conquistadores saw it only as an example of idolatry to be scorned and destroyed.

The Rock of the Sun, as the Aztecs called it, is carved from an enormous slab of basalt weighing over 20 tons and measuring close to 13 feet in diameter. The head in the center with its protruding tongue, represents the sun. Surrounding the face are four squares, symbols of the seasons and the Ages of Fire, Earth, Air, and Water. Outer circles indicate the number of years, the twenty days of the month, and the sixteen hours of the Aztec day and night. Originally, according to the native historian Zezozomoc, the entire surface of the stone was painted red, to denote its consecration to the sun.

THE WONDER OF HONEY

Your enthusiasm for the taste of honey may not match Pooh Bear's, but all will agree that the gift of the bees is as remarkable as any nature offers.

Ancient Greeks and Romans considered mead, honey wine, as nectar of the gods. The drink combines honey, water, and brewers' yeast, requires a full year to ferment, and must age three years more to reach full flavor. Mead was enjoyed by Anglo-Saxons and delighted medieval royalty and peasants as well. When sugar from the West Indies became available in the late 17th century, mead making lost favor, but honey from the comb continued to be cherished.

Today the golden liquid is a valuable ingredient in barbecue basting sauces, especially when combined with lemon juice. More unusual and equally delicious is a blend of honey and whipped cream to top waffles or fresh fruit.

Another honey treat is sure to please guests for afternoon tea.

Honey Orange Bread
2 tablespoons butter
1 cup honey
1 egg, beaten
2 tablespoons grated orange peel
2 and 1/2 cups sifted flour
2 and 1/2 teaspoons baking powder
1/2 teaspoon baking soda
1/2 teaspoon salt
3/4 cup orange juice

Preheat oven to 325 degrees. Cream butter, add honey and stir. Mix in egg and orange rind. Sift flour, baking powder, soda and salt together. Combine with the honey mixture, slowly adding orange juice to smoothly blend. Turn into a greased nine-inch loaf pan and bake for an hour and ten minutes.

Not only is honey a heavenly culinary sweetener, it serves as a household remedy as well. Honey disinfects and heals minor wounds; spread a thin layer and cover with a sterile bandage. It is successful in treatment of coughs and colds, indigestion, insomnia, and is an aid to hay fever sufferers, who are advised to use the product of local hives. And if all this isn't enough, a tablespoon of honey calms the mind and restores flagging spirits.

Illustrations by Ernest H. Shepard for A.A. Milne's Winnie-the-Pooh, 1926.

When witches gather rain . . .

Witches have always known the special meaning of nature's acts. They are warnings, blessings and magic guides to our living in the world around us. Rain is a special gift from the sky and its powers should be used wisely. Try never to shelter yourself from its fall, but rather accept the rain as we should accept life with all of its trials and blessings.

- Rain while the sun shines is a healing rain. Catch and store it in blue glass. Use the water for all manner of healing magic. Place in the bath for an overall body cleansing.
- The blessing of fairies is upon anyone who catches rain in a silver spoon after the rain has bounced off a flat stone. Place some of this water on any object that is frequently misplaced. Keys are always a good choice.
- Place midnight rain of a New Moon on the third eye to bring visions and see future events.
- The first rain gathered in May is symbolic of May Day dew and holds much power. It is used when very special favors are needed. Do not gather this rain in a metal container or its power will be lost. A glass or wood container would do much better.
- When rain runs off a gravestone, gather carefully and use with caution.

- Rain gathered during a thunderstorm holds much energy and can be used to enhance spells and potions. But be aware that the energy does not last long, and the spell should be completed before three days and three nights have passed or the rain water will be of little use.
- Houseplants enjoy the outdoor rain— this cleanses their leaves and helps to purify the indoor air when they are brought back in the home. This is especially good to do when you are in need of a clear mind and strong thought.
- Jewelry, charms, and other objects can be purified by standing in the rain, facing west and tossing the object into the air three times, catching it in your hands each time.
- The sound of the rain carries the voices of the water spirits. Listen to the sound of the rain and enjoy the gifts of the undines. They will speak to you of love and friendship.

The wise also realize that rain is just one aspect of nature. We should look to the wind, trees, lightning, fire, stones and other forms of nature's expression for clues to the magic of our world.

—THEITIC

SCARABS

Among the many amulets and ornaments worn by the ancient Egyptians during the historic period, the most important are the scarabs. These little objects are made of stone or glazed ware and are in the form of the scarabaeus-beetle (hence the modern name of scarab). The actual beetles appear to have been sacred in the prehistoric times, for they have been found, carefully preserved, in many of the early graves.

The scarabaeus is a dung beetle; it lays its eggs in the droppings of animals, then rolls the dung into a ball and pushes the ball with its hind-legs into a hole in the ground. These beetles can be seen in full activity in any part of Upper Egypt in a sunny place over which animals have passed. But the beetles will also lay their eggs in the dead body of one of their companions, and this is perhaps the reason why the scarab was taken by the ancient Egyptians as the emblem of the resurrection, for they saw life coming out of death as the young beetles emerged.

The Egyptian word for the beetle is Kheper, and the deity who takes his name from the creature and is represented as a beetle is Khepri, He of the Beetle. Kheper, however, means also To be, to exist; therefore Khepri can also mean the Existent One. In the theology of the Egyptians he was Existence itself and could therefore give existence to others; as a beetle he pushes the ball of the Sun into the Other World in evening; as a beetle he waits in the Other World to revivify the dead Sun, when the soul of Ra and the soul of Khepri are united; and in the morning he as a beetle pushes the ball of sun over the horizon of the earth. Khepri the god appears to be merely a theological abstraction, but the beetle was a popular form which conveyed to the common people the idea of eternal existence.

Scarabs begin as early as the first dynasty, become increasingly common throughout the historic period, and disappear under Ptolemies. These little objects are carefully carved in the shape of a beetle, but the underside, where the legs should occur, is left flat and engraved with a name or with some magical design. The earliest scarabs have royal names only and were possibly used for a double purpose, to protect the wearer by the power of a divine name and to show that he held some office under the royal god. In the Middle Kingdom (c. 3000–2780 B.C.)

design scarabs become frequent, the designs are often spirals arranged in intricate and beautiful patterns. In the New Kingdom (c. 1590–1370 B.C.) designs and the names of gods and goddesses are common, so common in fact many of the scarabs were sold as souvenir—charms at various shrines. In the ate period scarabs are merely charms.

Scarabs were at first made of stone—steatite of schist—glazed blue or green. In the Middle Kingdom carnelian and amethyst scarabs were made; as these stones were very hard and difficult to engrave, the base was covered with gold plate on which the appropriate signs were cut. Cheap scarabs were made in glazed ware, not in stone.

Scarabs used as amulets for the dead were differently made from those for the living. Instead of the flat base with engraved signs, the legs of the insect were carved, showing that it was the actual beetle that was represented. In the late New Kingdom and succeeding dynasties it was customary to make large scarabs with wings to be laid across the breast of the mummy, as signifying the belief in eternal existence. Large scarabs in dark stones, chiefly basalt, were also made for the dead. Those have a flat base on which was engraved the Chapter of the Heart from the Book of the Dead.

Scarabs were so popular that in countries adjacent to Egypt they were copied locally. The most important of these are the scarabs made in Palestine by the Hyksos long before they invaded Egypt. Such scarabs are distinctive, the hieroglyphs are clearly copied by people who could not read them, and the backs of the beetles show no division of the wing-cases as do the Egyptian examples. In the 16th dynasty the Greeks of Naukratis had a regular trade in scarabs for export to the Aegean.

—MARGARET A. MURRAY

This article was published as an appendix in Dr. Murray's *The Splendour That Was Egypt*. Her famed work, *The Witch-Cult in Western Europe*, was an essential factor in the establishment of Wicca as a bona fide religion.

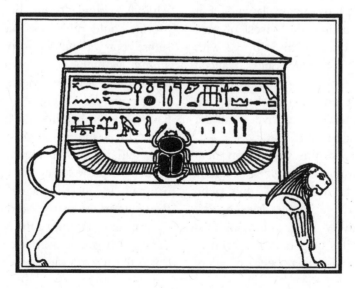

Merlin and Vivien

IN THE RICH mythology of King Arthur's court, the downfall of Merlin is one of the most bizarre legends. For once upon a time the wisest of men became besotted in his old age with Vivien, still in her teens but advanced in wickedness. It is a cautionary tale of a young enchantress holding an old man amorously captive—and the magician magicked.

The story begins on the mystical island of Avalon with Queen Morgana le Fay, sister of King Arthur, who nursed a grudge against Merlin. She had been lovely in her youth, and had used her wiles to persuade Merlin to teach her. Morgana became adept at potent sorcery second only to her mentor, but one secret was withheld. Although blind to his own destiny Merlin could otherwise see into the future, but was unable to pass on the ability. Morgana considered this lack an affront. As the queen brooded, Vivien arrived at court and no one had ever seen her like for bewitching beauty. But she was both shrewd and evil, and more than anything Vivien burned to possess secrets of sorcery. Morgana le Fay calculated how to use the avid girl to destroy Merlin.

One sunny afternoon the two strolled the fragrant garden overlooking the sea. Since the wizard was so vulnerable to beauty, Morgana suggested that Vivien approach him seeking wisdom. Sure of her power to inspire passion, Vivien deemed that she could attain such an end. "In this I shall play my wit against his wisdom and my beauty against his cunning, and I believe I shall win at that game," she said. Delighted at such assurance, Morgana believed that Vivien could indeed enchant the enchanter. But the enterprise was fraught with danger; men have been known to turn chilly as ardor wanes. Since Merlin might regret imparting such power and later harm his lover, Morgana provided a protective charm. "Whoever wears the ring with the red stone shall love with such a burning that you may do whatever you will of him," she assured.

Vivien arrayed herself in scarlet satin embroidered with silver and gold, her long red curls brimming within a golden net, and presented herself to King Arthur at the Pentecost feast. Luminous in her splendor she slipped the ring on Merlin's finger by a clever ruse. Immediately "a wonderful passion seized upon his heart and wrung it so that it was pierced as with a violent agony." From that day he was a man obsessed. To the amusement of the court the old wizard behaved like a lovesick youth. Wearied of his constant pursuit and embarrassed by the derision, Vivien hated Merlin with all her heart although she pretended great friendliness.

But Merlin had enough left of his

addled brain to question Vivien's sincerity and declare that he would do anything to secure her love. "Sir, if you would only impart to me your wisdom and cunning," she replied, "then I believe I could love you a very great deal." Merlin promised, despite misgivings. But he explained that he could indoctrinate her only in a secluded place. "There I will build a habitation by means of my magic and we shall abide there while I teach you wonders." They made their way to the Valley of Joyousness, where Merlin conjured up a castle more marvelous than is beheld even in a dream; The walls were of ultramarine and vermilion with gold adornments that gleamed in the moonlight "like a pure vision of great glory."

Now Vivien kneeled before the magician and said that the castle was the most wonderful thing in the world. And Merlin promised, "I will teach you not only how to create such a structure out of invisible things, but will also teach how you may with a single touch of a wand dissipate that castle instantly into the air even as a child dissipates a bubble with a straw. And I will teach you how to change and transform a thing into the semblance of a different thing. And I will teach you spells and charms such as you never heard tell of before." But Vivien still hated Merlin, for her heart was evil and his heart was good, and evil will ever hate good.

The pair dwelled in the valley for a year, and Merlin declared that now she had power almost as profound as his. Vivien was filled with joy and prepared a great celebration. In a gold chalice she poured wine laced with a magical poison and presented it with honeyed words of flattery. The sorcerer drank cheerfully, and immediately realized that he was betrayed. "Woe! Woe! Woe!" he cried, but was unable to rise. The supreme sorcerer was as enmeshed by invisible filaments as an insect floundering for life in a silvery spiderweb. Vivien laughed and conjured up a heavy stone coffin, in which courtiers placed the rigid body and covered it with a stone slab that ten men could not lift. Merlin lay beneath the stone like one who was dead. Vivien caused the castle to vanish and in its place a mist arose so dense that no human eye could ever penetrate the enigma within. And the young sorceress went on her way rejoicing in the destruction of Merlin. So it happens down the ages, sinister forces sometimes prevail.

—BARBARA STACY

The tale derives from *The Story of King Arthur and His Knights* by Howard Pyle, who also created the vivid illustrations.

Students of occult literature soon learn the importance of names. From Ra to Rumpelstiltskin, the message is clear—names hold unusual power.

The tradition of naming full Moons was recorded in an English edition of The *Shepherd's Calendar*, published in the first decade of the 16th century.

Aries—Seed. Sowing season and symbol of the start of the new year.

Taurus—Hare. The sacred animal was associated in Roman legends with springtime and fertility.

Gemini—Dyad. The Latin word for a pair refers to the twin stars of the constellation Castor and Pollux.

Cancer—Mead. During late June and most of July the meadows, or meads, were mowed for hay.

Leo—Wort. When the sun was in Leo the worts (from the Anglo-Saxon wyrt-plant) were gathered to be dried and stored.

Virgo — Barley. Persephone, virgin goddess of rebirth, carries a sheaf of barley as symbol of the harvest.

Libra — Blood. Marking the season when domestic animals were sacrificed for winter provisions.

Scorpio — Snow. Scorpio heralds the dark season when the Sun is at its lowest and the first snow flies.

Sagittarius — Oak. The sacred tree of the Druids and the Roman god Jupiter is most noble as it withstands winter's blasts.

Capricorn — Wolf. The fearsome nocturnal animal represents the "night" of the year. Wolves were rarely seen in England after the 12th century.

Aquarius — Storm. A storm is said to rage most fiercely just before it ends, and the year usually follows suit.

Pisces — Chaste. The antiquated word for pure reflects the custom of greeting the new year with a clear soul.

Libra's Full Moon occasionally became the Wine Moon when a grape harvest was expected to produce a superior vintage.

America's early settlers continued to name the full Moons. The influence of the native tribes and their traditions is readily apparent.

AMERICAN	**Colonial**	**Native**
Aries / April	Pink, Grass, Egg	Green Grass
Taurus / May	Flower, Planting	Shed
Gemini / June	Rose, Strawberry	Rose, Make Fat
Cancer / July	Buck, Thunder	Thunder
Leo / August	Sturgeon, Grain	Cherries Ripen
Virgo / September	Harvest, Fruit	Hunting
Libra / October	Hunter's	Falling Leaf
Scorpio / November	Beaver, Frosty	Mad
Sagittarius / December	Cold, Long Night	Long Night
Capricorn / January	Wolf, After Yule	Snow
Aquarius / February	Snow, Hunger	Hunger
Pisces / March	Worm, Sap, Crow	Crow, Sore Eye

– ELIZABETH PEPPER
Moon Lore

MASQUERADE

The November Eve sabbat is a night of illusion and fantasy. Strange notions of fear, beggary, mischief; guises of ghosts, goblins and monsters have been imposed on a sacred and beautiful holiday. Clear your mind and return to the time when witchcraft had a life of its own; before the Church ruled, before the Renaissance, before the Age of Reason. November simply marks the prelude to winter's dark chill. The ancients sensed a need for courage, a ray of hope. Imagination can spark both.

"Dressing-up" is fun, still a child's favorite pastime, and appropriate to this sabbat. Have you dreamed of finding an old trunk full of wonderful costumes in a dusty attic? The extraordinary Lady Ottoline Morrell, hostess to the literary lights of England's Bloomsbury set, recognized this common fantasy. She would invite her guests to choose costumes from a chest filled with exotic garments: a mandarin's robe of heavy silk, a Turkish vest encrusted with jewels and gold ornament, the elaborate headdress of a Balinese dancer, masks, fans, and all manner of fripperies. Shyness was soon forgotten as artists, writers, statesmen and philosophers dressed up and enjoyed themselves enormously.

Witches are keenly aware of the psychological lift to the spirits a visual transformation can bring. A new persona enlivens what may appear to be a hopeless situation. Whimsy and a light heart are keys to joy. Witchcraft in America is the fruit of a tree transplanted from Europe centuries ago. Its truth is ancient and profound. November Eve celebrates the death of the year and welcomes the delights of a new cycle. Within the magic circle of death and renewal is the hidden challenge to change. Take a night off from rigid reality. Free your imagination. Whether you attend a fancy-dress ball, spend a quiet evening at home with family and friends, or perhaps alone in front of a mirror, perform a transformation just for the fun of it.

Aubrey Beardsley

The Watchers

The legend of the Watchers relates how two hundred sons of heaven descended to earth and took as wives the daughters of men. The celestial beings, angels, taught their mates the forbidden arts of magic, botany, astronomy, astrology and the use of cosmetics. Azazel, leader of the Order of Watchers, instructed mankind on the manufacture and use of weapons in the art of war.

The most complete version of the tale is given in 1 Enoch, part of the Apocrypha, works not included in the Old Testament. A possible reference to the Watchers is found in Chapter 6 of Genesis: "The sons of God saw that the daughters of men were fair; and they took to wife such of them as they chose…their wives bore them children which were the mighty men of old, the men of renown." The myth is apparently a remnant of ancient Hebrew folklore. Negative elements would emerge over time. Azazel became linked to the planet Mars and warfare. The mating of angels and mortals produced giant offspring, monsters of evil. The sleepless ones, another name for the Watchers, were punished for their sins of pride and lust, sentenced to torment and eternal damnation by the all powerful Lord.

The theme of visitors from outer space is hardly unusual. Literary fantasy of science fiction has numerous examples, but folklore worldwide, oddly enough, has few. Nevertheless, the tale of the Watchers was popular during the Middle Ages. Their arrival date of June 5 was noted on calendar manuscripts of the period.

A Loaf for Lammas

Lammas, the Great Sabbat of harvest, takes its English name from the Anglo Saxon *hlaf-maesse*, meaning "loaf mass." The old custom of baking bread from the first ground grain and presenting it at the place of worship was an expression of spiritual thanks for a bounty. Our present-day harvests are likely to be metaphorical, but expressing gratitude for our blessings is a graceful and appropriate gesture. With that theme in mind, we offer a modern version of a harvest loaf.

1 large loaf French or Italian bread
3 ripe tomatoes, peeled and chopped
1/2 cup black olives, pitted and sliced
1/4 cup pimiento-stuffed olives, sliced
4 scallions, thinly sliced
A handful of parsley, chopped
A generous pinch of dried mint leaves, crumbled
A sprinkling of dried thyme
A scattering of capers
1/4 cup Parmesan cheese, freshly grated
1 tablespoon olive oil
A dash of lemon juice
Salt and freshly ground black pepper to taste

Cut one end from the loaf and with a long knife loosen the bread within, leaving about a half inch of crust.

Scoop out the crumb into a large bowl and combine with the tomatoes, olives, scallions, parsley, mint, thyme and capers. Add the cheese, olive oil, lemon juice, salt and pepper. Mix thoroughly with a wooden spoon. Stuff the mixture firmly into the empty loaf, wrap in aluminum foil, and chill overnight.

Slice and serve as picnic fare, hors d'oeuvre or as a part of the lammastide celebration.

Note: If the tomatoes are especially juicy, you may have to add additional bread crumbs. The object is to get the stuffing moist enough but not so wet as to soften the outside crust. A delicate problem.

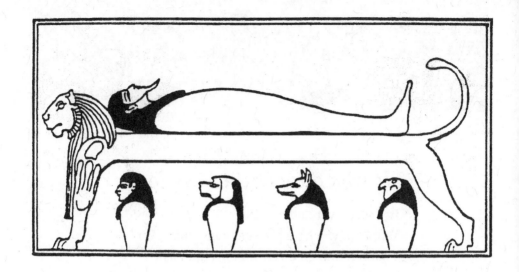

THE SONS OF HORUS

In Egyptian tombs the internal organs of the deceased were stored in four canopic jars, named after an ancient town in the Nile Delta. The receptacles, intended to preserve the viscera, were in early times plain covered vases of marble, earthenware or wood. Later, during the Middle Kingdom, the lids had human heads, often portraits of the dead. But Egypt's funerary customs became decidedly more elaborate with the advent of the New Kingdom. It was then that the covers of the canopic jars portrayed the four sons of the great solar god Horus and represented the cardinal points of the compass. The heads depicted were human, baboon, jackal and falcon. These primary guardians were in turn watched over by four goddesses.

✳   ✳   ✳   ✳

IMSETY'S head represents the human guardian. His compass point is South, Isis is his safeguard. The greatest of all Egyptian goddesses, Isis is called the "Lady of Enchantments" and "mother to all who worship her."

HAPY has the head of a baboon, an animal highly revered by Egyptians for its intelligence. He represents the North and his protector is Nephthys. While Isis symbolizes light, her sister Nephthys denotes darkness, a darkness without evil aspects. If Isis is substance, Nephthys is shadow.

DUAMUTEF is portrayed as a jackal and belongs to the East. Guardian Neith is one of the oldest deities of Egypt, her worship extending back to predynastic times. Associated with hunting, her emblems are a bow and arrows. The art of weaving is one of Neith's domains.

QEBEHSENUEF bears the head of a falcon. His cardinal point is West and Selket, the scorpion goddess, watches over him. The benevolent Selket, despite her poisonous symbol, is noted for her magical healing powers.

It was a lover and his lass

It was a lover and his lass,
With a hay, with a hoe and a hay nonie no,
That o're the green corn fields did pass,
In spring time, the only pretty ring time,
When birds do sing, hay ding a ding a ding;
Sweet lovers love the spring.

Between the acres of the rye,
With a hay, with a hoe and a hay nonie no,
These pretty country fools would lie,
In spring time, the only pretty ring time,
When birds do sing, hay ding a ding a ding,
Sweet lovers love the spring.

Then pretty lovers take the time,
With a hay, with a hoe and a hay nonie no,
For love is crowned with the prime,
In spring time, the only pretty ring time,
When birds do sing, hay ding a ding a ding,
Sweet lovers love the spring.

—THOMAS MORLEY (C.1557-1602)

BAROQUE WIT AND WISDOM

The 17th century in France is called Le Grand Siècle, The Great Century, one of the high points in Western civilization. Duc Françoise de La Rochefoucauld (1613-1680) typified the brilliance of the era and lives on today, for his words appear in every book devoted to memorable quotations. Some of his thoughts:

Grace is to the body what clear thinking is to the mind.

Nothing is rarer than true goodness.

There is more self-love than love in jealousy.

To love but little is in love an infallible means of being beloved.

Absence diminishes moderate passions and increases great ones, as the wind blows out candles and fans fire.

Judged by most of its results, love is closer to hatred than to friendship.

Few people know how to be old.

It is less dangerous to injure most people than to treat them too kindly.

The greatest fault of a penetrating wit is to go beyond the mark.

The pleasure of love is in loving. We are happier in the passion we feel than in that we arouse.

We frequently forgive those who bore us, but cannot forgive those who we bore.

A man who finds no satisfaction in himself, seeks for it in vain elsewhere.

Confidence contributes more than wit to conversation.

Midsummer Fire

bonfire, n. (ME. bonefire, banefire, orig. a fire of bones.)

Webster's Dictionary, 1934

Ceremonial bonfires celebrated holidays throughout Europe and the British Isles. The events began in pagan times and have persisted to the present. Folklorist Jacob Grimm believed them to be the survival of a once dominant religion which sought to waken latent psychic power and perception by means of ritual.

Summer solstice, the moment when the sun reaches its zenith and appears to stand still, was always an occasion for building great fires. Midsummer Night, or St. John's Eve as it came to be known under Christian domination, was observed in Britain with strict rules. A chronicle of 1515 records that "in the worship of St. John, the people make three manners of fires: one of clean bones and no wood, and that is called a bone fire; another of clean wood and no bones, and that is called a wood fire; and the third is made of wood and bones, and is called St. John's fire."

A Cornish version of Midsummer Fire occurs annually on June 23rd. When darkness falls, a beacon fire is kindled at St. Ives. Then all through the night a chain of bonfires blazes forth, one after another, across the length of the land. As each fire is lit, a master of ceremonies recites a blessing in the old Cornish language that roughly translates to:

Now set the pyre at once on fire, Let flames aspire in his high name!

A woman chosen to be Lady of the Flowers tosses a bouquet of herbs, wildflowers and leafy boughs on the fire with the invocation:

In a bunch together bound Flowers for burning here are found, Both good and ill;

Thousandfold let good seed spring, Wicked weeds fast withering.

The floral tribute contains vervain, rue, lavender, meadowsweet, St. John's wort, yellow and white daisies, or pine, feverfew, red clover mixed with branches of oak, ash and rowan.

Villagers merrily dance, young couples in love join hands and leap over the flames for good luck. The ashes of each fire are collected in a sack to form the base for the beacon fire the following year.

The Seven Deadly Sins

Gregory the Great, pope of the Roman Catholic Church from 590 to 604, may have been the first to define the medieval concept of the Seven Deadly Sins. The pontiff was renowned as a popularizer of ideas often originally pagan: angels, demons, devils, relic worship, miracles, the doctrine of purgatory and the use of allegory. Gregory, later canonized a saint, produced *Dialogues* and *Pastoral* for centuries essential in the education of the clergy.

Piers Plowman, a 14th-century English literary work, gives the Seven human form. Only Pride is feminine. Of the rest, Anger has "two pale eyes, and a sniffling nose" and Greed is "beetle-browed and flabby-lipped, with two bleary eyes." The German artist, Hans Baldung-Grien, depicted them as monsters. The Seven are identified below.

ENGLISH	GERMAN	LATIN
Pride	*Hochfart*	*Superbia*
Envy	*Neid*	*Invidia*
Anger	*Zorn*	*Ira*
Lust	*Unkeuscheit*	*Luxuria*
Greed	*Beitikat*	*Avaritia*
Gluttony	*Fressery*	*Gula*
Sloth	*Tragkait*	*Acedia*

PROMETHEUS

The romance of fire inspired poets from earliest time. Four thousand years ago Egyptians hailed the coming of the Phoenix. The fabulous bird symbolized enduring life by suffering a fiery death only to arise again from its own ashes. The Homeric Hymn to Demeter tells how the goddess placed the infant Demophoön in the heart of the hearth fire to grant him everlasting life. Perhaps the most potent story of fire derives from Greek myth as told by Hesiod:

> *Zeus would not give the power of fire to the race of mortal men who live on earth. But Prometheus outwitted him and stole the far-seen gleam of unwearying fire in a hollow fennel stalk.*

Prometheus was a resourceful Titan who stole fire from the sun and gave it to humans. His deed infuriated Zeus, who had Prometheus chained to a rock and made to suffer unspeakable torture. His punishment would end only when he disclosed the identity of the woman who would bear the son destined to depose Zeus. It was a secret known only to the Titan and one he refused to disclose.

Prometheus would become an archetypal figure in Western culture—the defiant rebel, humanity's champion, refusing to bend to the will of a supreme power. Aeschylus, the great Greek dramatist, wrote of the Titan's nobility in *Prometheus Bound*. The Roman poet Ovid told the tale again some four hundred and fifty years later. Centuries passed before England's Shelley defined the hero in his preface to his lyrical drama, *Prometheus Unbound*, as "the type of the highest perfection of moral and intellectual nature impelled by the purest and the truest motives to the best and noblest ends."

A giant gleaming statue of Prometheus dominates the plaza of Manhattan's Rockefeller Center. The bronze figure covered in gold leaf is by Paul Manship, a sculptor noted for his skill in expressing vitality and movement. The Fire Giver floats above a wide circular band upon which appear the twelve signs of the zodiac.

Manship often found inspiration in classical myths. His original sketches for the monument show a torch in the hero's right hand. The final version, however, adheres to Hesiod's words about preserving fire in the pithy center of a plant stem, a primitive way to carry fire from place to place. The noble character of the Titan is evident in the sculptor's tribute: *Prometheus brought the fire that hath proved to mortals a means to mighty ends.*

In Memoriam

With great sadness we announce to readers that Elizabeth Pepper, 79, passed away on July 14. Elizabeth was the publisher, executive editor and graphics designer of *The Witches' Almanac* as well as a number of books on the occult. She was a highly regarded member of the Craft community and enormously beloved by friends and colleagues. Elizabeth, a widow, died of a digestive ailment after months of a prolonged illness attended with devotion by a circle of close friends.

A longtime Newport, Rhode Island resident, Elizabeth was born in Providence and was a graduate of Pembroke College, Brown University, and the Rhode Island School of Design. After college she moved to New York, studied advanced type design, and became the Art Director of *Gourmet* magazine for seven years during the fifties. At that time Elizabeth married Martin Da Costa of Philadelphia. The marriage was a particularly felicitous union, loving and mutually respectful According to Elizabeth's wish, their ashes have been merged and cast into the sea from an excellent boat at a small private ceremony.

The couple were animal lovers, and dogs and cats in varying numbers were regular residents of their Manhattan home. Martin was an excellent sculptor and painter. His subjects were animals, sculpted and gilded or perceived in meticulously drawn detail much in the style of the medieval artists Elizabeth venerated and featured in the Almanac. She was one of the few remaining

Illustrations by Elizabeth Pepper

artists working with etchings, and her classic press has been donated to the Newport Historical Society.

In 1971 John Wilcock, an English journalist friend, aided her in publishing *The Witches' Almanac*. John was one of the co-founders of *The Village Voice*, and for some years ran a lively column within its

pages. Now a California resident, he has been a close friend and contributor down the years. John Wilcock changed her life, Elizabeth often said – the Almanac was doubtless her true calling, and she worked zealously every day, year in and year out, on the annual and the related book publications.

Elizabeth's impact on friends was notable. She was an incomparable source of wisdom dispensed in an unassuming manner, and we relied on her sweetness of character, affection and humor to enrich our lives. Staff and regular contributors, close friends all, tended to remain constant through the years. A visit with Elizabeth was a pleasure, tea and charm at the ready.

Elizabeth wished for the work to continue, and she has passed along The Witches' Almanac, Ltd., to her longtime friend and managing editor, Theitic. He is committed to maintaining the quality of the Almanac and other publications, and brings to the table his own talents and affinity for the company. All members of the staff and regular contributors are still on board, dedicated to keeping alive the unique spirit of the company.

Gentle Wind, Angry Wind

THE YORUBA OF NIGERIA have long honored a pantheon of deities called Orisa that often embodies natural elements. Chief among them is Oya, the ruler of the winds. A female divinity of many masks, she is recognized for her principal attribute as a warrior god riding the turbulent skies. But sometimes she manifests as Afefejeje, Gentle Breeze, revered for her ability to give respite from the heat of the day. In this role she fans her child, keeping the little one's head cool. Some devotees of Oya include in her shrine a toy windmill and a beautiful fan as tributes to her gentle aspect.

In her more fierce manifestation Oya is the goddess of howling winds, tornadoes, squalls and hurricanes. She is the wife of the equally ferocious Sango, Orisa of lightning and fire. Oya often foretells his appearance by blowing the roofs off houses and uprooting trees, and she is the wind that fans the flames of destruction wrought by Sango's lightning.

In Yorubaland where Oya is recognized—Benin and Togo as well as Nigeria—changes of the winds mark the changes of seasons crucial to these old agrarian cultures. The western wind brings the wet season, the northeastern wind brings the dry season. And as the ruler of winds, Oya also represents change in our lives. Cycles like summer breezes may pass quietly through our days. But often Oya is associated with the swift, devastating shifts like tornadoes that occasionally wreak havoc. Yet always in her wake we find quiet recovery. Without change there would be only stagnation.

Oya's dominion includes justice. Her strong, angry winds are tools for punishing the unrighteous. She is not only concerned about people abiding by law, but by their morality and compassion. The marketplace

Oya Sigil — the firma (signature) of Oya used in the Diaspora

also receives her attention, an important arena of change. Yoruba women are the dealers of food and textiles, and here fortunes may alter from poverty to riches, from riches to poverty—swift winds of drastic loss or breezes of affluence. Oya is the chief guardian of these women, and woe to the man who tries to control his merchant wife.

The deity is also known as Iyansa, mother of nine. Among those nine children which she birthed is the masquerade of the dead, the Egungun. Throughout Yorubaland masked member priests of the Egungun Society celebrate annual festivals for the ancestors. Through such masquerades the forebears may manifest among the living. In this way Oya appears again as an element of vast change, from the living to the guardian ancestor. Where the yearly festival has elapsed, Oya is regarded as the deity of the doorway to the cemetery. This manifestation is also associated with a mask—a face that cannot be seen and terrifying to those who have not been initiated.

Oya's winds, drastic or subtle, angry or balmy, always transform circumstances. May her winds blow gently in your life! As the Yoruba would say "let it be blessed"—ASE!

—IFADOYIN SANGOMUYIWA
Nigerian Priest to Sango and Babalawo "Father of Secrets"

Traditional Praise Poem for Oya
(Recited to Oya on her day of prayer)

Woman who grows a beard because of war
Powerful wind that tears down trees from their tops
She who threatens to rain with cloudy weather, yet never rains
Of the sixteen goddesses competing to have Ñàngó as a husband
It was Oya who won Sàngó as a husband
By virtue of her charming personality,
Her grace, and her elegance of movement
Oya covers herself with fire as if fire were a dress.

Spring Egg Spells

THE HARE, not the fuzzy bunny of cards and decorations, has long been a symbol of fertility. The hare excels at reproduction and provides an impressive number of offspring in a speedy mode. Since ancient times eggs also represented new life, welcome by implication. Children were essential to family survival, sharing the backbreaking work of farming. But symbols extolling human fertility were less enthusiastically viewed after the Industrial Revolution. With the prevalence of factories, the offspring of city-dwellers were now more liability than asset, especially after the law prevented child labor.

But the use of fertility symbols survives. Faced with the desire for children, some people continue to use eggs in rituals to aid conception. Some modern pagans and witches make use of symbols not as literal aids of physical reproduction, but to focus on the fecundity of mind, spirit, and the land. Many look upon spring and the humble Ostara Egg as yet another method of spell-work. Using magical correspondences, witches color and decorate eggs according to a wish or desire to be manifested. Choosing egg colors appropriate for your intention works similarly to choosing candle colors – the correspondences are generally the same. For example, many people choose red for healing because red is the color of blood, and blood represents vitality. The ancient Chinese opted for red eggs. Others choose green because it is the color of growing things, and growth of new cells is important in healing. Some prefer pink, the hue of healthy cheeks in light skin color, the source of the expression "in the pink" to describe good health. Those who use the yogic chakra system might select pink because it is associated with the heart chakra. The heart, or self-love, is often considered necessary for healing.

If you colored eggs as a child, you probably boiled them or tapped a small hole in each end and blew out the contents. But for magical spells you want raw eggs with the contents intact. Fertilized eggs, available in health-food stores or from farms, are better for spells than unfertilized commercial eggs. For best coloring results, start with a white egg, although brown eggs will do. Some chickens lay colored eggs. The Auracana chicken lays blue or green eggs, and you may be lucky enough to find eggs in the natural color needed for your spell.

Ritual preparations

To prepare the egg for coloring, wipe it with white vinegar or dip it in a solution of white vinegar and water; rinse with water. This makes the surface of the egg more porous, which helps it absorb the dye. For dye, use standard food coloring, available year-around in the baking section of your local grocery, or use an Easter egg kit. You can even use colored markers and crayons to avoid dye altogether. But for more authentic magical eggs, choose natural food coloring with dyes from nature.

For red, use the juice of raspberries, cranberries or blackberries. If you can't find fresh berries, look for frozen berries in the freezer section.

For pink, use beet juice and vinegar, the juice of pickled beets or red grape juice.

For green, a handful of carrot tops or spinach leaves yield a pale yellow-green.

For yellow, a color often used for spells regarding success, try ground turmeric.

For dark blue, the color associated with expansive Jupiter, slice red cabbage thinly and cover with water in a non-aluminum pot. (Because this color can stain, it's best to use a dark enamel pot or an old pot you don't care about.) Boil until tender. Pour into a jar, add the egg and leave overnight.

Drawing the magical symbols

You can add magical symbols after you color, using your choice of marker, paints, colored pens or whatever you choose. Or use crayons before you color, then remove the wax with a paper towel dipped in hot water.

For success, draw an icon of the sun or your hope of success. For example, for successful completion of a college degree, draw a diploma scroll or write the actual words that will be on your diploma.

For health, you may draw the staff of Aesclepias, the Greco-Roman god of medicine, a staff with a single snake twined around it.

For love, self-love or otherwise, decorate your pink egg with heart symbols and the word "love" in your own language or in all languages you can find.

For prosperity, use the sign of your local currency: a dollar sign, a pound sign, the euro sign, and so on.

Use your imagination. Draw whatever symbolizes your intention. After your egg is dry, find an appropriate place for burial, perhaps a site near your house or where you walk frequently. Or use a flowerpot filled with rich soil; you may want to decorate the pot with appropriate colors and symbols. Hold the egg in both hands, send your intent into the egg and bury it as you would a seed.

– MORVEN WESTFIELD

THE SOLAR HOUSES

1. Image
2. Finance
3. Relations
4. Family
5. Children
6. Health
7. Marriage
8. Death
9. Philosophy
10. Fame
11. Friendship
12. Sacrifice

The Queen Bee

Arthur Rackham

THREE PRINCES once set off in search of adventure. The two elder brothers mocked the youngest, whom they called Blockhead, for his nature was simple. As they traveled, they came across an anthill. The elder brothers wanted to destroy it, but Blockhead made them leave the ants alone. Then they saw some ducks swimming, and wanted to roast them, but Blockhead made them leave them alone. When they spied a beehive, they wanted to light a fire so that they could take the honey, but Blockhead made them leave the creatures in peace.

Finally the three came to an enchanted castle. A little man told them that three princesses lay asleep within. If the brothers could do three tasks, they would win the princesses. If not, they would be turned to stone.

The first task was to gather a thousand pearls that lay hidden in the moss of the forest. The first two brothers failed, and were turned to stone. But when Blockhead tried, the ants he had saved brought the pearls to him. Then he had to get the key to the princesses' room. The key lay at the bottom of a lake, and Blockhead despaired until the ducks he had saved got the key for him. For his final task, Blockhead had to determine which of the princesses was youngest and sweetest. They all looked the same. The only difference was this: at their last meal, the youngest had eaten honey, while the others had eaten some sugar and some syrup. The queen of the bees Blockhead had saved flew into the room and alighted on the lips of the youngest and sweetest princess, for she could still taste the bit of honey. When the prince awoke her, his brothers revived. Blockhead married the youngest and sweetest. Never again did his elder brothers make sport of him.

– FROM THE BROTHERS GRIMM

The buzz on honeybees

BEES RELATE to humankind on both ends of the pain/pleasure continuum, from sting to honey. We forgive the bees their occasional hostility for providing us with honey, one of the most delicious of foods, a sticky substance that makes endorphins dance. We love honey on toast in the morning, Brits spread it on scones in the afternoon, Greeks enjoy flaky baklava as dessert. Fermented honey becomes mead, created before wine and the most ancient alcoholic drink, discovered in Scottish tombs from the Iron Age.

The world has more bees than you may imagine – twenty thousand species buzz around, although we take honey from only four types in the U.S., principally *Apis mellifera*. Honeybees long have played an important role in mythology and folklore almost everywhere. In the Near East and Aegean worlds, people believed that honeybees could travel to the underworld and buzz messages to the gods. The Minoan *tholos* tombs took the form of beehives; bees and honey were arranged in graves. Alexander the Great rests in a honey-filled coffin.

Perhaps this divinity connection accounted for bees' status as the "wisest of insects" in many cultures, credited with esoteric powers. The Pythian pre-Olympian priestess remained the "Delphic bee" long after Apollo had usurped her role as oracle, and the Homeric Hymn to Apollo acknowledges that the god's gift of prophecy derived from three bee-maidens. Apollo's sister Artemis shared his bond with bees. In her later role as Diana of Ephesus, beehives symbolized the deity's fertility rites. Her cult was called the "hive," her priests and priestesses "worker bees." Demeter's priestesses were similarly termed, and their goddess was the "queen bee."

The Greeks offered libations of honey to their gods, and believed it to be the food of muses and poets. As for honey fermented into mead, in the classical Greek language "honey-intoxicated" was a pleasant term for drunk.

Bees lost none of their symbolic meaning with the rise of Christianity. Mary, like Demeter before her, was known as the "queen bee," Christ the

Dawnsio, dawnsio, little bees –
keep to your hives and do not roam.
– From a witch's blessing for honey

"honey." Christian tradition kept up the bees' connection to the underworld, too, calling them "little winged servants of God" and comparing their springtime emergence from hives to Christ's emergence from the tomb. New stories about bees also arose, such as the Welsh legend that they originated in Paradise, where they were white, and turned brown only after Adam and Eve ate the forbidden fruit.

Modern beliefs emphasize the bond between bees and beekeepers. Bees will not stay with a bad-tempered keeper. Bees must know everything that happens to the owner's family; births, illnesses, deaths. Some cultures go as far as including bees in weddings or funerals, tying red or black cloths to the top of hives and bringing sugary food to the bees while guests are feasting. Cornish tradition warns that you will get stung if you move a hive without telling the inhabitants. In many parts of the world a keeper's heir must inform the bees of the keeper's death by knocking three times on each hive with an iron key. If the bees buzz response, they are assuring their new owner that they will remain.

Bees also remain creatures of prophecy, but only single bees signify luck. Swarms of honeybees are ill omened and associated with bereavement. A honeybee landing on a hand means money coming in. A honeybee landing on a head indicates great future success. In Wales, a bee flying around a child's head foretells a happy life. A bee in the house assures good luck in Cornwall, as long as it is allowed to fly away or remain of its own will.

Nine thousand years of history and impressive powers indicate that the "wisest of insects" deserve respect. Little wonder that at one time you could only purchase bees with gold, and to gift a friend with a hive assured both honey and good luck.

– MOONDANCER

Charms for Neptune's Favors

THE URGE TO GIVE one's self up to the wonders of water has long been a source of joy. A cool dip on a hot summer day is a childhood memory cherished by many, and most of us still enjoy a day at the beach. Just a breeze from sea, river or lake offers refreshment. Evidence exists that contact with the crystals in salt water as well as negative ions generated by waterfalls have the ability to heal the mind as well as the body.

Once our feet leave the shore we are forever visitors in another realm, and there is another side to our pleasure. A deadly rip current, high winds or attack from Jaws can quickly turn the idyllic experience into a nightmare.

Early mythology always recognized the sea as a living, conscious entity. Prayers to Neptune for safe passage as well as charms against sea serpents have been recorded for thousands of years. Sailors often carried a seashell from their home ports to assure a safe return.

For swimming or boating, emulate the time-honored sailors by making personal shell charms:

When the Moon is new in a water sign, collect or purchase a shell pleasing to you. Find one with a natural hole or drill one. String the shell on a cord and reverently chant the name of Neptune or another favored water deity. Bury the shell in a dish of sea salt to be charged with protective forces until the Full Moon rises, then remove the charm. Toss the salt into the water you are about to enter as an offering and hold the shell aloft in the moonlight. The shell charm will be ready to wear as you enter the water.

Surfers at Florida's Sebastian Inlet usually possess a special charm. The waves at the inlet are notoriously shark infested. A shark's tooth added to a choker of puka shells is worn as a warning. The idea is that the sharks will stay away, sensing what happened to the last one who bothered the surfer. Puka shells are the small tops of the Pacific Island conus shell. They have a natural hole and were collected in Hawaii to be worn by island queens and princesses as adornments and talismans. Pisces Elizabeth Taylor was given puka shells as a ceremonial gift from the sea during a 1974 visit to Hawaii. She wore them publicly often. With or without a shark's-tooth pendant, a puka choker is a beautiful and powerful talisman to wear against the perils of the briny deep.

— ESTHER ELAYNE

Merry Meetings

A candle in the window, a fire on the hearth,
a conversation over tea…

From time to time, *The Witches' Almanac* will offer interviews with noted members of the Craft community. The first such to grace our pages is the conversation below with the late Elizabeth Pepper:

Although one must admit that it's a subtle declaration, you have been referring to yourself obliquely as a "witch…from New England" on the title page of The Witches' Almanac *since its first publication in 1971. How did you come to define yourself as a witch or associate yourself with witchcraft?*

My parents and other members of our family practiced the Craft. All of them, in one way or another, taught me. The training was informal. You learned as you grew, selecting or rejecting whatever came into your scope. Speaking from my own experience, magic is something that is learned day by day in an indirect fashion. It can't be formally taught. And because there is no dogma, you evolve your own pattern.

That would place you in the somewhat controversial camp of hereditary, family, or traditional witches. Since authenticity is often called into question for those with this background, would you mind sharing some information regarding your lineage?

I was an only child; *the* only child on my mother's side of the family. I grew up in Providence, Rhode Island, on the East Side.

My father's family, the Peppers, came to this country in the sixteen-hundreds and there were English, Welsh, Scottish, Irish, Dutch and German surnames on the family tree. I gather that at least one member of each succeeding generation had an interest in or displayed an aptitude for witchcraft. The trait surfaced again and again.

My maternal grandmother was Spanish Basque. She met and married my grandfather, an Anglo-Irish sculptor whose specialty was gravestone angels, in London. They immigrated to America, settled in New England in 1887 and raised seven daughters and one son. I think it's unusual for an entire family to follow a single

occult path, but my mother's did. Six of my aunts lived within walking distance. Each one had a particular occult interest or talent. The mainspring of Craft traditions as I know them comes from them.

I think it is safe to say that growing up with an entire family that practices witchcraft is a rather unique experience that would place you in a minority among today's witches. Looking back on your childhood, what would you say are some of your greatest lessons or favorite memories?

It was fun. The Craft educates the heart and the spirit as well as the mind. Imagination is constantly encouraged and stimulated. I learned to recognize how commonplace things could be touched with magic. I have so many lovely memories — like being given my first kitten or watching the full moon rise for the first time. These were like sacred ceremonies, very solemn occasions.

Can you describe some of the magical work that you did with your family?

Dark of the Moon was the time for healings and forming rings of protection.

Tide Turnings, that's changing a run of bad luck by ritual, took place after the first quarter of the waxing moon. If someone had a near accident, a close call, and was haunted by it, the group would get together to remove the fright at full moon. Something was always happening—a disagreeable boss giving trouble, a love affair that wasn't working out—we'd concentrate to make it right, turning negatives to positives.

How old were you when you were allowed to participate in magical workings?

As soon as I could comprehend the nature of the problem to be solved or turned right, even in very simple terms, I joined my mind with the rest. Young children often bring a surprising amount of mental energy to the case at hand.

You say that the training was informal, unstructured, and that there is no dogma. If all of this is true, how does one come to define oneself as a witch? Is there an underlying moral or ethical code that you were taught to follow as a member of the Craft?

The first thing that comes to my mind is the deep and abiding love for animals. This is the one attribute every member of my family, all their friends, every single person we knew and associated with shared in common. I feel it is central to the recognition and practice of witchcraft. I realize that this is a sweeping statement, certain to provoke dissent. However, I'm absolutely convinced of its truth. Second is a sense of humor.

It's like a balance wheel. We should be serious in our work, or Craft undertakings, but not pious. "A witch isn't self-righteous" is the theme. Third – there is always a third, which is a tradition in itself – you can never refuse a cry for help. And when a gift is given or a favor done, the recipient is expected to pass the goodness along – not to necessarily repay the giver but to respond in a similar manner when the occasion arises. Other than that, I can only say that I think witchcraft is far more mysterious than anyone realizes.

You are far too engaged in the world around you to be accused of remaining aloof and unaware of the resurgence in witchcraft during the last five decades. How would you compare contemporary Craft to the Craft you were taught as a child?

Much of the lore and flavor is similar. Religion is far heavier a focus today than the Craft I grew up to know. That is not to say our work wasn't considered sacred, for it was very serious indeed. The structure of beliefs and ethical considerations were of an entirely different framework.

Elizabeth, you have always chosen to keep your personal life private. You've always denied having students, stating simply that your teaching is done through your writing. You have no coven and you claim no initiates. You choose instead to be who you are and practice the Craft as a way of life, in the same manner that is was handed down to you. Why then, do you expose yourself to public scrutiny by publishing The Witches' Almanac?*

I wanted to rid the Craft of its reputation of evil, horror, chicanery. I wanted to make it elegant; present its beauty, gentle nature, deep wisdom and simple good sense. I wanted to show that the Craft, like the Tao, is a way, an attitude toward living.

Finally, do you have any parting thoughts or words of advice?

Witchcraft fills a need for beauty, faith, romance, and a sense of the larger pattern. It's as simple as this — a sense of witchcraft is as elusive as a sense of humor. It can't be defined or taught. But if you've got it, you know it. You'll know if you belong to us. It's a lovely world full of joy and surprises, rewards beyond imaging.

Prometheus

✳ the fixed stars

NASHIRA – THE FORTUNATE ONE. Long ago, as the first horoscopes were being drawn, ancient astrologers divided the celestial bodies into three groups. There were the luminaries, the "bright lights," the Sun and Moon. The stars that moved rapidly were called "planets," from a word which means "wanderer." The last group, by far the most numerous, are the fixed stars. There are many thousands of them. Each one glittering in the night sky is a Sun, glowing by generating its own light. Many may be surrounded by a solar system of planets like our own. Variations in distance and chemical composition give the fixed stars different colors and magnitude, or brightness. Astrologically this means that each creates unique cosmic energies, some positive and some sinister. The term "fixed" is rather a misnomer. The stars do move, but very, very slowly. Astrologers took a long time to recognize this movement because the distance covered in a century is barely perceptible.

Nashira is a star whose name means "She Who Brings Good News," or "The Fortunate One" in Arabic. Currently located at 20 degrees of Aquarius, 33 minutes 52 seconds, Nashira is truly a lucky star. The legendary astrologer Ptolemy related the nature of Nashira to that of the benevolent, generous planet Jupiter stabilized by Saturn. When active in the horoscope of a person or in an event chart, Nashira's presence turns hardship to success. Evil is overcome by goodness. Success in government matters as well as a gift for writing come to light when Nashira shines. However caution prevails regarding wild or large animals. Especially at this time they must be handled with thought and skill or injury tends to occur.

Those born from February 8 to 14 have Nashira conjunct the Sun. Many important and powerful individuals, including Abraham Lincoln and Charles Darwin, were born during this time. However Nashira impacts other birthdates as well. Check your horoscope for planets positioned from 19 to 25 degrees of Aquarius. These are within orb of being positively affected by this angel among the stars. According to the nature of the planet in question and its house position, Nashira will stimulate a realization of its highest and best potentials.

From spring 2007 through early 2008, Neptune will transit from 20 to 22 degrees of Aquarius, in exact conjunction with Nashira. Neptune relates to all that is fanciful and illusionary as well as beautiful, including elves and fairies. Overall spiritual awakening can be expected. Those who meditate and study yoga can make great progress. Mediumship, tarot and other esoteric subjects can provide new levels of enlightenment. The fine arts, especially music and dance, will be favorably affected. New types of music and dance forms can emerge. Neptune in Aquarius is in mutual reception with Uranus in Pisces. This cosmic shape shift brings a Uranian element to Nashira's message. New technologies are perfected to solve old problems.

Remembering the ancient caution this star gives regarding animals, it's important to note that Neptune rules marine life. Swimmers, divers, fishermen and sailors would be wise to respect the ecology of the sea and to exercise caution when they encounter the creatures of the deep.

From March 24 to 30, 2007, Mars will transit in conjunction with Nashira. This time period favors athletes and all kinds of adventurous undertakings. Military matters will take a fortunate turn. Those who handle animals must use special caution, especially advisable at competitive events such as dog shows and horse shows.

From March 4 to 12, 2008, Mercury and Venus will conjoin Nashira. The release of new works of visual art, films or books is favored. It's a time when writers, students, travelers and artists will all find that their undertakings are blessed.

– DIKKI-JO MULLEN

Arabian astronomer constructing a celestial globe, from Alboul Hassan Ali's *Praeclarissimum in Juditijs Astrorum*, Venice, 1519

Buddha's Magical Numbers

Four Noble Truths – an Eightfold Path

IN OUR ACTION-DIRECTED world, most people think there's no point in sitting still. Modern witches, magicians and pagans might feel that we are more in touch with a slower, more cosmic rhythm – but are we? Even in metaphysical circles our lives may be overly busy, filled with daily obligations that seem to leave no time for calm reflection. For improved concentration, clearer connection to our inner selves and a deeper sense of compassion, one Buddhist teacher offers excellent advice: "Don't just do something, sit there!"

Although in the West we think of Buddhism as a religion, it is essentially a technique for understanding our essential nature and ending suffering. Substitute the phrase "true will" for "essential nature" and you will begin to see that the traditions of East and West might not be so far apart. In Greece, the famous inscription at the temple of Delphi advised, "Know thyself." The journey of the Buddha, Siddhartha Gautama, followed just that directive. Through the technique of sitting meditation he attained four insights, now called "The Four Noble Truths," and an "Eightfold Path" – fundamentals of every form of Buddhism worldwide.

The Noble Truths:

1. Nothing lasts forever. Expecting to be miserable when things come to an end. This is called "impermanence," often stated as "life is suffering."

2. This suffering starts because we are attached to the idea that things will last forever or that if we can just find the magic formula, we can make things the way want them to be, always. This is called "craving" or "attachment."

3. We don't have to be miserable. We can teach ourselves to let go of our cravings and attachments so that we don't have to suffer as much when things change, as they inevitably will. This truth is called "freedom from confinement" or "extinction." It is like getting the key to our jail cell or blowing out a candle burning us.

4. There is a path to liberation from suffering and getting burned by our expectations. This path runs between the extremes of hedonism and asceticism.

The Eightfold Path: Right Understanding, Right Intention, Right Speech, Right Action, Right Livelihood, Right Effort, Right Mindfulness, Right Concentration.

Meditation techniques

In the Buddhist view, the way to work on these techniques must be grounded in meditation, the eighth branch of the Path. Through sitting still, bringing full attention to what transpires mentally, a practitioner comes to understand how to embody the other parts of the path and attain freedom. When you temporarily remove the distractions of a busy life, you come to see how reactive your mind really is. It is quite shocking to realize how many activities you do almost in your sleep.

The basic technique given to Buddhist students is to simply sit, for perhaps five minutes a day in the beginning, just being aware of your breath as it moves in and out of your body. Thoughts seem to fill your every moment, demanding that you do their bidding. *Get up! What are you doing here, doing nothing? Feed the kids! Pay the bills! Did you remember to turn off the stove? Maybe the house is on fire. Go look. Get up! Get up!* You might think of this as "getting on the train."

Whenever you find yourself on the train, get off without adding more thoughts to the baggage. Like the demons that wrestled with the Buddha in his quest to awaken, your thoughts wrestle you. The impressions might get darker, scarier, more intense, but still, just get off the train. Keep going back to noticing your breath, a simple act always in the present moment.

After a long period of awareness about how many "worry, scurry" concerns race around, you begin to notice their ebbing. Perhaps you're not entirely made up of anxiety, anger and obligation. When fears begin to recede, detachment begins. This is when meditation becomes fruitful. You learn how to let go of disparaging attitudes toward yourself and others, and compassion springs up like grass after the rain. Anger, greed and ignorance loosen their grip. The negative actions of others seem less important and the small everyday moments in life are revealed as beautiful. You focus more on making better choices and forgiving yourself for mistakes. You are no longer a prisoner of your thoughts.

If you devote yourself firmly to this process, a deeper connection to life emerges. In this awareness lie the seeds of enlightenment or awakening – "Buddha" simply means "one who is awake." How do we assess a spiritual or religious path unless it makes us more compassionate, more grounded, focused and aware? If your personal path seems to be lacking these elements lately, you might want to try just sitting there.

– ELIZABETH ROSE

From Ming dynasty porcelain: the "eight Buddhist symbols"

Crystal Balls

Visions in smoke

WE'VE ALL SEEN the image of the fortune teller with her headscarf, peasant blouse, broomstick skirt. Her fingers are covered with rings, her forearms decked with gold bracelets. She sits at a round table passing her hands in circular motions over a ball. A client may be listening to her say, "I see a tall, dark stranger..." Perhaps you've wondered if you too could see visions in a crystal ball.

The process begins with the right material. Many balls are now made of acrylic and much more affordable than the traditional quartz crystal. Whatever material you choose, select your crystal carefully to make sure it is free of scratches, bubbles, or occlusions. Use the crystal in a darkened room. The only light should be a candle, positioned so that the flame does not reflect in the ball. Bring yourself into a relaxed state and gaze at the ball. Blink naturally. Clear your mind.

After a time the ball will appear to fill with smoke and then gradually clear, leaving behind a scene. Allow your mind to make free associations. Note the spatial relationships and movement of images. Ascending clouds are believed to answer questions in the affirmative; descending, negative.

You may not see anything at first. Try passing your hands over the ball. Passes with the right give power, while passes with the left increase your sensitivity to the crystal's messages. If you do not see anything after ten minutes, put the ball away and try again later. Even with daily practice it may take as much as a week to see something.

When the ball is not in use, swaddle it in silk or velvet and store it away. Some crystal gazers feel that only the owner should handle the mystical ball. Other adepts have the querent hold the ball and meditate on a question.

If you're not sure you want to invest in a crystal ball, try one of the traditional substitutes – a mirror, a bowl of ink, or even a dark bowl of water. Practice gazing as described above. Be patient. Sooner or later you have a good chance of encountering visions in smoke.

– MORVEN WESTFIELD

The Bald Man and the Fly

Aesop's Fables   Illustrated by Arthur Rackham

THERE WAS ONCE a Bald Man who sat down after work on a hot summer's day. A Fly came up and kept buzzing about his bald pate, and stinging him from time to time. The Man aimed a blow at his little enemy, but – whack – his palm came on his head instead; again the Fly tormented him, but this time the Man was wiser and said:

"You will only injure yourself if you take notice of despicable enemies."

Hathor at Dendera

with the sistrum – a metal rattle thought to echo a papyrus stem being shaken. The sound was considered protective, symbolic of Hathor's divine blessings.

The goddess is known as Eye of the Sun, the daughter of Ra, and she dances to charm the sun god when he is in a stormy mood. In her fascinating Distant Goddess myth, Hathor clashes with Ra and wanders away from Egypt. Grief falls over the land and Ra, lost without his Eye, decides to fetch her. But the benevolent Hathor has turned feral, into a raging wildcat, and no one knows how to catch her. Thoth eventually manages to coax her home with stories, and back in Egypt she bathes in the Nile to calm the flames of rage. Eventually the waters cool Hathor down to her usual gentle demeanor, but not before the waters of the river turn red – emblematic of divine rage shed.

– LENURA BARD

ON THE EDGE of the Egyptian desert lies the ancient city of Dendera. Behind the mud brick walls in this isolated area are a cluster of well-preserved temples from antiquity. The site was paramount to the worship of Hathor, the female deity par excellence in the earliest pantheon. Her temple rises magnificently from foundations that date to the fourth millennium. Hathor is most often associated with the Celestial Cow, one who protects calves, and in her motherly aspect safeguards pregnant women and children. The temple compound includes a birthing house. Hathor is depicted with cow's ears, as seen on the temple pillars, or horns cradling a sun disk.

The deity meant everything to women of the era. She is the patron of beauty, love, sexuality, joy, dance and music. Hathor enjoyed a large female priesthood performing during temple rituals as dancers, singers and musicians. At Dendera Hathor is also associated

Notable Quotations
Prophecy

Every dream is a prophecy.

– George Bernard Shaw

The difference between heresy and prophecy is often one of sequence. Heresy often turns out to have been prophecy – when properly aged.

– Hubert Humphrey

To see clearly is poetry, prophecy and religion – all in one.

– John Ruskin

The best qualification of a prophet is to have a good memory.

– The Marquis of Halifax

If you can look into the seeds of time, and say which grain will grow and which will not, speak then unto me.

– William Shakespeare

She is the Sybil;
    days that distant lie
Bend to the promise that her
    word shall give.

– Thomas Gordon Hake

Prophecy, however honest, is generally a poor substitute for experience.

– Benjamin Cardozo

And it shall come to pass afterward, that I will pour out my spirit upon all flesh; and your sons and your daughters shall prophesy, your old men shall dream dreams, your young men shall see visions.

– Joel 2:28, King James Version

For I dipped into the future,
    far as human eye could see,
Saw the vision of the world, and
    all the wonder that would be.

– Alfred, Lord Tennyson

My interest is in the future because I am going to spend the rest of my life there.

– C.F. Kettering

This is the first age that's ever paid much attention to the future, which is a little ironic since we may not have one.

– Arthur C. Clarke

Why Wisdom Is Everywhere

A LONG TIME ago, Anansi the spider had all the wisdom in the world stored in a huge pot. Nyame, the sky god, had given it to him. Anansi had been instructed to share it with everyone.

Every day Anansi looked in the pot and learned different things. The pot was full of wonderful ideas and skills. Anansi greedily thought, "I will not share the treasure of knowledge with everyone. I will keep all the wisdom for myself."

So Anansi decided to hide the wisdom on top of a tall tree. He took some vines and made some strong string and tied it firmly around the pot, leaving one end free. He then tied the loose end around his waist so that the pot hung in front of him. He then started to climb the tree. He struggled as he climbed because the pot of wisdom kept getting in his way, bumping against his stomach.

Anansi's son watched in fascination as his father struggled up the tree. Finally Anansi's son told him, "If you tie the pot on your back, it will be easier to cling to the tree and climb." Anansi tied the pot to his back instead, and continued to climb the tree with much more ease.

When Anansi got to the top of the tree, he became angry. "A young one with some common sense knows more than I, and I have the pot of wisdom!"

In anger, Anansi threw down the pot of wisdom. The pot broke and pieces of wisdom flew in every direction. People found the bits scattered everywhere, and if they wanted to they could take some home to their families and friends.

That is why, to this day, no one person has *all* the world's wisdom. People everywhere share small pieces of it whenever they exchange ideas.

– *Author unknown*
Motherland Nigeria

Decoration from Hausa people, Nigeria

196

The Bear Who Married a Woman

ONCE UPON A TIME there lived a widow of the tribe of the Gispaxlats. Many men tried to marry her daughter, but she declined them all.

The mother said, "When a man comes to marry you, feel of the palms of his hands. If they are soft, decline him. If they are rough, accept him." She meant that she wanted to have for a son-in-law a man skillful in building canoes.

Her daughter obeyed her mother's commands and refused the wooings of all young men. One night a youth came to her bed. The palms of his hands were very rough, and therefore she accepted his suit. Early in the morning, however, he had suddenly disappeared, even before she had seen him.

When her mother arose early in the morning and went out, she found a halibut on the beach in front of the house, although it was midwinter. The following evening the young man came back, but disappeared again before the dawn of the day. In the morning the widow found a seal in front of the house. Thus they lived for some time. The young woman never saw the face of her husband; but every morning she found an animal on the beach, every day a larger one. Thus the widow came to be very rich.

She was anxious to see her son-in-law, and one day she waited until he arrived. Suddenly she saw a red bear emerge from the water. He carried a whale on each side, and put them down on the beach. As soon as he noticed that he was observed, he was transformed into a rock, which may be seen up to this day. He was a supernatural being of the sea.

– FRANZ BOAS
Tsimshian Mythology

✢ The Doctrine of Signatures ✢

WHEN YOU BITE a carrot, examine its cross-section – lines radiate outward from its core like the pupil of an eye. Popular folk myth claims carrots are good for eyesight and Western research has come to back this up. This is a survival of the wisdom called "the doctrine of signatures."

The doctrine of signatures is popularly regarded as a medieval herbalist belief that God left signs in plants to reveal their medicinal uses. A plant's properties, including its appearance, taste and smell, governed its virtues. Many of these claims have been supported by modern research.

Common examples of the doctrine include lobelia, the stomach-shaped leaves of which indicate emetic

qualities, and bloodroot, the blood-red roots of which treat toxic blood diseases. The milky sap of mature lettuce leaves has been prescribed for lactation, beets to build blood, and kidney beans to strengthen the kidneys. Stinging nettle's hairy leaves are a common ingredient in hair concoctions and liverwort's liver-shaped leaves promote hepatic functioning.

Because yellow also indicated plants useful to the liver, the yellow roots of goldenseal, Oregon grape and barberry plants were used for jaundice. The yellow-flowered dandelion remains a popular liver tonic today.

The sixteenth-century alchemist, Oswald Croll, reportedly said of walnuts that "these have the perfect Signature of the Head: the outer husk or green Covering represent the Pericranium, or outward skin of the skull...and therefore salt[s] made of those husks or barks, are exceeding good for wounds of the head....The kernel hath the very figure of the brain, and therefore it is very profitable for the brain." Research shows walnuts are rich in Omega-3 fatty acids, an essential nutrient to brain functions.

To accompany the walnut, herbalist William Coles recommended for balding a "decoction of the long Mosse that hangs upon Trees."

Spiritual roots

Although the term "doctrine of signatures" was first published in medieval Europe by Paracelsus in the sixteenth century, it undoubtedly began as a spiritual philosophy, perhaps as part of the concept of magical sympathy – the belief in a symbolic universe with vibratory patterns that link objects endowed with similar qualities.

Paracelsus appears to be the first to write about the "language of nature," but he certainly didn't invent it. In the first century C.E., Balinus published an alchemical work claimed to be of great antiquity entitled "The Emerald Tablet." A portion of its translation reads, "Whatever is below is like that which is above, and whatever is above is like that which is below, to accomplish the miracles of one thing."

Schooled in these mysteries, Paracelsus claimed that a consistency existed between the outer and inner worlds: "All of nature signifies, all is purposive, once our eyes are opened to it." Known as the "German Hermes," he claimed nature left signs in all earthly things – just as the number of tines on a stag's antler showed the animal's age, so did plants symbolize in their shape, color, smell or taste their healing properties.

Although much hated by the medical establishment, Paracelsus' methods were effective. In one conflict he was forced to treat syphilis brought back by Columbus' crew from the New World that had proved resistant to local doctors. Paracelsus cured nine out of fourteen cases.

Evidence of the doctrine of signatures exists worldwide. In India, peasants cure venomous bites with snakeroot. A Chinese document dating back as early as 1000 B.C.E. breaks plants down into five elemental correspondences and then goes a step further, recommending only the upper parts of herbs to treat the upper half of the body and the lower half for the lower extremities.

Today flower essence and homeopathic medicine has added to the doctrine. Through blind tests, where the source substance was revealed to neither researchers nor subjects, homeopathic remedies have supported the doctrine of signatures' effectiveness in not only plants, but also minerals and animals.

Mark Twain said that "Cauliflower is nothing but cabbage with a college education." Who's to say he wasn't right? After all, what other vegetable looks more like a brain?

– NIALLA

ASCLEPIUS

Deity of healing arts

PRINCESS Coronis of Thessaly was among the mortal women lucky enough (or unlucky enough) to mate with a god – the mighty Apollo. Unfortunately the beautiful Coronis lacked the good sense to stay faithful and was subsequently slain by Apollo's ever-loyal twin sister, Artemis. As Coronis began to crackle on her funeral pyre, Apollo took pity on the son still inside her womb. From this act of mercy was born Asclepius, god of healing.

Asclepius took pity on suffering mankind as his father had taken pity on him. With the knowledge he acquired from the wise centaur Chiron, his adoptive father, Asclepius set out of his boyhood cave and began to cure the diseases that ravaged his mortal brethren. He traveled extensively, absorbing local healing practices. As time passed Asclepius became famous as the most knowledgeable healer in Greece. Wherever he went, the region became healthier.

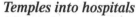

Temples into hospitals

People began to regard Asclepius as a deity. Temples sprang up in his honor where he had relieved the suffering. Over time the temples pervaded Greece and the sick flocked to the steps seeking help. Beds were placed in front of Asclepius' altars to accommodate patients. His temples became the first hospitals.

Asclepius' methods of determining the cause of ailments and the treatments he prescribed ranged from the practical to the mystical. Among the most fantastic of his methods was to give his patients a soporific potion and then divine the cause and cure for their ailments based on dream interpretation. Asclepius also often sought the advice of snakes, which he believed possessed secret knowledge of the earth's cures. Asclepius therefore found snakes good company. He kept two with him at all times, curled around his staff at the ready to dispense their secret wisdom. This attribute survives today as the Asclepian staff or caduceus, the universally recognizable symbol of modern medicine.

Cheating Hades

The curing arts of Asclepius eventually became so advanced that he was actually able to bring the dead back to rosy-cheeked life. This was all well and good for mankind, but Hades was becoming rather irked. Every body that was saved from death by the healing art of Asclepius equaled one less soul in the underworld. Soon the flow of souls over the river Styx ceased. To Hades this was a perversion of the natural order. He demanded immediate action be taken by his brother Zeus. But Zeus failed to see a problem with the behavior of Asclepius. The good he did mankind greatly outweighed the disservice to Hades. And happier, healthier mortals meant more jubilant feasts and sacrifices to the Olympian gods. Zeus allowed Asclepius and his offspring (notably daughters Hygieia, goddess of health, and Panacea, goddess of the cure-all) to continue their good work undisturbed. But one day Asclepius accepted gold in exchange for his services.

To Zeus, this was outrageous. Asclepius had always seemed to act out of love for his mortal brothers; by accepting coin, Asclepius now seemed to act for personal gain. Fearing an escalation of this selfish practice, Zeus struck Asclepius with a lightening bolt. And so the life of Asclepius ended where it had begun – in a pile of ash.

Despite his untimely end, the influence of Asclepius can still be felt. His godly form was placed in the sky by Zeus and still hangs there as Ophiuchus, the serpent bearer, watching over ailing humanity even today. The Greek doctor Hippocrates, from whom modern medicine received the edict "first do no harm," claimed to be a direct descendent of Asclepius. Should that be true, the lineage of Asclepius could take credit for the multitude of advances effected by Hippocrates and his followers.

– SHANNON MARKS

201

Roger Bacon

The Wise Enchanter

DESPITE everything that Apuleius of Madaura, Cornelius Agrippa, Pico della Mirandola, or indeed Éliphas Lévi and Aleister Crowley could do to raise "magic" out of the mire of disrepute it has lain in for centuries, ultimately, so far as the general public is concerned at any rate, their efforts have not paid off. To most people outside the neo-pagan community, the word "magic" describes at best something out of fairy tales, at worst the craft of stage illusionists or the scams of charlatans.

The word *"magia"* was coined by Greeks and Romans as a term to describe supernormal acts performed by mortals. But even then it carried a pejorative stigma implying something *"nefas,"* not quite proper and indeed outlandish – the Magi were after all originally a priestly caste serving a remote Persian religion. Magic has labored in vain off and on over the years to acquire respectability, and during the first millennium C.E. the Christian Church only compounded the problem by adding the Devil into the mix. According to Church doctrine,

anything "supernatural" was, by definition, either stage-managed by angels or by devils, and seeing that the Church had sole charge over angelic matters, that left only devils for magicians to work with.

Friar Roger Bacon was a thirteenth-century Franciscan monk who over the years also garnered a legendary reputation as a magician. Historian Claire Fanger has recently demonstrated that

The Evil Spirit figured as a black bird whispering into the ear of a magician. Hortus Deliciarum, *eleventh century*

Bacon was not only actually quite interested in magic, but probably had experimented with it, too. However he took pains to avoid applying the term "magician" to himself, for by this point in history magicians had already been defined by the Church as folk dependent on diabolical assistance. Bacon, however, appears to have studied the non-Christian Arabic occult philosophy that began filtering into Europe between the eleventh and thirteenth centuries. Seeking to take the "super" out of "supernatural," he came to the conclusion that "properly performed" ritual acts and incantations resulting in apparently miraculous results were in fact quite "natural" and therefore fell within the purview, not of religion, but of what would later be known as "science," something that today we might label psychic research or psi. So when writing about such acts and those that performed them, Bacon prudently opted to use the word *"sapienter,"* "sage," or "wise man," rather than *"mage."*

"When words are uttered with deep thought and great desire and good intention and firm confidence, they have great virtue," he wrote, with enormous understatement, in his *Opus Tertium.* "Then they are philosophical and the work of a sage, wisely enchanting...."

Bacon had, for the first time in the English language, articulated the first rule to be learned by the would-be apprentice, "wise" enchanter.

– PAUL HUSON

---

from Opus Majus

"If in other sciences we should arrive at certainty without doubt and truth without error, it behooves us to place the foundations of knowledge in mathematics."

"Mathematics is the gate and key of the sciences....Neglect of mathematics works injury to all knowledge, since he who is ignorant of it cannot know the other sciences or the things of this world."

"Argument is conclusive, but it does not remove doubt, so that the mind may rest in the sure knowledge of the truth, unless it finds it by the method of experiment. For if any man who never saw fire proved by satisfactory arguments that fire burns, his hearer's mind would never be satisfied, nor would he avoid the fire until he put his hand in it that he might learn by experiment what argument taught."

土
牛

Illustration by Ogmios MacMerlin

YEAR OF THE EARTH OX
January 26, 2009 to February 13, 2010

The gentle and patient Ox, actually a symbol for the ancient Water Buffalo, is beloved in legends and art throughout the Orient. Uncomplaining and hardworking, Ox reaches its goals through sheer endurance. Occasionally an Ox will become enraged and charge an adversary in frustration, but that's a rare occurrence. Usually this faithful one can be found pulling a plough or turning the water wheel. Ox is a good friend who provides sustenance for others. During an Ox Year, sincerity and hard work will earn respect. Make it a successful cycle through diligence and perseverance. Those who are mild mannered and modest tend to attract the attention of powerful and helpful associates.

People born during an Ox Year are contemplative and industrious. A surprising eloquence surfaces as they explain positions and subjects they feel strongly about. They often have an exceptional vocabulary and language skills. Quite persuasive, they can use subtle humor to make a point. Strong opinions concerning right and wrong are firmly held. Loyalty is important and a certain stubbornness is present. Because those born in the Year of the Ox are careful observers, they develop outstanding accuracy and proficiency. They leave a lasting impression on their surroundings and upon their acquaintances.

If you were born during one of the years of the Ox, as listed below, you will be starting a new cycle of growth and opportunity this year.

1913   1925   1937   1949   1961   1973   1985   1997   2009

Return of the Green Fairy

We took a glass of absinthe to compose our nerves.

– Thackeray

ABSINTHE IS BACK behind bars in the U.S., the fabled herbal liquor banned here since 1912. At that time the villain of the drink, according to the Department of Agriculture, was its content of wormwood, a bitter herb deemed to have a drastic effect on habitual users. The feds may also have had their knickers in a twist because of the raffish cultural backstory of the drink. Its abuse can provoke hallucinations, convulsions and psychoses.

During the Belle Epoch and the early twentieth century, absinthe was all the rage in Paris, other European sites and in major U.S. cities, especially New Orleans. In bistros absinthe seemed to be the choice intoxicant of painters, musicians, poets, journalists, philosophers, aristos, ne'er-do-wells, drunks, prostitutes, chronic troublemakers – anyone with the time and inclination to hang out and do some serious drinking. The list of famous devotees is extensive, including at random Gauguin, van Gogh, Manet, Toulouse-Lautrec, Degas, Verlaine, Baudelaire, Rimbaud, and Picasso. Roaring around France, Spain, Cuba and the U.S., Hemingway knocked back his own manly share.

Although it is not a psychedelic, absinthe is reported to induce clarity, a heightened state of mind and mood. Its abuse is believed to provoke mental deterioration.

The biblical "bitter gall and wormwood" has become proverbial. But the drink was consumed for thousands of years, sometimes as medication, sometimes for pure pleasure. Ancient absinthe, generally just wormwood leaves soaked in wine, has been the subject of diverse health claims. Hippocrates advised it for jaundice and anemia, Pythagoras claimed that it eased labor in childbirth, Pliny recommended it as a cure for bad breath. Onward to seventeenth-century France, a court lady wrote the definitive word to Mme. de Sévigné, "My little absinthe is the cure for all diseases."

Then as now, absinthe has its own ritual. It is prepared by slowly pouring icy water through a lump of sugar on a slotted spoon over a glass holding a small amount of absinthe. The solution trickles into the glass until the liquor turns "louch," generally a pale green, dubbed the "Green Fairy" – a spirit recently revisiting America.

A Garland of Seasonal Festivals

WHILE modern Wiccans and Neo-Pagans celebrate all eight seasonal festivals of the Wheel of the Year, most books and articles on the subject seem to concentrate on the four major ones – Imbolg, Beltane, Lughnassad and Samhain. These are of Celtic origin while the other four, the equinoxes and solstices, are older and probably date back to Neolithic times. The megalithic culture that built the stone circles in Britain and Europe used these monuments to mark the solar and lunar seasonal alignments. We still observe various folk customs associated with the equinoxes and solstices – the dates when day and night are equal and the shortest and longest days – which originated with pagan beliefs and rituals.

Spring and summer

March 21st is the vernal or spring equinox (the date is approximate as the equinoxes and solstices move from year to year by a few days). This festival usually coincides with the Easter period in the Christian calendar, set each year by the ancient calculation that it is the first Sunday after the first full moon after the spring equinox. The celebration retains many of the pagan elements of the old spring rites. For instance, on Good Friday people eat hot-cross buns, which originated with the small cakes used by the Greeks, Romans and Saxons as sacrificial offerings at the spring festival.

In ancient Rome a small cake with an equal-arm-cross decoration was offered to Diana, the goddess of the moon and hunting. This pagan origin is reflected in the popular belief that preserved pieces of hot-cross bun can be used as a protective charm against fire or for healing purposes.

Easter Eggs also have a pagan source. It was a widespread pre-Christian custom to give painted eggs as a gift for fertility at the spring festival. The egg in ancient times was a well-known symbol of the life principle. In many cultures Creation was believed to have

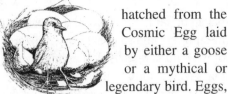

hatched from the Cosmic Egg laid by either a goose or a mythical or legendary bird. Eggs, especially golden ones laid by a golden goose as in fairy tales, were also symbols of the sun. On Easter morning they were rolled down hillsides in imitation of the solar orb's progressions through the sky. A folk belief also discloses that at sunrise on Easter Sunday the sun can be seen to dance with joy. In folklore hares were supposed to lay eggs to give birth to their young. They were the sacred animal of the moon goddess Eostre, the Saxon deity who gave her name to Easter. This is possibly the origin of the Easter Bunny, really a hare.

Midsummer or the summer solstice (approximately June 21st), the shortest day of the year, was celebrated in the West Country and Scotland with the burning of fires on the hills. People leaped through the flames "for luck," and cattle were driven through the burning embers to protect them from disease. The ashes were scattered on the fields to increase the fertility of the crops and bring a good harvest. The farm workers also carried blazing torches lit from the Midsummer fires around the fields for the same purpose. This reflects an ancient magical and pagan belief in the fertilizing power of fire as symbolically representing the sun's rays. In some parts of Britain a blazing "sun wheel," made from a wooden cartwheel tied with straw, was set alight and rolled down a hillside to imitate the sun.

Midsummer's Eve was a magical time, one of the three "spirit nights" with May Eve and Halloween, when the veil between the worlds was thin. It was a time for divination and gathering magical herbs like St. John's wort to hang above the door to ward off thunderstorms and evil influences. Fern seeds collected on this date were also magically potent. They warded off the unwelcome attentions of the Good Folk or fairies who were abroad at this time, and also had the power to make their carrier invisible.

Autumn and winter

The autumn equinox (approximately September 21st) coincided with the end of the harvest, and the ancient belief in the corn spirit survived in folk customs. The last sheaf was ritually cut and formed into a human-shaped image known variously as the Corn Maiden or Corn Mother, the Kern Baby, the Mare, the Old Wife, the Old Hag or the Old Witch. This was carried in procession back to the farm and placed above the hearth to bring fertility and prosperity to the household. In January, when the early ploughing began, the corn dolly was buried in the first furrow to bring a good harvest in the summer.

The last of the minor seasonal festivals of the Wheel of the Year is, of course, the winter solstice or Yule (approximately December 21st), which coincides with Christmas. Before the early Christian Church adopted it as a suitable date for the birthday of Jesus,

the Romans celebrated it as the Saturnalia. They decorated their houses with evergreens, the Lord of Misrule reigned, masters waited on slaves and anarchy replaced the rule of law. The Scandinavians celebrated Yule (literally "wheel," referring to the turning of the year) in honor of the god Frey, whose sacred animal was a golden boar. This may be the pagan origin of the medieval custom of a boar's head as the central feature of the Christmas Day feast. Decorated with the magical herbs of rosemary and bay and with a sacred apple in its mouth, the boar's head was carried to the table accompanied by minstrels preceded by a dancing fool or jester (the Lord of Misrule).

To encourage the sun to return after the winter solstice, the Yule Log was burned during the Twelve Days from Christmas to Twelfth Night (January 6th). It was always of oak, the sacred solar tree. The log had to be lit from a piece of the previous year's wood and was not allowed to burn out during the Yuletide season. Mistletoe, the sacred plant of the druids, was also placed prominently in the house. Garlands of holly and ivy represented the male/female polarity, and yew represented everlasting life. Finally, the evergreen Yule Tree was decorated to symbolize the Cosmic World Tree of pagan mythology.

Traditionally, the Twelve Days of Yule is one of the times when the Wild Hunt rides out from the Hollow Hill, gathering in the souls of the dead. This pagan belief is reflected in the seasonal mumming plays re-enacted by "guizers" dressed up in ragged clothes and bizarre masks. Customs such as the Mari Llwyd ("Grey Mare") in Wales and the Hoodening Horse and Christmas Bull in England also honor this concept. The Mari Llwyd and Hoodening Horse use a real horse's skull attached to a pole and carried by a human operator concealed under a white sheet. Accompanied by its attendants, the Horse was taken around the village and farms; any house it visited was blessed with good luck for the coming year.

The winter solstice celebrations end on Twelfth Night, the Christian festival of Epiphany. At this time black-faced performers caper around the orchards. They bless the tree spirits with libations of cider and offerings of apple cake, singing the traditional wassailing songs. The celebrants fire shotguns into the branches to ward off disease and evil influences. This is the climax of the folk celebration of the four minor seasonal festivals, which as we have seen are deeply rooted in the ancient past and the pagan beliefs inherited from our ancestors.

– *The Sacred Ring: The Pagan Origins of British Folk Festivals and Customs*
MICHAEL HOWARD

Scarborough Fair Duet

BOTH

Are you goin' to Scarborough Fair?
Parsley, sage, rosemary and thyme,
Remember me to one who lives there,
For (she/he) once was a true love of mine.

MAN

Tell her to make me a cambric shirt,
Parsley, sage, rosemary and thyme,
Without any seam nor needlework,
And then she'll be a true love of mine.

Tell her to wash it in yonder dry well,
Parsley, sage, rosemary and thyme,
Which never sprung water nor
rain ever fell,
And then she'll be a true
love of mine.

Tell her to dry it on
yonder thorn,
Parsley, sage, rosemary
and thyme,
Which never bore blossom since
Adam was born,
And then she'll be a true love of mine.

Ask her to do me this courtesy,
Parsley, sage, rosemary and thyme,
And ask for a like favour from me,
And then she'll be a true love of mine.

BOTH

Have you been to Scarborough Fair?
Parsley, sage, rosemary and thyme,
Remember me from one who lives there,
For (she/he) once was a true love
of mine.

WOMAN

Ask him to find me an acre of land,
Parsley, sage, rosemary and thyme,
Between the salt water and the sea-strand,
For then he'll be a true love of mine.

Ask him to plough it with a lamb's horn,
Parsley, sage, rosemary and thyme,
And sow it all over with one peppercorn,
For then he'll be a true love of mine.

Ask him to reap it with a sickle of leather,
Parsley, sage, rosemary and thyme,
And gather it up with a rope made
of heather,
For then he'll be a true love
of mine.

When he has done and fin-
ished his work,
Parsley, sage, rosemary
and thyme,
Ask him to come for his
cambric shirt,
For then he'll be a true love of mine.

BOTH

If you say that you can't, then I shall reply,
Parsley, sage, rosemary and thyme,
Oh, let me know that at least you will try,
Or you'll never be a true love of mine.

Love imposes impossible tasks,
Parsley, sage, rosemary and thyme,
But none more than any heart would ask,
I must know you're a true love of mine.

The Charm of Henna

HENNA ranges from a reddish brown to a brownish red, depending on its mix and one's own visual perception. On the hair, henna adds a ravishing frame to every skin color and leaves tresses shiny and healthy. But for millennia the plant also has been used for bodily adornment on ritual occasions. And with our own recent taste for such ancient practices as tattoos, studs and rings in odd places, can henna be far behind? Apparently not. Madonna, now sort of English and sort of Jewish, has always been a harbinger of the trendy; she and other pop icons are now lauding henna.

The plant's botanical term is *Lawsonia Enermis*, and the shrub grows from four- to eight-feet high. The flowers, leaves and twigs of henna are ground into powder with natural dying properties and mixed to a paste with hot water. For hair dye of various exotic shades the henna teams with companionable fruits and leaves, including cloves, lemon, indigo, tea and coffee. For body adornment, the powder is mixed with sugar and oil to intensify the color and encourage the art to last longer. Designs are applied without the use of needles and cannot be removed by scrubbing. Henna remains until the skin exfoliates, from three to four days on thin parts of skin and up to eight weeks on the soles of the feet. But its beauty is more than skin deep. Henna cleanses and conditions the skin. The plant is also a natural coolant, and worked into the hair keeps the scalp cool in hot weather. Cooling the soles of the feet, it is known as "henna shoe."

The plant thrives in hot spots through southern Africa, Asia, the Middle East and Europe and is used by religious groups for a variety of purposes. Henna has been prized for at least five thousand years in its guise as cosmetic, healer and spiritual aid. Many ancient cultures believed that natural red substances such as blood, ochre and henna had virtues that intensified awareness of the earth's energies. Archaeologists tell us that henna stained the fingers and toes of pharaohs about to be mummified. A widow adorned herself with henna before she hurled herself into her husband's funeral pyre. And the plant's medicinal use over much of the world is so broad as virtually to constitute a panacea. Somewhere or other healers have used it for burns, wounds, leprosy, smallpox, scabies, headaches, blisters, eye ailments, and in the Middle East, "congruity with nerves when used in poultices."

But from earliest times henna body designs, known as "*mehndi*" (main-dee), have had erotic connections, and the perfume from henna flowers was believed erotic. The Queen of Sheba made herself irresistible with henna fragrance and adornment as she journeyed toward King Solomon, passion, and immortality. "My beloved is to me as a cluster of hennas in the vineyards of En-gedi," sang the bewitched king.

Women make use of henna to mark ritual occasions – engagements, marriages, pregnancies, childbirths, baptisms. But henna reigns supreme most at weddings. In India and in the Islamic world, applying the art is a ceremonial party; the bride's attendants gather, singing, dancing, doubtless giggling, and adding to the beautification.

Either nuptial or religious, miniature body art turned up in little Minoan figurines from 1800 B.C.E., found with spiral henna adornment. Since the twelfth century Indian brides have decorated their hands and feet, sometimes forearms and shins, in complex lacy designs of paisleys, dots, geometrics. Sometimes the *mehndi* features fertility symbols such as the peacock, mango or lotus. In many places the marriage couple's initials are worked into tangled designs, and the honeymoon can't wend its sexual way until the groom finds them. Middle Eastern brides choose sensual vines and florals. Saudi woman are hennaed several times in the days preceding the nuptials, and their little sisters "play wedding" embellished with hennaed flowers, stars and trees. In the Sudan the bride, once decorated, dances a slow, swaying dance like a courting bird for her groom. Moroccan women believe that traditional henna designs protect them and avert evil. Odalisques of the Turkish harems used henna just about everywhere, as did Moorish courtesans in medieval Spain.

Henna adornment knows no boundaries, transcending all cultures, religions, and spiritual creeds. The designs are gorgeous, high decorative art of an ephemeral nature. Dilxoz, an eighteenth-century poet, sees it from a dreamy perspective: "When she puts henna on her hands and dives in the river/ One would think one saw fire twisting and running in the water."

– BARBARA STACY

The floral vocabulary

Love held a central role in the language of flowers, but the garden aided the verbally challenged on a wide variety of subjects.

- buttercups – *riches*
- camellias – *excellence*
- chrysanthemums – *slighted love*
- daffodils – *uncertainty, unrequited love*
- dahlias – *elegance*
- daisies – *affection*
- dandelions – *coquetry*
- dogwood – *indifference*
- forget-me-nots – *true love*
- geraniums – *stupidity*
- hollyhocks – *ambition*
- honeysuckle – *bonds of love*
- jonquils – *desire*
- lavender – *mistrust*
- lilacs – *fastidiousness*
- lilies-of-the-valley – *return of happiness*
- lime blossoms – *conjugal love*
- love-lies-bleeding – *hopelessness*
- magnolias – *love of nature*
- marigolds – *trouble*

- narcissus – *selfishness*
- nasturtiums – *patriotism*
- orange blossoms – *chastity*
- pansies – *thoughts*
- passion flowers – *belief*
- peonies – *shame*
- poppies, red – *dreams*
- poppies, white – *dormant attention*
- scarlet pimpernels – *appointment*
- sunflowers – *lofty thoughts*
- sweet william – *scorn*
- tiger lilies – *cruelty*
- touch-me-not – *impatience*
- tulips, red – *true love*
- tulips, yellow – *hopeless love*
- violets, white – *candor*
- violets, purple – *modesty*
- water lilies – *growing indifference*

Saffron Robes of Virtue

THE AUTHORITY of Buddha himself settled the question for the monastic community. Taking the robe became one of the outward indications of monkhood, along with the tonsure and begging bowl. Buddhist scripture and commentaries provide precise details about the simple garment – color, fabric, cut and style of wrap. Bright primary colors were proscribed, and the subtly glowing yellow of saffron, *Crocus sativa*, was adapted as the official color. Saffron robes were particularly embraced in the Theravada tradition of Thailand, Cambodia and Sri Lanka.

The plant transforms into the most expensive of cooking spices, requiring 75,000 blossoms to make a pound of the dried pistils, at one time worth their weight in gold. Ironically, the luxurious spice has long been associated with austerity in the religious world – but it is the essential oil crocin from *Crocus sativa* that provides the approved dye.

Monks wear the triple robe, an inner garment from waist to knee, an upper robe from the torso and shoulders, an outer robe for cold weather. The fabric may be made from plants, cotton, silk, wool or hemp. The laity donates new material at a ritual ceremony during the rainy season in East Asia, thereby gaining merit. The Buddha recommended that the design should be patchwork, based on the pattern of rice paddies in Indian fields, laid out in strips, lines, embankments and squares.

Sect and country determine how the monk wraps his *civara*. Generally he covers both shoulders when making his public rounds for alms. In the monastery the robe is usually worn with the right shoulder bare, leaving the arm free for working. The same wrap is secured for meetings with senior monks, the custom considered a gesture of respect – although ancient texts reveal that the wrap was arranged on the right shoulder when disciples approached Buddha with a question.

It is mind-boggling to consider that this precise ritual of attire has been passed down from generation to generation of monks for two thousand, five hundred years. It is the world's oldest robe pattern – golden, ascetic, abiding.

Dr. Nicholas Culpeper

Astrologer, Author,
Physician, Magician
and Herbalist,
1616-1654

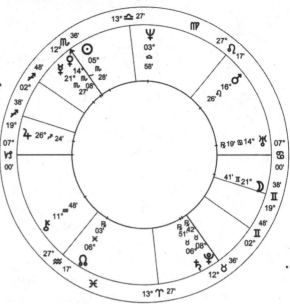

MODERN astrologers still honor the remarkably eclectic legacy left by Nicholas Culpeper, adept at ritual magic and science as well as astrology. He was an expert researcher, with the Sun in Scorpio in the 9th house of his horoscope, born on October 18, 1616 (Old Style calendar) at 12:12 p.m. in Ockley, England. Culpeper was versed in languages and healing arts, educated at Cambridge and apprenticed to an apothecary. Disillusioned with doctors when his mother died, he broke with the medical community of the day. Culpeper's Moon was in Gemini, quincunx Mercury and in the 6th house. This shows elements of fate at work through his family background and his emotional attachment to health matters. The disseminating lunar phase at his birth shows his ability to guide, teach and to learn from experience.

In Culpeper's time, London's medical care was in a crisis rivaling the current health-care system in the U.S. The outspoken Dr. Culpeper denounced other physicians as "insolent and incompetent." He obtained medical supplies from the forests and fields and encouraged patients to listen to "Mother Nature, and the Drs. Diligence, Experience and Reason."

Culpeper's Venus-Mercury conjunction in the 10th house describes his piercing rhetoric, charm and prominence. He maintained a busy professional practice in Red Lion Street, just outside of London, earning support for his wife Alice and their seven children. Beloved for his generosity and skill, Culpeper often provided free medical advice to poor people after seeing forty or more paying patients during the morning hours. Jupiter in Sagittarius in the 12th house shows his devotion to charity as well as keen intuition.

Myrten.   Roßen.   Strauß basilien.

Astrological rulers for herbs

Eventually Culpeper was condemned and denounced as a witch by jealous rival physicians when his unorthodox cures worked. His Uranus in Cancer and Mars in Leo are in the 7th house, which relates to open enemies. He retaliated with actions perceived as radical. Culpeper translated medical texts from Latin into language everyday people could understand. He opposed the bloodletting and other toxic practices supported by his critics. A mutual reception involving Pluto in Taurus and Venus in Scorpio shows that Culpeper was able to elude his enemies and continue with his good work.

Culpeper's books, *The English Physician* and *Complete Herbal*, relate the curative virtues of herbs to their astrological rulers. His Capricorn ascendant exactly trines a close Saturn-Pluto conjunction in Taurus, revealing his affinity for nature. Throughout the years many colonists carried treasured copies of his books with them around the world. Today the use of the foxglove plant in making digitalis for heart medicine, for instance, is one of the remedies that can be traced directly to Culpeper's work.

Neptune in the 8th house in Libra shows an affinity for magic and prophecy. Culpeper was a close friend of the astrologer and mystical prophet William Lilly, with whom he worked closely and published astrology tracts. Lilly predicted the Great Fire and Great Plague in London. Culpeper sustained a wound fighting in the English Civil War and was unable to completely recover. He died of pneumonia at only thirty-eight years of age. It is interesting to examine the indicators of the passing of Nicholas Culpeper, recognized as one of the greatest astrologers and healers of all time. Culpeper's natal Uranus oppose the ascendant describes the accident. This is supported by the hard angular aspects to his natal Mars, the planet of military conflict. In medical astrology the 3rd house, the planet Mercury and sign of Gemini all relate to the lungs. Glancing at Culpeper's chart, we can see his natal Saturn in the 3rd house in a nearly exact opposition to the Sun. The Sun is always the source of life and vitality. Gemini rules the 6th house of health. The Gemini Moon in the 6th is oppose Jupiter in Sagittarius in the 12th house of sacrifice.

– Dikki-Jo Mullen

Dill and Mercury

THE COMMON dill groweth up with seldom more than one stalk, neither so high nor so great, usually, as fennel. The tops of the stalks have four branches. It is most usually sown in gardens and grounds for purpose but is also found wild. Mercury hath the dominion over this planet, and therefore to be sure, it strengthens the brain.

It stayeth the hiccough when boiled with wine, and but smelleth unto, being tied in a cloth.
– *Complete Herbal*
Nicholas Culpeper

Dr. Nicholas Culpeper

October 18, 1616 OS (Old Style) at 12:12 p.m. Ockley, Surrey, England

(Culpeper's birthday is recorded in the Old Style Calendar, which is about eleven days different from the contemporary calendar. That's why he's a Scorpio, not a Libra. Data sources: Erlewine's *Circle Book of Charts* and "American Astrology Magazine" files.)

Data Sheet

Sun 5 Scorpio 28 – 9th house

Moon 21 Gemini 41– 6th house *(Moon is waning in the disseminating phase)*

Mercury 21 Scorpio 27 – 10th house

Venus 14 Scorpio 08 – 10th house

Mars 16 Leo 26 – 7th house

Jupiter 26 Sagittarius 24 – 12th house

Saturn 6 Taurus 51 (retrograde) – 3rd house

Uranus 14 Cancer 19 (retrograde) – 7th house

Neptune 3 Libra 58 – 8th house

Pluto 8 Taurus 42 (retrograde) – 3rd house

North Moon Node 6 Pisces 03 – 2nd house

Ascendant (rising sign) is 7 Capricorn 00

Magpies

Good birds, bad birds

MAGPIES often receive a bad press, perhaps because of an ancient belief that seemed to spring out of nowhere. Some people were convinced that magpies, of all God's creatures, were the only ones to forego the comfort of the interior Ark. They opted for perching by themselves atop the vessel, chattering maliciously at the animals huddled within. Add to this a legend that magpies were the only *Corvidae* refusing to don full mourning dress on the day of Christ's crucifixion. Their kin, ravens and crows, attended in sober black; magpies as usual were pied with white.

From such folklore we can see why these birds are met with some ambivalence. It is considered unlucky to kill magpies, and in certain areas of Europe the birds are honored for the chattering that warns of approaching wolves. In Scotland, however, they are regarded as the Devil's own bird, believed to have an unholy drop of his blood under their tongues. In Scotland and England it is unlucky to see one flying away from the sun. Whoever does so should grab the first object that come to hand, throw it after the bird and say, "Bad luck to the bird that flies widdershins."

Old ways exist believed to avert a malevolent magpie sighting: Raise your hat in salutation. Form a cross with your foot on the ground (or as many crosses as magpies).

Wet your forefinger with spittle and make the sign of the cross on your shoe. Spit on the ground three times and say, "Devil, Devil, I defy thee! Magpie, Magpie, I go by thee!"

A single magpie is especially associated with bad luck. Only one bird croaking persistently around a house, for instance, sounds the death knell of an occupant. Two magpies foretell good luck, although it is still necessary to salute the duo by bowing or spitting to ensure that the auspicious omen will be fulfilled.

A childhood rhyme indicates the ambivalent and magical nature of the magpie sightings: One for sorrow/ Two for joy/ Three for a girl/ Four for a boy/ Five for silver/ Six for gold/ Seven for a secret/ Never to be told.

— SARAH SIMPSON ENOCK

Creature Kinship

If you really understand an animal so that he gets to trust you completely and, within his limits, understands you, there grows up between you affection of a purity and simplicity which seems to me peculiarly satisfactory. There is also a cosmic strangeness about animals which always fascinates me and gives to my affection for them a mysterious depth or background.

— LEONARD WOOLF

❧ Goats Nibble on Trees ❧

In a play of the fifth century B.C.E., a chorus of goats boasts of its appetite:

On arbutus, oak, and fir we feed, all sorts and conditions of trees,
Nibbling off the soft young green of these, and of these, and of these;
Olives tame and olives wild are theirs and thine and mine
Cytisus, mastich, salvia sweet and many-leaved eglantine,
Ivy and holm-oak, poplar and ash, buckthorn, willow and heather,
Asphodel, mullein, cistus, thyme and savory all together.

– Eupolis (tr. Edmonds)

Window on the Weather

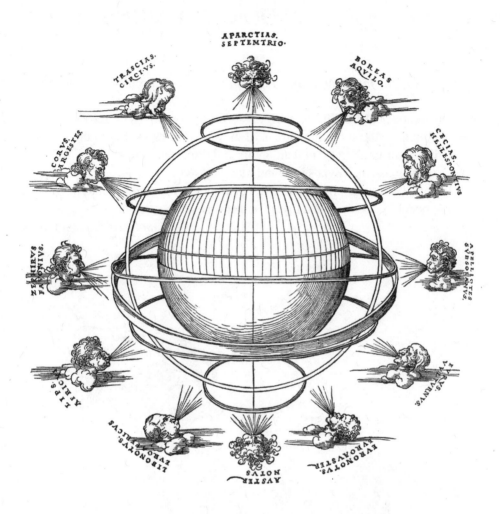

The weather-cock on the church spire, though made of iron, would soon be broken by the storm-wind if it did not understand the noble art of turning to every wind.

– HEINRICH HEINE

Hell-Broth

*Hecate and the Weird Sisters
stir up a steaming pot of wickedness*

Fillet of a fenny snake,
In the cauldron boil and bake;
Eye of newt and toe of frog,
Wool of bat and tongue of dog,
Adder's fork and blind worm's sting,
Lizard's leg and owlet's wing,
For a charm of powerful trouble,
Like a hell broth boil and bubble.
— SHAKESPEARE, *Macbeth* (IV.i)

Hot Cross Buns, Sweet Pagans

Hot cross buns, hot cross buns, one a penny, two a penny, hot cross buns.

— Traditional street hawker cry

IT IS A familiar oddity that many customs, myths and foods enjoyed at Christian holidays have their origins in pagan traditions. Traditionally eaten on Good Friday, hot cross buns are thought to predate Christianity. The "hot" in hot cross buns is a relatively new development. Before heating became customary, they were just "cross buns" – buns marked with a frosting of cross. The cross of Christianity had been added as a blessing to protect those who ate them. Many people believed that if they failed to eat a crossed bun on Good Friday ill luck would pursue them throughout the year. The belief in the protective power of the buns, however, predated the cross.

According to nineteenth-century historian Thomas Wright, "The Christians, when they seized upon the Easter festival, gave them the form of a bun, which, indeed, was at that time the ordinary form of bread; and to protect themselves, and those who eat them, from any enchantment, or other evil influences which might arise from their former heathen character, they marked them with the Christian symbol – the cross."

The former "heathen character" of the buns refers to their history as sacred cakes purchased at the entrance to the ancient Temples of Irqata in northern Lebanon. The honey-sweetened consecrated bread would be offered to the gods or eaten for their healing or protective properties. These buns were associated with the celebration of Eostre, a dawn goddess, from whose name we derive the word Easter.

You may wish to celebrate the goddess of spring with an offering of these special buns or to avail yourself of their protective and healing properties. Further your enjoyment with the knowledge that the cross was also considered to represent the four quarters of the moon or the four corners of the earth. The typical hot cross bun is a standard yeast-bun recipe enhanced with spices and currants or raisins; form your own symbolic decoration with the frosting. Whatever the topping, the hot cross bun is a seasonal celebration with an ancient sacred food.

– MORVEN WESTFIELD

Dana

Goddess of the Fey

THE Tuatha Dé Danann are an ancient race of people in Irish mythology, the fifth race to colonize and conquer the Emerald Isle. Their name, which means "Children of Dana," pays tribute to a primordial goddess. The Tuatha Dé Danann, Dana's Children, were eventually conquered by the Gaels, the present Irish people. In response, they retreated underground, inhabiting barrows, mounds and hills. The Tuatha Dé Danann transformed into the Sidhe (pronounced *shee*), the Irish name for the fairy folk or the fey. As befitting these powerful spirits, their ancestress Dana is a grand and powerful goddess.

Dana (pronounced *Dawn-uh* or *Day-na*) is the ancient Celtic goddess of the fairies. Throughout the Celtic world, she is the special friend and caretaker of the fey. Sometimes called Danu (*Dawn-oo*), this deity is also equated with the Welsh mother goddess Don. Her name may be the inspiration for the great Danube River, a region once inhabited by Celts.

Dana is associated with handicrafts, fire keeping, and manifestation ritual magic. A tremendous source of inspiration, she can be invoked for general creativity as well as for fertility. Dana is a High Priestess who shares and transmits profound spiritual teachings. Dana is a goddess of alchemy, revealing secrets of transmutation – perhaps she is responsible for the Tuatha Dé Danann's transformation into fairies.

Dana's tarot card is The Empress. Amber and all stones with natural holes are her talismans. A perfect summary of her archetypal attributes is suggested by the Old Irish root word "*dan*," which translates as "knowledge." In Sanskrit and Pali, which are Indo-European languages as are the Celtic tongues, Dana means "generosity" and "giving" whereas among the Scandinavian *vitki* and rune casters, Dana means "woman of Denmark."

– ELAINE NEUMEIER

In Memoriam

An age has passed... but a tradition continues

AS fate would have it, two young, intelligent and spunky women crossed paths in New York City in the late 1940's. They were none other than Elizabeth Pepper and Barbara Stacy. Elizabeth was the art director at *Gourmet Magazine* and Barbara was writing and editing magazines for Ideal Publishing. Soon thereafter, Barbara also joined the staff at *Gourmet* and a friendship that would last a lifetime was formed – reaching into the 21st century and halted on this plane only by death. Elizabeth passed in July of 2005 to be joined by Barbara on May 5th of 2010.

Barbara Stacy, charming, intelligent and gifted with wit sharper than a razor's edge, had an indomitable spirit. Born in New Haven, CT in 1926, she briefly attended the University of Connecticut and the Yale School of Drama, and in Barbara's own words, "hastily achieved dropout status in both." Nothing less than the Big Apple could satisfy Barbara's thirst for life and craving for adventure. She spent the fifties on the editorial staff at *Gourmet Magazine* and then took a copy writing position for a public relations firm. *The Witches' Almanac* made its debut in 1971 – Barbara's myriad contributions as a writer and editor enlivening its pages from its earliest days. In 1980 Barbara accepted a position as copy editor with the *PacificSun* and moved to Marin County, California. She finally moved to North Miami Beach, Florida with her husband, musician Eddie Caine.

By the time Barbara "retired" to Florida, she had already authored *The Alitalia Book of Authentic Italian Cookery*, *Ancient Roman Holidays*, and the original *Magical Creatures* with co-author Elizabeth Pepper. If anything, the two became closer in their later years; their joint venture, *The Witches' Almanac*, providing endless fodder for debate and countless reasons to keep in touch on a regular basis. When Elizabeth passed, Barbara made a choice each and every day to keep the legacy alive. Few readers know that Barbara was struck by illness in her twilight years, bedridden most of the day for close to a decade. Yet she never faltered in her responsibilities as an associate editor and even researched and authored an entire new work single-handedly – her last published book titled *Greek Gods in Love.*

Barbara could edit an entire paragraph – over the phone – in less than a minute; deleting nothing more than the 17 characters that just couldn't be squeezed onto the page and leaving the meaning intact. She took great pride in her research for each and every piece she wrote. Barbara delighted in humor and found it around every corner. She was endlessly fascinated by ancient myths, traditional stories and literature of every shape and size. Language was her playground, and Barbara Stacy was always "king of the hill."

We will miss her contributions as our esteemed Associate Editor, but most of all we will miss Barbara and the unexpected turn of phrase that was part of every conversation, certain to evoke a lingering smile or a full-fledged belly laugh that had to be shared with another member of the staff as soon as possible. We know that she missed Elizabeth dearly and we are convinced that they are reunited, watching over the legacy that is The Witches' Almanac, Ltd. Our lives are enriched for having known these two amazing women and we dare to believe that they have reached beyond the pages of our publications to enrich your lives as well. Indeed, an age has passed... but we will continue the tradition by striving for authenticity, integrity and quality in all of our future publications.

Brief Encounter with a Higher Power

AT AGE TEN I corner my mother in the kitchen to tell her that I do not believe in God. She yells that if I talk like that, God will strike me dead. I walk into the dining room where there is a rug, thump to the floor, and remain immobile. My mother comes running and lets out a scream, real fright. Now I get scared, not of the wrath of a God I don't believe in but of the wrath of my mother, which I have good reason to believe in. I am too frightened to move, because as soon as I get up I know I am in for it. And the longer I lay there the more hysterical my mother grows. Finally I stand up and she gives me one hell of a smack on the tush. It does not renew my faith in the Almighty, but it does renew a healthy respect for a higher power.

– BARBARA STACY
from Brief Encounters

Divine White Mare

In stables, garlands of roses

A FEW MILES south of Uffington, incised into the chalk bedrock of the hilly English countryside, stretches the gigantic figure of a horse at full gallop. Angular and abstract, elegant and mysterious, the white form measures 374 feet from muzzle to tail. Experts believe it dates from the late Bronze Age, about 1000 BCE, and may be a tribute to Epona, the ancient Celtic horse goddess. Now largely shrouded by time, the "Divine White Mare" had epochs of glory.

Epona worship arose in Gaul, flourished with the conquering Romans and traveled with the legions throughout Britain. The goddess was especially worshipped by the cavalry and turned up everywhere in Roman stables and barracks. Somewhere in the rafters an icon of Epona and her horses would turn up, sometimes depicted with foals on her lap. She often holds a basket of corn or fruit, especially apples. Sometimes Epona is riding, always "lady style," never astride. She may be lying back along the horse but never sidesaddle – the goddess sits the horse on the side

as if on a chair, legs dangling over the animal's flanks.

The deity loved roses, and soldiers believed that decked with garlands of the fragrant flower she worked protective magic. Tiny clay images of Epona were available for travel, tucked into tunics or saddle trappings for luck in battle.

Charioteers were the athletes of the military, and they too relied on Epona to keep them safe in the perilous sport. Eight annual Equirra celebrations in holiday-mad Rome honored horses, the chief festivity dedicated to Epona on December 18. The daredevils drove two- or four-horse chariots around a tight oval in the Circus Maximus, cheered on by over two thousand bloodthirsty spectators. It

took immense skill not to be hurled out on the turns; an official on the sidelines threw water on the smoking wheels. For the victor, a laurel wreath, palm and glory. For Epona, adoration.

On horseback or off, mother for all

Other than as battle goddess, the White Mare has profound dominions especially appealing to women. Epona also personifies an early fertility goddess, a protective deity, in icons offering the symbolic horn of plenty. Sometimes Epona is depicted as a goddess of rivers and thermal springs, a naked water nymph in such shrines. When an Epona image holds a key, she is honored as a psychopomp – guide to the underworld land of the dead. As a crossroads symbol, the goddess is conceived as an intermediary between the living and the dead or between day and night. And especially in Ireland she has a connection with nightmares. Beyond the horse, she is especially protective of oxen, cattle and donkeys, a lover of dogs and birds.

Some viewers perceive the Uffington figure as a dragon rather than a horse, perhaps the site of the battle with St. George. Who knows? It is difficult to reconstruct the mind set of Iron Age people and the purpose of such quirky vestiges. But we do know the prodigious figure has inspired awe down the ages. Since ancient times, every seven years the local lord hosted a three-day festival at the spot, fun and games, including wrestling and cheese rolling down the hillsides – how Merrie England is that? The basic purpose of the event was to clean up overgrowth and scour the horse to the whiteness of new blizzard. The celebrations lapsed about a hundred years ago, but the English Heritage is responsible for the site and keeps things nicely pristine, thank you.

– Barbara Stacy

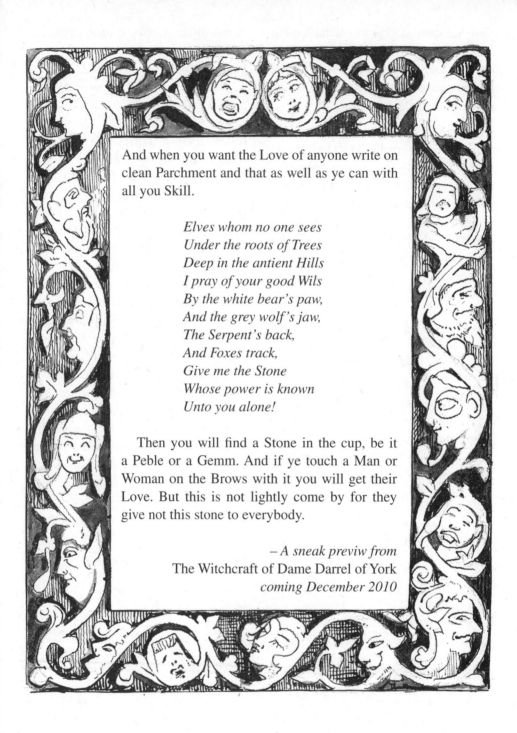

And when you want the Love of anyone write on clean Parchment and that as well as ye can with all you Skill.

> *Elves whom no one sees*
> *Under the roots of Trees*
> *Deep in the antient Hills*
> *I pray of your good Wils*
> *By the white bear's paw,*
> *And the grey wolf's jaw,*
> *The Serpent's back,*
> *And Foxes track,*
> *Give me the Stone*
> *Whose power is known*
> *Unto you alone!*

Then you will find a Stone in the cup, be it a Peble or a Gemm. And if ye touch a Man or Woman on the Brows with it you will get their Love. But this is not lightly come by for they give not this stone to everybody.

– A sneak previw from
The Witchcraft of Dame Darrel of York
coming December 2010

September

The goldenrod is yellow,
The corn is turning brown,
The trees in apple orchards
With fruit are bending down.

– HELEN HUNT JACKSON

White Alligators

The legend of living swamp ghosts

A SOUTHERN LEGEND tells us that people who can stare into the bright blue eyes of a rare kind of alligator will be blessed with incredible good luck. The evidence for this legend is strong enough so that for generations many have ventured into dangerous territory, risking life and limb to seek out these creatures.

About once in a century they do actually appear. This is just often enough to remain a part of living memory before it dissolves into myth and folklore. In 1987, deep in the bayous of Louisiana, a miracle occurred. A Cajun fisherman discovered a nest of eighteen newborns, only one of which was female. Today

twelve are still alive. Four are housed in a comfortable, secure compound at Gatorland near Orlando, Florida. (The other eight are at the Audubon Zoo in New Orleans.)

The four Floridians have Cajun names, with English translations listed below on celebrity-style nameplates posted outside the private doors. Blan Bouya (White Fog), Jeyan Kwok (Giant Fang), Feros Zanbi (Fierce Ghost) and the last and largest of all, The Nameless One. They are pure white alligators. Because of a rare genetic trait called leucism, they are white without being albinos. Albino gators are quite common and they have pink eyes. But albinos tend to be fragile with deformed jaws and spines, and don't survive long.

The leusistic gators are completely unlike their weakling cousins. The true white alligators are exceptionally strong. Large and long lived, with striking electric-blue eyes, they are dangerous and bad tempered, even by alligator standards. They don't dwell in harmony with either each other or the commoners, those familiar brownish alligators. Visitors to the Orlando tourist corridor who have the opportunity to seek the vintage attractions of Old Time Florida can make a spiritual pilgrimage to see the white leusistic alligators and even exchange a lucky stare.

Where did the mysterious white alligators come from? Why are they so very rare? The wise ones of the bayou offer an interesting explanation. Long ago, when the world was younger, all the alligators were white. Arrogant and warlike, they felt invincible. Wily Rabbit was fed up with the situation and decided to play a trick.

Rabbit saw a swamp fire burning. He called out to the King of the White Gators and said, "There's the devil over there, I bet you're afraid of him."

Gator turned his cold blue eyes on the rabbit, telling Rabbit how stupid and ridiculous he was. "Of course I'm not afraid, the devil can't hurt me."

"You'd be afraid to go and see," answered Rabbit.

"Would not."

"Would too."

With that Gator walked straight into the flames, relentlessly ignoring the smoke and heat. He caught on fire, and yelped and screamed as he turned a toasty brown. Even his eyes became brown and murky. Ever since then, almost all alligators have been brown, humbled and fooled by wily Rabbit.

– MARINA BRYONY

Sixty Years of the Museum of Witchcraft

A Diamond Jubilee

ON 14 May 2011, England's historic Museum of Witchcraft celebrated its sixtieth anniversary, as well as fifty years at its present location in the village of Boscastle on Cornwall's north coast. This is no small accomplishment, as the Museum has survived fire bombs, decades of abuse from Christian fundamentalists, and the flash floods that swept through Boscastle on 16 August 2004. The Museum of Witchcraft currently houses the world's largest collection of witchcraft-related artifacts and regalia and serves as a showcase, repository, and archive of the magical history of witchcraft.

The brainchild of Cecil Williamson, a brilliant occultist, former film producer, and MI6 agent, the Museum first opened its doors in 1951 in Castletown on the Isle of Man. Gerald Gardner, who is widely considered to be the father of modern Wicca, served as the Museum's resident witch, until he and Williamson had a falling-out.

Over the next ten years, the Museum moved to several locations, with consistently unhappy results, as locals did not welcome a museum devoted to witchcraft. For example, during a brief stay in Bourton-on-the-Water, in the Cotswolds, a local vicar preached against the Museum, which was then fire bombed. Dead cats were hung from trees on its grounds. Finally, in 1961, the Museum found its home in Boscastle, where it remains. Controversy continues, however, and the current owner still receives death threats from those who consider witchcraft to be evil.

Williamson ran the Museum, until – at midnight on Halloween of 1996, three years before his death – he passed his mantle to Graham King, the current director. Under King's careful watch, the Museum continues to flourish and to serve as a precious resource to students of witchcraft and the occult. It is also a tremendous tourist destination: the Museum of Witchcraft attracts visitors from around the globe and its collection has a five-star Trip Advisor rating. Further information may be found at www.museumofwitchcraft.com.

– JUDIKA ILLES

Oak Apple Day, May 29th

His Royal Highness Up a Tree

OAK TREES have been considered sacred since pagan times, but we doubt that King Charles II kept that much in mind as he shinnied upward, fleeing for his life. The king, evading Cromwell's soldiers, took refuge in a lofty, bushy oak, perfect for camouflage. The ruse saved the king's life, and to this day a descendant of that tree is honored as the Royal Oak, its name the third most common in pub signs.

Kings don't usually go in for arbor sports, but Charles was hard pressed, fleeing to Boscobel Castle after defeat at the Battle of Worcester. His hosts cut his fashionably long hair, dressed him in rough clothes, and propelled him upward. Here the king stayed the whole day, fortified by bread, cheese and beer.

The account has all the earmarks of an historical legend. But years later Charles related the details of his arboreal experience to the diarist Samuel Pepys, and so we have the story – including sight of a soldier under the tree as the king was "peeking from the wood." Would a diarist prevaricate?

King Charles escaped and the tree seemed to deserve celebration. In 1660, Parliament declared May 29 Oak Apple Day, and the Royal Oak came to national attention. The tree standing today is not the original, which languished in the nineteenth century, as too many tourists snapped off souvenir leaves, twigs and bark. It has been succeeded by the Son of the Royal Oak, and, a few years ago, Prince Charles planted a sapling grown to the present Grandson of the Royal Oak. English tradition dies hard.

The "apple" referred to a gall resembling the fruit, reddish or brownish, formed on branches by larvae of hornets. In parts of England, where oak apples were known as "shick-shacks," the holiday was also known as Shick-Shack Day. Celebrants wore sprigs of oak, and the royal association also resonates with the pagan tradition of tree worship. But another connection is less lofty. Although Oak Apple Day was abolished in 1859, here and there children still have their own festive ways, although the origin of the holiday has been lost to them. On May 29, they challenge each other to show their oak sprigs. Kids lacking the leafy symbols are fair game for having their bottoms pinched, and the holiday is also termed Pinch Bum Day. Children tend to have a rhyme for every occasion, and so for this peculiar arbor day they chant: "The 29th of May is Oak Apple Day. If you don't give us a holiday, we'll all run away."

– BARBARA STACY

A Séance Invocation

There is a land where we all go,
Whence ne'r the frost nor cold wind blow,
And friends remembered reunite,
And those who hate, forget their spite.
In glow surround these gentle beings,
We call you now to bless our meetings,
Heaven's promise, our spirits thrive,
So now for the living, let the dead come alive.
Greetings Spirits… Speak thee to us?

– from The Spirit Speaks
Weekly Newspaper, 1901

Ghost Friendly Lavender, Flowers and Music

LAVENDER IS KNOWN to attract spirits. A dish of lavender flower clusters, either dried or fresh, is an invaluable aid for the medium in the séance room. Lavender will relieve depression or negativity and heighten spirituality.

A traditional Victorian séance is held by candlelight. When the candle flame turns blue, a ghost is present. Fresh flowers for the table and music are other helpful elements to ensure a successful séance.

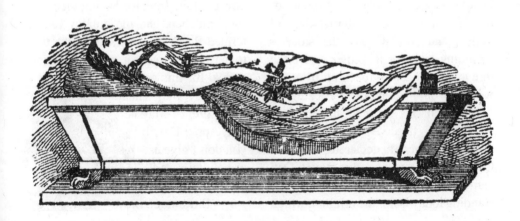

Hymn to Lucifer

Jera Runesinger

Andante

Lord of the new-born day fill my heart with cou-rage joy and might. Lord of the liv-ing flame fill my heart with ra-dient sun_light. Shine forth in__ all I see. Shine forth in__ all that I may do. Lord of the new-born day help me grow to__ be more like__ you.

*Go to www.TheWitchesAlmanac.com/AlmanacExtras/
to hear this song sung by the composer.*

Mirror, Mirror...

Reflections on myth and magic

HUMANS are among a select group of animals capable of recognizing their own reflections. Most animals, when confronted with their image in a mirror, react as though another animal is just beyond the glass: they run and cower or scratch and yowl at the newly manifested imposter. Humans, on the other hand, will sit transfixed, preening and pouting at their perfect double. We not only recognize ourselves in the mirror but we ascribe great significance to the power of the mirror's gaze. Mirrors have the power to transfix us, to terrify us, and to offer us a glimpse into other realms.

Seven Years Bad Luck

Mirrors have long held supernatural significance in a variety of cultures. One of the most commonly held beliefs is that the reflection which appears in the mirror is actually the gazer's soul. Vampires do not show up in mirrors because they are soulless creatures. If one's image in the mirror appears distorted in any way it is taken as a sign of a corrupt or troubled soul. Damaging a mirror is really damaging ones soul – which explains why breaking a mirror is considered tremendous bad luck (if you happen to break a mirror and wish to avoid the associated seven years bad luck, try submerging the pieces in a south-running stream or grinding the pieces into powder).

There are a variety of other ways in which a mirror can act as a conduit of bad luck. For example, seeing your reflection in a mirror that belongs to someone else might give that person power to influence your actions; infants younger than one year should not be allowed to look at mirrors for fear their soul could become lost in the reflection; if someone dies in the presence of uncovered mirrors, their soul may accidently cross over into the mirror instead of the next life.

Into the Looking Glass

Mirrors are also considered portals to other realms. Narcissus was pulled into the underworld when he became unable to look away from his own reflection in a still pond. In Jewish folklore, every mirror is an opening to the demon Lilith's cave, where she mates with all manner of beast and births a multitude of monstrous offspring. Vain young girls who stare at their own reflections for too long can be sucked through the mirror into Lilith's cave, never to return. Those who stare too long at their own reflection also open themselves to demonic possession – the demons pass through the mirror and enter through the eyes of the victim. This is believed to be especially true around the Hallows, when the veils between the worlds begin to thin and all sorts of creatures look for a gateway from one world to another. Mirrors are especially desirable for this purpose.

Matrimony and Mirrors

Mirrors are not all bad luck and trapped souls, mind you – there are many positive associations with mirrors as well. Anyone wishing to glimpse the face of their true love should sleep with a mirror under their pillow: at night, they will dream of their future husband's or wife's face. It is also supposed that anyone who sees their true love for the first time through the reflection of a mirror is destined for a lifetime of happiness.

Black Mirrors

Mirrors also bestow the power to look into the future. The Black Mirror is a divination technique heavily influenced by the moon, visions being most clearly defined at the full moon. The original black mirrors were highly polished pieces of obsidian stone, but nowadays any piece of glass with a black backing will do nicely. The technique requires the practitioner to clear their minds and stare deeply through the mirror, focusing on a central point somewhere behind the surface. As the mind clears the mirror will begin to fill with visions of the future. At first, all the diviner will see will be clouds. As the diviner's skill progresses, clearer visions will emerge from the fog.

Whether opening a window to the soul, a gateway to other dimensions, or a glimpse of the future, mirrors are powerful supernatural objects. Next time you find yourself staring at your reflection, try to remember what might be lurking beyond – maybe our animal compatriots see something we don't, after all.

– Shannon Marks

Athena turns spiders into living shuttles

ATHENA was both the goddess of war and goddess of the arts. She delighted in weaving and provided the Olympians with shimmering garments, their colors exquisite beyond description. Athena was astounded to learn that Arachne, a peasant girl, declared her own work to be superior. Athena descended and arranged a contest. Looms were set up and piles of wondrous fabrics evolved, all colors of the rainbow, shot through with silver and gold threads, unmatched for silkiness and elegant designs. Finished at the same moment, Arachne's weaving was in no way inferior. Anger the goddess of war at your peril... Athena beat Arachne's head with a shuttle. The girl crept away, disgraced and humiliated, and hanged herself. But repentance crept into Athena's heart. She removed the noose, sprinkled Arachne with a magic potion, and the girl morphed into a spider. The weaver and others of her kind are classified as *Arachnida*. What geometric wonders they conceive and weave!

– Barbara Stacy

Apollo, God of Poetry and Music, and Hermes, God of Eloquence,
from Moretus' Philomathi Musea Iuveniles, *Antwerp, 1654.*

Merlin. *Illustration by Aubrey Beardsley*
Roundel on contents-page verso of
Le Morte Darthur, *Vol. 1,*
published by J.M. Dent & Co., London, 1893.

The Ballad
of the White Horse

Before the gods that made the gods
Had seen their sunrise pass,
The White Horse of the White Horse Vale
Was cut out of the grass.

Before the gods that made the gods
Had drunk at dawn their fill,
The White Horse of the White Horse Vale
Was hoary on the hill.

Age beyond age on British land,
Æons on æons gone,
Was peace and war in western hills,
And the White Horse looked on.

For the White Horse knew England
When there was none to know;
He saw the first oar break or bend,
He saw heaven fall and the world end,
O God, how long ago!

– excerpt of "The Vision of the King"
from The Ballad of the White Horse
by GK Chesterton

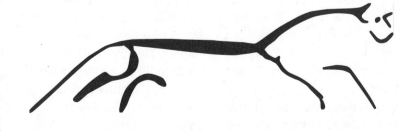

The Mirror of Matsuyama

CENTURIES ago on the island of Shikoku lived a man, his wife, and their little daughter. One day the man decided to undertake a pilgrimage to Matsuyama, hoping to secure good fortune for his family. The man promised to be careful and to return soon and to bring presents back from the city. He put on his traveling clothes and set off down the road.

He returned two weeks later bearing gifts. For his little girl, sweets gathered from each stop on his pious journey, and for his wife, a gift of rare splendor: a finely embellished bronze mirror. When he handed the mirror to his wife, she shrieked! She had never seen her own reflection before and was clearly confused, but she came to treasure the mirror as her most prized possession.

Years passed and the family lived on happily together, until one day the wife grew gravely ill. As it became clear that she would not recover she asked her daughter to sit by her bed. She handed the little girl the prized mirror.

"Take this, dear child. Whenever you miss your mother just look here and you will see my spirit." With this final declaration the wife passed into the next life.

The little girl was overwhelmed with sadness, but when she looked into the mirror she found her mother was right! There, staring back, was the face of her mother – not pale and gaunt from sickness but once more young and beautiful. She kept the mirror in the sleeve of her kimono so that she could carry her mother's spirit everywhere.

More time passed and the man remarried – but his new wife was suspicious of the little girl. The girl was secretive, aloof, and never smiled at her new mother. One day she caught the little girl huddled over something, whispering. When she asked what she was doing the little girl slipped something in her sleeve and ran away. The new wife became convinced the little girl was cursing her and begged her husband do something.

So the man found his daughter and demanded the little girl surrender the object. Reluctantly, she handed him the mirror.

Her father was puzzled. "Dear girl, where did you find this?"

"Mother gave it to me on her deathbed. She told me that whenever I missed her I could look into the mirror and see her spirit."

The man understood at once what had happened. The little girl mistook her own reflection for the spirit of her mother. The man and his new wife were touched by the girl's innocence and begged her forgiveness for doubting her. The girl forgave instantly and the new family lived the rest of their lives in serenity.

– TENEBROUS RAE

The Cornish Yarrow Spell

ON THE NEW MOON or even on the evening before, a young girl shall place a piece of yarrow herb under her pillow with the intention of knowing her true love. Recite the spell:

Good night, fair yarrow,
Thrice good night to thee;
I hope before tomorrow's dawn
My true love I shall see.

If a marriage to one she already knows is in the stars, the girl shall see her intended true love on the following morning.

Devils, Demons and Angels

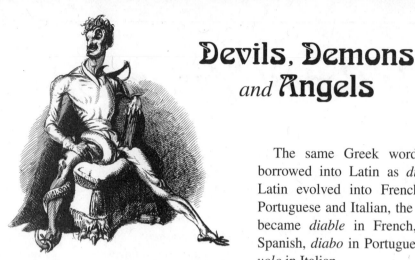

THE WORDS *devil* and *demon* are not English words originally, but were borrowed from Greek. The English word *demon* was taken directly from the Latin *daemon*, which, in turn, goes back to the Greek *daímon* or *daimónion*. In Pagan Greece, a demon was a kind of immaterial or spiritual being who occupied a position in the universe midway between humanity and the Gods and could travel into either realm. Among other things, demons could serve as messengers between the two realms. These demons were not always malevolent, but quite often were benevolent or indifferent toward humanity.

The English word *devil* has a slightly more complicated history, going back to Old English (Anglo-Saxon) *deofol*, which is related to German *Teufel* and Dutch *duivel*. All three of these words can be traced back to the Gothic *diabaulus*. The Gothic word, in turn, was borrowed from Greek *diábolos*, which originally meant a slanderer, a liar, a perjurer, and so forth. That is, a *diábolos* is just a person – any ordinary person – who cast aspersions on others or spoke falsehoods.

The same Greek word was also borrowed into Latin as *diabolus*. As Latin evolved into French, Spanish, Portuguese and Italian, the Latin word became *diable* in French, *diablo* in Spanish, *diabo* in Portuguese and *diavolo* in Italian.

Angels are demons, too

Like so many other things, the meanings of these two words – *demon* and *devil* – were greatly changed by the coming of the monotheistic religions, Judaism and Christianity. The Hebrew Scriptures – including some books that the rabbis would later reject – began to be translated into Greek by Greek-speaking Jews, as early as the fourth century before the Christian era. This old Greek translation of the Hebrew Bible is usually called the Septuagint. It had an enormous influence on all the books of the New Testament, which were also written in Greek.

In the Septuagint, the kind of immaterial or spiritual Being that the Pagan Greeks called a demon is sometimes still called a demon (*daímon* or *daimónion*), More often, however, it is called an angel (*ángelos*). The Greek word *ángelos* just means a messenger, and it originally referred to ordinary people who carried messages. Applied to demons, the word just emphasizes one of the functions that those Beings have.

In the Septuagint, as in the New Testament, there was no moral difference whatsoever between a demon and an angel: an angel can be either good or evil, just as a demon can. The New Testament speaks in one place of "the devil and his angels" (Matthew 25:41). In another place, it describes a coming war in heaven, which the Archangel Michael and his angels will wage against Satan and his angels (Revelation 12:7, 9). The popular view that such Beings are called angels when they are good and messengers of the Christian or Jewish God, but demons when they are evil and messengers of the Devil, has no basis in the Bible. It is a somewhat later development, as we shall see below.

Satan, the adversary

In the Hebrew Scriptures, there is also the occasional mention of a being called *ha Satan*. This phrase just means "the adversary." In the Septuagint, however, Hebrew *ha Satan* is usually translated as *ho diábolos*, literally, "the slanderer, the liar." This is something of a mistranslation, but it seems to have been a traditional one. (In these phrases, the Hebrew *ha* or Greek *ho* simply means "the.")

The New Testament, being written in Greek and heavily influenced by the Septuagint, most often uses the same phrase, *ho diábolos*, "the Devil," to refer to the same Being. In a few places, however, he is called *ho Satanas*, which is simply a transcription (with a Greek ending added) of the Hebrew phrase *ha Satan*. Very rarely, he is simply called *Satanas*, without the word *ho* (meaning "the"). In these cases the word seems almost to be used as one of the Devil's proper names, Satan.

Demonizing the old gods

For monotheists, naturally enough, the many Gods and Goddesses of the Pagan Greeks could not be thought of as actual Gods, but had to be called by some other word. The early Christians, like the Jews, had no doubts about the existence of these Beings, but they saw them as subordinate Beings under their One God. Since the word *demon* originally referred to spiritual Beings subordinate to the Pagan Gods, Jewish monotheists, naturally enough, extended its range to cover the Pagan Gods as well. "For all the Gods of the Pagans are demons" – so claims the Septuagint (Psalm 95:5). (In the Hebrew and English Bibles, this is Psalm 96:5.)

Christians easily followed suit, beginning with Paul: Pagan sacrifices before images of their Gods are sacrifices "to demons (*daimónia*), not to God" (I Corinthians 10:20). Christians were to shun these sacrifices, which are a form of idolatry, as they would shun any sin. It is not too great a jump from all this to the notion that all the Pagan Gods are themselves evil Beings, and one small jump further turns every demon into an evil Being. And, of course, if all demons were evil, what should Christians call Beings of the same kind who serve their God? The word *angel* was at hand, and so it acquired its present, more limited meaning: angels good, demons bad.

– ROBERT MATHIESEN

Notable Quotations
THE EARTH

And forget not that the earth delights to feel your bare feet and the winds long to play with your hair.

– Khalil Gibran

It suddenly struck me that that tiny pea, pretty and blue, was the Earth. I put up my thumb and shut one eye, and my thumb blotted out the planet Earth. I didn't feel like a giant. I felt very, very small.

– Neil Armstrong

The true object of all human life is play. Earth is a task garden; heaven is a playground.

– Gilbert K. Chesterton

Earth laughs in flowers.

– Ralph Waldo Emerson

Earth and sky, woods and fields, lakes and rivers, the mountain and the sea, are excellent schoolmasters, and teach some of us more than we can ever learn from books.

– John Lubbock

The earth is the mother of all people, and all people should have equal rights upon it.

– Chief Joseph

Shall I not have intelligence with the earth? Am I not partly leaves and vegetable mould myself.

– Henry David Thoreau

Trees are the earth's endless effort to speak to the listening heaven.

– Rabindranath Tagore

The longer one is alone, the easier it is to hear the song of the earth.

– Robert Anton Wilson

Quotes compiled by Isabel Kunkle.

Atlas in Starry Affliction

Crouching Figure of Atlas, Baldassare Peruzzi (1481–1536)

PEOPLE STRESSED OUT and overburdened may be haunted by Atlas, for the Greek god held aloft the heavens, "shuddering and shifting the weight upon his trembling shoulders." A Titan fighting on the losing side of the giants' battles with Zeus, his burdens are the thunder god's punishment. The hero Heracles, questing for the Golden Apples of Hesperides, seeks the aid of Atlas, for the magical fruit is guarded by the Titan's starry daughters, the Pleiades. But Heracles will have to hold the vault of the sky while Atlas performs the task. Heracles sustains the burden, but when Alas returns with the apples he refuses to resume the celestial globe. Heracles groans at his ill fortune and pleads for some cushions to pad the strain on his aching shoulders. Atlas, more brawn than brain, lifts the globe to place the pillows, Hercules slips away with the golden prizes, and Atlas again quivers under his starry affliction.

Ganesh and the Milk Miracle

A contemporary paranormal phenomenon

IT BEGAN in New Delhi, where, during the predawn hours of September 21, 1995, a devout, but otherwise ordinary man dreamt that Ganesh, Hinduism's beloved elephant-headed god, thirsted for a drink of milk. Waking from the dream, the man rushed to a nearby temple. Although the resident priest was skeptical, he permitted the man to offer a spoonful of milk to a small statue of the deity. As both men watched in amazement, the milk vanished immediately, just as if consumed by Ganesh. That was only the beginning. What followed over the next twenty-four hours was astonishing

Word of this miracle spread at breakneck speed. The news that a statue of Lord Ganesh was drinking milk first passed locally from temple to temple, but was soon seized by the national and international news media. CNN and the BBC were among the television stations that broadcast news of the miracle. The Washington Post, The Daily Express, The Guardian and The New York Times sent journalists to investigate. All reported that the incredible event was real.

A great soul is born
Soon millions of awestruck devotees in virtually every Hindu household, temple, and shrine all over the world began to offer milk to their own statues. For twenty-four hours, Ganesh reputedly sipped this milk all up, drop by drop. A bride and groom married on that day offered Ganesh milk during their marital ceremony, requesting that he bless their nuptials. Witnesses from India to Trinidad to the United States and throughout Africa and South America testified that they saw Ganesh drink. Thousands of gallons of milk were consumed. The miracle seemingly proved that a divine force is active in our universe. Some devotees believe that the miracle indicates that a great soul – a saint – was born on that day.

Scientists, attempting to debunk this miracle, insisted that it was surface tension, capillary action, or even mere hypnotic suggestion created by mass hysteria, but they could not explain why the milk miracle had apparently never previously occurred and why it abruptly ceased just twenty-four hours after the dream.

Lord of Obstacles
Ganesh, also known as Ganesha and Ganapati, is among Hinduism's principle deities. With his benevolent expression, elephant head, and round belly, the image of Ganesh typically

raises a smile. His huge fan-like ears reputedly hear all pleas for his help and assistance. The snake that appears at his waist represents divine kundalini energy. Lord Ganesh represents success in all endeavors. He sweeps away obstacles, destroys evil, and brings wealth and wisdom.

Many-handed Ganesh holds a noose that snags and captures all difficulties, a goad to gently propel humanity forward, and a broken tusk that has been transformed into a pen. Ganesh is the special patron of writers. Books printed in India often feature his image on the title page. Ganesh rides a mouse, suggesting that his influence is pervasive and that he possesses the power to transcend desire.

– GRANIA LING

Jovial and benevolent, Lord Ganesh is renowned as the master of new beginnings. Chanting his mantra invokes his aid in removing all obstacles that prevent one's progress: *Om Gum Ganapataye Namaha.* Miraculous results are reported. Request that Ganesh sweep all obstacles from your path, perhaps also burning a candle or incense in his honor. Small silver spoons may also be placed on Ganesh's altar in commemoration of the miracle of milk.

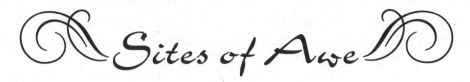

Sites of Awe

Niagara Falls

IT IS IN THE AFTERNOON when my partner and I reach the parking lot near the Falls. From the car, I can hear a thunderous sound – a deep roar that seems to surround me from all directions. I can see people lined up along the edge of the parking lot. Cameras are flashing and people are posing in front of the Niagara River, which flows from Lake Erie to Lake Ontario – two of the fresh water lakes which are part of the Great Lakes of North America. Niagara Falls is actually made up of three waterfalls: the American Falls, the Horseshoe Falls, and the Bridal Veil Falls. As I rush to the rail and look over the edge – I gasp!

I am terribly excited to finally be here. As a child, I learned of the Falls that embodied the power of the element of Water, and I had always hoped to visit one day. It is my goal to gather a scant amount of water from the river and take it home to place in one of the quarters of my altar.

We quickly got the lay of the land, learning that there was an available helicopter tour, as well as a boat ride, walking tour of the tunnels, cable car ride over the whirlpool, and countless souvenir shops. Okay, just one more look over the edge – I gasp again!

Although the drop seems to go on forever, I know that it is just over 160 feet from where I am standing to the water level below. But, over one hundred thousand cubic feet of water pass over the falls every second – a gasp without looking!

Eye of the cyclops

The helicopter ride would be first – I wouldn't want to miss any part of this majestic expression of the Water element. I spot a sign for the helicopter ride. "Let's give it a whirl," I say. After paying our fare, we head to the platform where we climb into the helicopter. Up we go and firmly my hands grip the bar in front of me. I never did like heights, but I would not miss this for the world. We ride down the river, a rather simple excursion so far.

Then, rather abruptly, we find ourselves turning around and coming back the way we went. Then, hovering just briefly, we seem to plunge over the Falls. Yikes! For an instant, my inner organs seemed to all gather up around my throat for a mini-convention to discuss my obvious demise. Without remaining here very long, thank Neptune, we continue down to the whirlpool.

The whirlpool is enormous; its center reminds me of the eye of the Cyclops. Although the water appears to be moving very slowly from where we are, it is actually moving quite fast, about 30 feet per second. The river takes a rapid near 90 degree turn and we follow it from above. The subtle, soft power of nature's river turns so quickly and violently, as we see it make the turn from the whirlpool and head toward the Horseshoe Falls. Once here, our pilot descends into the center of the Horseshoe Falls – mist is rising all around us. It is so thrilling to feel air and water in harmony and such a powerful manifestation of the two.

The Maid of the Mist

What can I say about the *Maid of the Mist*? These wonderful boats, which have transported thousands of visitors throughout the past decades, travel from calm water to the rougher water beneath the Falls. Here the boat pauses for a while. Some of us are holding on to the edge of the boat as it rocks, while others are reaching for their cameras. Although the view from here is spectacular, the camera images are not very good. This is principally due to the mist that surrounds us. I decide to put the camera away and look into the mist. The faces of water nymphs are visible everywhere. I am not surprised and you wouldn't be either. There is water beneath us, splashing down all around us, and the air that we are breathing is as moist as air can be. Truly, this is one of the greatest elemental wonders of our world.

After an experience like this, I am redirected, as I find myself assessing a very different type of adventure – entering a cave in the earth to better experience the Falls. The tunnels behind the Falls are pretty well cut out and wide enough for several people to walk through. As I walk in, I can hear the roar of the Falls. I walk for some time before the air becomes very thick and damp. Now the sound is once again nearing a deafening level. I have to speak very loudly for those around to hear me. As we reach the end of the tunnel, there is truly a sight to behold – the back side of the Falls. Standing back and looking at the opening of the tunnel, as it frames the water fall, it appears as a window into another world. This is a site that I will never forget.

One final gasp before I turn around and head back to our room.

The moonbow

After dinner, we are beginning to settle down into our room for the evening. It was an exhausting day, primarily because of the emotional excitement that surged through our veins. It is also a full moon and we are beginning to feel a bit restless. "I think we should go for one final walk," I say. So, we leave our room and head toward the Falls for one last look. I am just not prepared for the breathtaking experience that I am about to have. Looking up over the falls there is a rainbow at night! The light of the full moon combines with the mist of the falls and creates a perfect rainbow.

Later the next morning, we would learn that the rainbow at night over the full moon, formed in the mist of the falls, is known locally as a moonbow. It has been a very magical night. And I suggest that if any of you can ever travel to the renowned Niagara Falls… better it be when the moon is full!

– ARMAND TABER

The Cimaruta

AMONG THE MANY folk charms of Italy, we find one of particular significance and antiquity. It is commonly known as the cimaruta (pronounced chee-mah-roo-tah). In Italian, the word "cima" means the "top" of something. The word "ruta" translates into the English word for the herb rue. Putting the two words together, we find that cimaruta means the top of the rue plant, which is where the buds and flowers appear.

In Italy, during the 19th century, the cimaruta charm was quite popular. Among the common people it was most often used to protect against "envy" and the "evil eye" (particularly in the case of keeping infants safe). It was a common practice to place a silver cimaruta charm on the crib, and this was often tied with a strip of red wool. The magical power of the cimaruta lies, in part, with the old magical reputation of the rue plant itself.

Traditional uses of the cimaruta
One of the misconceptions about rue is that it is an herb specifically against witchcraft. But this sole assignment is untrue. Rue's reputation is that of an herb used against enchantments, which means its nature is counteractive against magic in general. Since magic is not exclusive to witchcraft we cannot diminish rue to an anti-witchcraft charm.

The traditional cimaruta charm is made of silver and worn as a necklace piece. Most of the antique pieces measure about three inches long and two inches wide. The charm is fashioned in the design of a sprig of rue divided into its three primary branches. Each branch terminates into a bud from which is suspended a symbolic charm. These charms differ depending upon from which region in Italy the specific cimaruta piece originated.

A similar Iberian charm
In Spain and Portugal we find a similar charm suggestive of a folkloric tradition behind the cimaruta that was more widespread than just throughout Italy. The charm is known as *cinco seimao*, and is comprised of five symbols: a pentagram, a figa hand, a human-faced crescent, and a key, all of which are grouped around a heart pierced by two arrows. Standing on top of the heart is the image of what commentators describe as the Virgin Mary. Of interest is the appearance of a flower on the wrist of the figa hand, which also appears on the cimaruta as a separate charm. Folklorist W.L. Hildburgh comments:

In the cinco seimao *we find combined the protective virtues of silver, of an image of the Virgin, of the lunar crescent, the key, the ithyphallic hand, the heart, and the pentagram, and possibly also those of the flower-like emblem, the arrow, and the cross. In the Neapolitan cimaruta we find embodied several of the same conceptions which are embraced by the* cinco seimao. *The cimaruta, literally the "sprig of rue," is a stem from which extend short branches, each of which holds an amuletic emblem or symbol at its extremity. It is worn as a protection against* Jetiatura *(the evil eye), it is almost always of silver, and usually roughly made, and it counts amongst its symbols the lunar crescent, the key, the ithyphallic hand (the* mano fica), *a flower-like emblem, and often the heart and the arrow. The number of coincidences between the two amulets appears too great to be the result of mere chance; in fact it is so great that we may fairly assume that the amulets themselves have had a common origin, and that one or the other has changed in form, and in some of its less valued symbols, during the centuries since their genesis.*

Protection of infants

Most of what is publicly known of the cimaruta comes from various writings of the late 19th century and early 20th century. Almost without exception the majority of writers of this period associate the cimaruta with the protection of infants. As previously mentioned in this article, protection involved hanging the charm on the crib of the infant. An additional practice was to fix garlic to the infant's chest and sprinkle rue around the mother's bed. Such practices arose as a protection against envy, which was viewed as a sinister force. The fear being that people visiting the newborn infant and its mother might be envious, which would contaminate the child and draw vitality away from its life force.

Some writers of the 19th century appear to be aware of the cimaruta as a charm of pagan origin associated with the goddess Diana and with witchcraft. This is supported through old oral teachings preserved among some practitioners of Italian witchcraft. Here we learn that the cimaruta contains lunar symbolism directly linked to the goddess of witchcraft. According to this lore, witches wear the charm as a token of their devotion to the triformis goddess of witchcraft. It is also worn by witches as a sign to others of their membership in her society. The association of Hecate-Diana-Proserpina with witchcraft is a long-standing tradition in pre-Christian literature.

Hecate-Diana-Proserpina

In ancient writings witches call upon Diana to aid their magic. The Roman poet Horace writes in his *Epodes* that Diana witnesses the deeds of witches in the night. He goes on to say she is the mistress of the silent hour when mystic rites are performed *(Epode 5, verse 50)*. Other writings list Diana in a triformis group with Hecate and Proserpina. One example appears in the works of Apollodorus whose opinion is that Hecate, Diana and Proserpina are all one and the same. Here the triple goddess is described as Hecate in the heavens (the moon), Diana on Earth, and Proserpina in the Underworld.

The beliefs connected to the cimaruta as they appear in common folk magic (protection of the infant) and that of witchcraft (connection to the goddess Diana) seem to not match, but this is due to a surface understanding. In ancient times the goddess Diana played an important role related to pregnant women and birthing. Her sanctuary at Lake Nemi was the site of an annual pilgrimage where women petitioned Diana for a safe and easy labor. Author Eustace Neville Rolfe, in his book *Naples in 1888*, wrote about the cimaruta in connection with Diana and infants.

Diana, Queen of Heaven

Rolfe writes that in her aspect of Diana Pronuba, the goddess oversaw maternity. Concerning rue, the author states "the rue plant is the herb of maternity, and clearly represents Diana Pronuba, while the key represents Diana Jana, the heart Diana Virgo, and the moon the Queen of Heaven." Folklorist Frederick Elworthy, in his book *The Evil Eye*, remarks that three branches of rue represent Diana Triformis or her prototype. He

equates Diana with Proserpina who he states is concerned for women in labor. Rolfe writes in conclusion:

Of all the many charms combined in the Cimaruta we find on close study that there is scarcely one which may not directly or indirectly be considered as connected with Diana, the goddess of infants, worshipped today by Neapolitans as zealously as ever she was in old times by the men of Ephesus and Rome; the only change is in her name. Many a Demetrius, who still makes her silver shrines, flourishes near the Piazza Margherita, though nowadays he knows her only as La Madonna; she is, however, his goddess, his 'regina del Cielo, della terra, del parto, ed anche del inferno.'

Thus far we have seen that the amulet contains no directly Christian emblem. There is no trace in it of a cross, a halo, a crown, or a palm branch. None of the emblems which we habitually see in the ancient catacombs, or in the modern churches, are discernible, and both catacombs and churches are accustomed to display symbols of various kinds with astonishing prodigality. We must consequently conclude that, after something like sixteen centuries of Christianity, an amulet exists in Italy in which heathen emblems only prevail. There is, in fact, nothing we can twist into a Christian symbol, excepting so far only as the worship of the Virgin Mary at Naples today is identical with, and a survival of, the worship of Diana Tifatina at Capua in the Roman times.

Symbols of the Cimaruta

Despite the obvious intimate connection of the cimaruta with pre-Christian symbolism, most modern scholars insist upon its use in Christian culture as an indication of its meaning (if not origin). As noted earlier, the cimaruta is regarded by modern academics as strictly an anti-witch charm used by superstitious Catholic peasants in 19th century Italy. However, when we examine the symbolism of the cimaruta it becomes difficult to understand how it meshes with Catholic beliefs in such a way that the charm reflects Christian tenets. We should expect to find only Christian symbolism in a charm designed to protect the Catholics of Italy who relied upon it. But in its earliest forms such symbols do not exist. In order to understand the cimaruta as a non-Catholic devise used by witches we must revisit the symbolism and see them through the eyes of the witch.

As we have seen, the 19th century cimaruta charm was most commonly comprised of several symbols that readily identified it. These were attached to the sprig of rue plant design, encircling it to form one complete amulet. All cimaruta pieces of this era contained the following symbols: hand, moon, key, flower,

horn or dagger, rooster (or sometimes an eagle), and the serpent. Later other symbols were added to the cimaruta. Among the most common were the heart, the cornucopia, and the cherub angel. The later addition of the heart (sometimes depicted as a flaming heart) and the cherub are the only ones to reflect Catholic theology. When we compare this cimaruta design with earlier ones, the heart or the cherub is always placed in areas that are empty spaces in the earlier cimaruta piece designs. What does that suggest?

The Triformis Goddess of Witchcraft

As noted earlier in the article, the branches of the rue naturally divide into three trunks. This we can regard as being representative of a triple nature, and therefore it can be connected with the triformis goddess of witchcraft. Most scholars argue that the concept of a triple goddess associated with witches or witchcraft is an entirely modern notion. But this is incorrect.

The Roman poet Ovid (in his work titled *Metamorphoses*) mentions "the sacred rites of the three-fold goddess" in connection to an oath sworn to the witch Medea, and portrays her as a priestess of the goddess Hecate. Lucan writes (in Book 6 of his *Bellum Civile*) of witches worshipping Hecate as a triformis goddess, with Persephone being the "lowest of the three aspects." The Roman poet Catullus writes of Diana as a "three-fold" goddess, and Horace associates witches with the goddess Diana who watches over their rites. Virgil refers to Diana as having three faces and names one as Hecate. Horace writes that witches worship Hecate, Diana, and Proserpina (Persephone). An Orphic tradition also joined Hecate, Diana, and Persephone (Proserpina) into one triformis goddess. None of this is proof that witches actually worshipped a triformis goddess in ancient times, but it is proof that the concept itself is not a modern invention.

Diana's Dart

One of the titles for Diana is Queen of the Fairies, and in accord with this the vervain blossom on the cimaruta gains even greater significance through its faery connection. The relevance of the moon is obvious, but in connection with the moon the appearance of the dagger requires further explanation. The dagger represents a moonbeam, the light of Diana directed as she wills. In this context it is known as the dart or arrow of Diana. With it, Diana bestows either enlightenment or lunacy – what a person is prepared on unprepared to receive beneath her emanation of mystical light.

Hecate has been associated with witches and witchcraft almost since her first appearance in ancient writings. Legends about her place Hecate as a goddess who rules over the crossroads. Since ancient times this site has been sacred and magical. An ancient common belief is that the dead who were unable to pass

into the Otherworld gathered at the crossroads. Here they came under the protection of Hecate. The key became a very important symbol related to Hecate, because she is the gatekeeper between the worlds. In this light, the key is an important symbol on the cimaruta. However, it is also a sign that the wearer (as a witch) is one to whom no mystery is ever closed.

No Stronger Symbol of Allegiance

The last aspect of the triformis goddess is Proserpina, a mystical form of Persephone. Her name is related to the serpent, which is one of the manifestations in which she presents herself. The serpent is a creature that moves below and above the earth. It passes through the portals between the realms. In this regard the serpent knows the secrets of the Underworld and is a messenger between the living and the dead. On the cimaruta, the serpent moves along the edge of the crescent, symbolizing its connections to the phases of the moon in a mystical shedding of its skin.

As a triformis goddess on the cimaruta, Diana resides in the night sky. Proserpina walks in the Underworld, and Hecate appears in the middle, here on Earth where she stands at the crossroads between the worlds. There can no stronger symbol of allegiance to the Triformis Goddess, and to the way of witchcraft, than the cimaruta charm.

– RAVEN GRIMASSI
Excerpt from *The Cimaruta:*
and Other Magical Charms
from Old Italy

PICKING THINGS UP:

Pins and pennies

See a penny and pick it up,
all the day you'll have good luck.
See a penny and let it lay,
bad luck you'll have all the day.
— Traditional rhyme

THE EARLIER VERSIONS of this popular nursery rhyme referred to pins, also called common pins, which are no longer very common, unless you sew or craft. They were made entirely of plain metal — no pretty glass heads — and were quite expensive. So expensive, in fact, that a "paper of pins" (a strip of paper pierced with pins) would be given as a gift. Women would allot a portion of the household budget to pins, necessary in making clothes. This practice gave rise to the phrase "pin money" and eventually covered not just money for items used in making clothes, but clothing itself, and eventually expanded to mean any money set aside for incidentals.

Finding an expensive item like a straight pin would be lucky in itself and even a sign that the gods were favoring you. To ignore a gift from the gods —  some believed that all metal was a gift from the gods — would be an insult, bringing down their wrath in the form of bad luck.

The position of the pin, when found, has significance. If the point is toward you, it can bring good luck, but only if you then either stick it in a piece of wood or pin it in your coat with the point toward the back. If you come upon it with the head facing you, a message awaits. If you find it crossing your way — that is, lying with its side toward you — then you will see your love that day.

The rhyme has evolved to use the word penny instead of pin, which still fits with the idea that finding a thing of value is good luck. A penny, like a pin, is also metal, signifying a gift from the gods. In 1793, the young United States of America began minting copper pennies. The British followed in 1797. Copper is ruled by Venus, which leads some to believe that the luck that comes with picking up copper is not financial, but related to love.

Once again, some say that the lie of the penny, when found, has an influence on whether the luck will be good or bad. A penny found heads up is always considered good luck, but a penny found head down is not. I always pick up pennies, even those laying tails up. To ward off any bad luck, I simply say this charm as I pick it up: "As I do will, so mote it be, any penny is lucky for me."

– MORVEN WESTFIELD

Monday's child is fair of face,
Tuesday's child is full of grace;
Wednesday's child is full of woe,
Thursday's child has far to go;
Friday's child is loving and giving,
Saturday's child works hard for its living;
But the child that is born on the Sabbath day
Is bonny and blithe, and good and gay.

– Mother Goose

Here's to thee, Old Apple Tree

WASSAIL is known today in the U.S. as a hot cider drink, commonly consumed at the mid-winter holidays. But to the knowledgeable U.K. resident, it is a festive brew made from most any type of fruit. The earliest known apple wassailing — also known as 'apple howling'— was in Fordwich, Kent in approximately 1585.

Stories and songs surround the Wassailing tradition:

"Drink the drink and
make an offering to the tree,
Wassail brings luck and
bounty for thee."

Custom has it that songs regaling the power of the Wassailing be sung over future crops. The last drops of the old drink are poured upon the roots of the oldest or most prolific fruit-bearing trees to ensure a good crop for the next year.

There are a great many old familiar Wassail chants and rhymes. An early example:

"Here's to thee,
old apple-tree,
Whence thou may'st
bud, and Whence
thou may'st blow,
And whence thou
may'st bear
Apples enow!
Hats-full! Caps-full!
Bushel, bushel, sacks-full!
And my pockets full, too! Hurra!"

Recipes for the old-style drink vary greatly, depending on location and according to each old family recipe.

Service of the Dead

IF YOU ARE FOOLISH ENOUGH to watch by the gate of a church's graveyard at midnight on All Hallows Night, you may be sufficiently ill-fated to see the Service of the Dead — a most disturbing sight indeed. A vision of those who will die within the coming year marching before you might be alarming in and of itself, but there is always the chance that you are in danger of being the first-comer yourself. Should you be the unlucky one, you will become the Churchyard Walker and the Guardian of the Graveyard, until another foolhardy person disturbs the Service of the Dead on this most powerful night of the year. The person who is clandestinely touched by the Church-Yard Walker (the sight of him alone could cause one to perish of fright) dies on the spot.

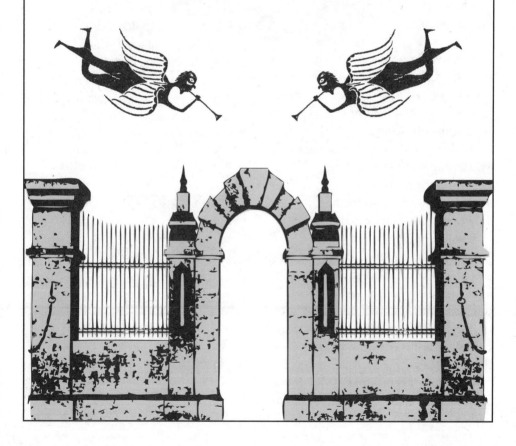

If they would eat nettles in March
And mugwort in May
So many young maidens
Would not turn to clay.

– ANONYMOUS
AND CENTURIES OLD

The Birds of Somerset

THE OLD FOLKS tell that crows are harbingers of evil, for, if one is seen flying alone, it betokens ill-luck and to see one perched in the path is a sign of wrath and dismay. Offer the crow respect when you see one, but at all costs, avoid crossing its path.

The screech of an owl is still heard with alarm: "the owl's screech is a sound of death to the body."

Cuckoos come in for their share of patronage, for when the cry of one is heard for the first time, it is usual to turn the money in the pocket and with children often sing:

> *Cuckoo, cuckoo, cherry tree,*
> *Catch a penny and give it to me.*

The robin is held in great veneration. To kill one is deemed unlucky. Before the death of a person, this bird is said to be seen tapping three times at the window.

The wren was sacred in the eyes of the Druids and therefore is also treated with great respect. The praises of both wren and robin are sung in the old couplet:

> *The robin and the wren*
> *are God Almighty's cock and hen.*

The Four Witches, Albrecht Dürer, 1497

Invocation to Diana

Diana, beautiful Diana!
Who art indeed as good as beautiful,
By all the worship I have given thee,
And all the joy of love which
  thou hast known,
I do implore thee aid me in my love!
What thou wilt 'tis true
Thou canst ever do:
And if the grace I seek thou'lt
  grant to me,
Then all, I pray, thy daughter Aradia,
And send her to the bedside of the girl,
And give that girl the likeness
  of a dog,
And make her then come to me
  in my room,

But when she once has
  entered it, I pray
That she may reassume
  her human form,
As beautiful as e'er she was before,
And may I then make love to her until
Our souls with joy are fully satisfied.
Then by the aid of the great
  Fairy Queen
And of her daughter, fair Aradia,
May she be turned into a dog again,
And then to human form as
  once before!

– *Aradia: Gospel of the Witches*
Charles Godfrey Leland, 1899

Aradia: Gospel of the Witches may be read in its entirety in *The Witches' Almanac* edition featuring an introduction by Professor Robert Mathiesen and new essays by notable modern Craft authors including Paul Huson, Raven Grimassi, Judika Illes and Dr. Leo Louis Martello.

Nyctophilia or the Love of Night

TRAFFIC NOISE dies down. Birds' song ceases and squirrels' chatter stills. The air becomes moist; you can feel it touching you. Night is falling and instead of mourning the dying day, you find yourself invigorated.

You may call yourself "night owl" or "child of the night," but there's another word for those drawn to the darkness, especially for those who feel sexual arousal when the black cloak of night descends: Nyctophiliac from the Greek *nycto*, meaning night, and *philos*, meaning fondness or attraction.

Is it surprising that many witches are nyctophiliacs? The notion that magic is more prevalent and magicians more powerful after the sun sets is an old and respected belief, so much so that the hour of midnight is called the Witching Hour.

Spirits are easier to communicate with after dusk, especially those who have gone before. Think of it: how many séances are conducted at high noon?

– MORVEN WESTFIELD

HERBALISTS' SYMBOLS

✠

Symbol	Meaning	Symbol	Meaning
℔·I·	pound	Σ	sugar
ANA	equal amounts	⚏	alcohol
℥·I·	ounce	⚭	honey
ʒ·I·	dram	⚻	mix
Ə·I·	scruple	⚼	boil
P·I·	pinch	℞	take
O·I·	pint	⚗	distill
ℳ	still	◇	filter
☽	retort	⚛	essence
	receiver	P	powder
⚴	vinegar	⚵	compose

266

Tomb Sweeping Day

A Chinese festival of the dead

EACH SPRING, on the fifteenth day following the Spring Equinox (typically April 4, 5 or 6), highway tolls in mainland China are suspended to make travel more affordable. Millions of people anticipate this annual journey, which is rooted in a tradition that began over 2500 years ago. The Chinese government reinstated the Qingming festival in 2008 and officially these people are taking time to go outside and revel in the greenery, while absorbing the wholesome energies of springtime.

Qingming, the name of the festival, may be translated as Pure Brightness Day, Clear Bright Festival as well as Ancestors Day or Tomb Sweeping Day. However, while enjoying the outdoors and 'treading the greenery' as  they are officially encouraged to do, some may also discreetly seek a spiritual awakening. They honor, remember and connect with their departed loved ones. Tombs and burial grounds are swept free of leaves and other debris left by the passing winter. Gifts of food, libations of wine and tea, chopsticks, flowers, candles, joss

(lucky burnt paper votive offerings), incense and firecrackers are presented to the deceased. Tomb Sweeping Day has elements reminiscent of both Halloween and Spring Equinox. It honors the processes of death, as well as the promise of rebirth. Chinese communities not under Communist control including those in Taiwan, Hong Kong, Vietnam and Malaysia are able to express the religious elements of Qingming. They celebrate their ancestors more openly.

This beautiful and bittersweet tradition, originally called Hanshi Day, might have begun as a memorial in 636 BCE when Jie Zitui died. He was a loyal follower of Duke Wen. Jie supported the duke during a difficult nineteen year exile. Once, when the duke was starving, Jie saved him by serving a nourishing soup. As he relished the delicious soup, Duke Wen was most appreciative, but could not understand how Jie found the ingredients to make it. It turned out that Jie had sliced off and stewed a piece of his own thigh. Duke Wen was so touched that he promised Jie a handsome reward. Jie sought no reward: he only wanted to help Wen become king.

Upon ascending the throne, Wen rewarded many loyal followers, but Jie disappeared into the forest, not seeking compensation. He had merely wanted to help Wen. Determined to find him,

Wen ordered the forest burned down in order to force Jie to come out of hiding. However, Jie perished in the fire. Overcome by remorse, Wen ordered the people to honor Jie by going three days without fire. Wen also established a place held sacred to his benefactor, naming it Jiexiu, meaning "the place where Jie rests forever." At first, the faithful would sacrifice a live rooster annually to honor Jie's death. Later, the holy day expanded to include other offerings to all of those who were mourned.

Another tradition credits the origin of Qingming to the Tang Emperor Xuanzong. In 732 CE, this emperor declared that Chinese citizens were becoming wasteful and extravagant. Ostentatious ancestor-worshipping ceremonies were being held too often and were used to try to outshine everyone else. The emperor declared that such parties could only take place on the one-hundred-fourth day after the Winter Solstice, which is also the fifteenth day following the Spring Equinox.

The Qingming festival has been firmly rooted in Chinese culture ever since. Family members of all ages gather to sweep tombs and have a party for their ancestors. This has expanded to include dancing, singing, and flying beautiful paper kites to honor and delight those who have passed away. Often willow branches are placed near household gates and doorways at the end of the day for protection. This turns away angry ghosts or other malevolent spirits. The willow branch is held as a healing implement by the benevolent goddess Kwan Yin.

Here is a traditional invocation to call upon Kwan Yin. Throughout the year as well as on Tomb Sweeping Day, it is said that she is infinitely compassionate and will always help whenever there is need, never turning her back on the living or the dead.

Homage to Kwan Yin
who holds the willow branch,

Homage to the vase hand
of Kwan Yin.

Bodhisattva of mercy
whose right hand heals.

She drives away illness.

Her left hand holds the vase
from which streams the nectar
of wisdom and compassion.

May it be sprinkled on me,
all merciful and divine mother
from the East.

– Marina Bryony

Magic that Works

FROM A PAGAN perspective, the visible world is the expression of a reality that both permeates and transcends it. From this it follows that behind its rich diversity lies a subtle unity, which, in turn, reflects the inter-connectedness of its myriad parts. As Hinduism puts it, these are but the million faces of Brahman. Herein lies the secret why magic — real magic, that is, not the smoke and mirrors kind — actually works.

For centuries, the words "magic" and "witchcraft" have been virtually interchangeable, although surviving records make it hard to distinguish between what witches got up to in the past and what their accusers invented or, for that matter, what witches themselves invented in order to satisfy their tormentors. Interestingly enough, among the lurid tales of orgies, curses, familiars and demons, well captured by Goya

Chick with infant head,
from *Los Caprichos,* by Goya.

in his paintings, there is mention also of nocturnal feasts, allegedly presided over by a goddess, where the serious business of magic was conducted. This last detail is sometimes overlooked by those who argue, not completely without justification, that modern witchcraft is the invention of an ex-colonial civil servant on the south coast of England close to seventy years ago. It is indisputable that without a touch of magic, there is no such thing as witchcraft.

The art of causing change

What has by now become a standard definition of magic was provided by Aleister Crowley, no saint, but no monster either, who defined it as "the art of causing change to occur in conformity with the will." Dion Fortune, his more respectable contemporary, called it "the art of causing changes to occur in consciousness" but this tells us little, as changes in consciousness can be induced by a variety of means, among them drugs, meditation and fasting, none of which requires us to put on ceremonial dress or, as the case may be, strip off and invoke Pagan gods. No, by 'change,' Crowley certainly meant more than a different state of awareness from our everyday one.

To understand the mechanics of magic, so to speak, we have to remind ourselves that reality is more, far more, than what our senses reveal. It is presumptuous to think otherwise, implying, as it does, that nothing can exist

unless it is perceptible. Even scientists believe otherwise, now that particle physics have demonstrated that the smallest components of matter straddle a frontier between the spatial-temporal world we occupy and another, no less real, in which neither space nor time exists. Not only is the latter beyond our understanding but also beyond our conceptual reach, given that our imagination is nourished by our environment and nothing outside it.

The miracle of the One thing

Only by analogy can we attempt to grasp what lies beyond, since, although both are manifestly different, the "here" that is familiar to us and the inconceivable "there" are essentially one and the same. It is this unity and the relationships among its myriad parts that magic seeks to exploit. In words attributed to the legendary Hermes Trismegistus "that which is above is like that which is below, to accomplish the miracle of the One thing."

The same principle applies as much to the world around, as to any hypothetical reality beyond it. It permits us to adopt what I call an "integrated" approach to the natural world, one that enables us to discern the implicit unity among its many parts. Thanks to this and, as Dion Fortune would maintain, to an appropriate change in consciousness, we are able, for example, to discern the hidden virtues of plants,

whether medical or magical, something witches have traditionally been doing for centuries. It explains why the local cunning man or woman is still esteemed in rural Wales where I grew up.

Eye of the soul

What he or she does, of course, is discern the very being of things, thereby observing the landscape with what Jakob Boehme, the Silesian mystic, famously called the "eye of the soul."

The technique can be mastered by anyone minded to do so. Yet, like many traditional practices, it is often overlooked by contemporary witches, either because most live in towns or cities and have lost touch with the countryside, even with Nature herself, or because they prefer working with fellow coven members at what they regard as more exciting stuff. For many, ritual and the company of others are preferable to a solitary walk in the woods. More's the pity.

But then the preference is understandable. Few would deny, after all, that magic is most vividly experienced in a semi-formal setting where it emerges from the collaborative effort of several people, all compatible and all prepared to work together more or less harmoniously. (I say "more or less" because a little rivalry, even a hint of tension, can sometimes add zest to the proceedings.) It then becomes far easier to gain access to supra-sensible reality, a condition — for we can hardly call it a "place" — that goes by a variety of names, one of the most popular being the Inner Planes.

Correspondences sympathetic and symptomatic

We reach this supra-sensible reality by attaining a higher level of consciousness, helped by the impact of symbols, colours, sounds and scents, as well as the overall "choreography" of the ritual proceedings. These elements will have been selected with an eye on the aim of the operation and on whatever supernatural being or force is to be evoked. Here, use is made of the "correspondences" sympathetic to it and, if you like, symptomatic of it. With their assistance, we aspire to exchange the conditioned reality we normally occupy for the unconditioned one beyond it and thereby "earth" so to speak, a specific impulse within it.

As the 19th century magus, Eliphas Lévi declared, "Analogy" — represented by the "correspondences" we've assembled — "is the last word of science and the first word of faith... the sole possible mediator between the visible and the invisible, between the finite and the infinite."

But magic is nothing if not practical and, as such, it has a purpose beyond passive enjoyment of a heightened awareness, always at risk of degenerating into mere self-indulgence.

Outward vesture

Lévi, whose given name at birth was Alphonse-Louis Constant, described ritual as the "outward vesture" of every magical operation, by which he meant that its function was to serve and stimulate the volitional and creative powers of the imagination, so that a specific objective might be attained. Experience does indeed show that the more involved participants become in what happens around them — seduced, as it were, by the "outward vesture" — the greater the energy available to realize a collective intention. In addition, should conditions be right, it may even contrive to render objective whatever is visualized, a process familiar to psychical researchers and known in the East as *kriyashakti*. It enables archetypal forms and other entities not of this world to take on form and substance in our midst, seemingly every bit as solid as ourselves.

A quasi-sacramental quality

It would nevertheless be wrong to think of Lévi's "outward vesture" as no more than a means to this end and devoid of any merit of its own. The truth is that through long association the elements which comprise it become imbued with the very forces they purport to represent, acquiring in the process a quasi-sacramental quality. (A sacrament is defined by theologians as the visible sign of an invisible grace.) Thus, a given symbol not only points to a supernatural reality, itself inexpressible, but, more importantly, contains something of its essence. That is why meticulous attention must be paid to getting the details of a magical operation exactly right. Failure to do so may not lead to catastrophe, although some people have come perilously close, but it does mean that one's magical efforts will have been in vain.

On the other hand, if one goes by the book, then success is guaranteed. Again this is due to the sacramental quality of the outward vesture, for success proceeds from the ritual itself and not from the merits of whoever performs it, a consequence theologians sum up rather well by distinguishing between the act (*ex opere operatis*) and the agent responsible for its execution (*ex opere operantis*). Certainly the lesson for ceremonial magicians and witches alike is to get the details right each and every time.

The educated will

All of which may seem far removed from the spells and good luck charms — let's not mention the curses — for which old-fashioned witches were long famed. In all cases, however, the principle remains the same, for as Lévi points out, "a practice, even though it be superstitious and foolish, will be efficacious because it is a realization of the will." Elsewhere he refers to it as the "educated" will and on this Aleister Crowley would later base his personal philosophy, opting to call it, with a brief nod to Rabelais, the Law of Thelema. (Crowley, born eight months after Lévi's death in 1875, declared himself to be none other than an incarnation of that magus.)

It makes sense, for, all things considered, it is indeed our will that ultimately sponsors the changes magic brings about, whether these occur inside our consciousness, as Dion Fortune maintained, or objectively in the world around us. Given the Hermetic connection between the microcosm that is each of us and the macrocosm that is everything, we are entitled to regard every informed act of will as a local manifestation of that supreme will which quickens and directs the universe itself.

Yes indeed, magic works.

– DAVID CONWAY

The Eve of the Fairy Queen

Radiance on a bleak winter night

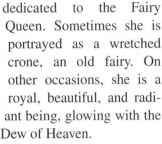

THE ANNUAL appearance on our Moon Calendar of Fairy Queen Eve, celebrated on December 16, has evoked the curiosity of those readers more familiar with seasonal Yuletide and Saturnalia celebrations. Numerous requests have been made for an explanation of this fey holiday, as well as for information on how to honor the occasion.

Fairy Queen Eve can be celebrated on many levels, true of many passages linked with the Old Ways. The days leading to the Winter Solstice mark a cycle when the gates to Fairyland, the Other World, are more accessible to mortals. A Celtic tradition exists with a connection to Queen Maeve (or Medb), who presides over her court, directing the preparations for the cross-quarter day of Yule, with its longest of nights.

The date specifically marks the beginning of a nine-day period of grace and waiting in early Catholic rituals dedicated to the Blessed Virgin Mary, Queen of the Universe. A time of reverie, of sacred anticipation, begins at 4 a.m. on December 16. For nine successive mornings, until Christmas Day, the enigmatic energies of a pre-dawn mass are dedicated to the Fairy Queen. Sometimes she is portrayed as a wretched crone, an old fairy. On other occasions, she is a royal, beautiful, and radiant being, glowing with the Dew of Heaven.

Fairy Queen Eve, among the holiest times of joy and penance, is now most familiar in the traditional Catholic cultures of the Philippines and Puerto Rico. December 16 is the start of the mass or *Misa de Aguinaldo. Aguinaldo* is a Spanish word meaning "a unique holiday gift." In Puerto Rico, this mass is completely musical and the *Aguinaldo* becomes the gift of holiday songs.

To call in the Fairy Queen, whether you see her as Maeve or Mary, withered or youthful, obtain a bell and a snow-white or silver-gilt candle. During the dark hours on December 16, ring the bell nine times and light the candle. Ask for her blessing. Be observant, for either the old woman or the lovely lady will probably appear to you. Most likely this will be briefly and from a distance, as you round a corner, during an outing, before Midwinter's day has passed.

– DANA N.

This Fairy Queen Eve feature is dedicated to the memory of Nadya, dear familiar and best friend, who, once upon a time, incarnated in this world on a Fairy Queen Eve.   – A.T.

A Hymn in Praise of Neptune

Of Neptune's empire let us sing,
At whose command the waves obey;
To whom the rivers tribute pay,
Down the high mountains sliding:
To whom the scaly nation yields
Homage for the crystal fields
Wherein they dwell:
And every sea-god pays a gem
Yearly out of his wat'ry cell
To deck great Neptune's diadem.

The Tritons dancing in a ring
Before his palace gates do make
The water with their echoes quake,
Like the great thunder sounding:
The sea-nymphs chant their accents shrill,
And the sirens, taught to kill
With their sweet voice,
Make ev'ry echoing rock reply
Unto their gentle murmuring noise
The praise of Neptune's empery.

THOMAS CAMPION

A Pagan Manifesto

1. Thou shalt always say, think and do what you truly desire, so long as it hurts no one else.
2. Thou shalt live in accordance with the laws of nature, not against them, and coordinate sleep, food, physical exertion and work with the ways of nature.
3. Thou shalt not destroy nature or take from it without restoring that which has been taken, and thou shalt keep the balance of nature intact at all times.
4. Thou shalt worship in any way that pleases thee and let others do likewise, even though ye may not understand their ways.
5. Thou shalt not take the life of another living thing, except for protection or for food.
6. Thou shalt not cage another living thing.
7. Thou shalt be free to love whomever thou pleasest, so long as thy primary obligations to family, home and community are not neglected.
8. Thou shalt express thyself through art, crafts, music, dancing, singing, poetry, for in so doing, thou shalt be in harmony with nature.
9. Thou shalt accept communication from the world beyond and the inner planes as natural, and thou shalt develop psychic abilities as a natural function of thy personality.
10. Thou shalt always strike a happy balance between mind and body, exercising both and developing thy inner self through the interplay of both selves, ever mindful that the spirit is above and beyond mind and body.
11. Thou shalt not forget the Spirit within and the Spirit without are the one and only true God/dess.

Paganism has one primary law – the law of Threefold Return, which states: Whatever you do, for good or for ill, returns to you threefold.

– The New Pagans, HANS HOLZER

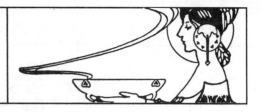

Glögg

GLÖGG, ALSO KNOWN as Svařené Víno in the Czech Republic, Glühwein in Germany and mulled wine in English speaking countries, is a customary drink of Sweden. It is traditionally enjoyed on St. Lucia's Day, a holiday that celebrates light over darkness. Evergreen trees and holly decorate homes as they maintain ancient Pagan traditions by representing life everlasting during the cold dark holiday season.

Historically, it was considered illfated for a visitor to leave a Swedish household during the holiday season without offering the guest some form of refreshment—usually Glögg. As a staple drink throughout the Yuletide season, it is generally enjoyed from December 13 through the Winter Solstice.

Every winter my Swedish grandmother would make Glögg (pronounced glerg)—a wonderful, traditional Nordic drink. It was usually served during the cold winter holidays to warm you, bring good fortune and cheer for the coming year. This recipe was handed down from my grandmother to my older brother and eventually to me.

To make Swedish Glögg:

¼ cup vodka

1 quart apple juice or cider

3 whole cloves

2 cups of dry red wine

3 cups water

2 cinnamon sticks or ½ tsp ground cinnamon

½ tsp ground cardamom

½ to ¾ cups of raisins or dried cranberries.

Bring all ingredients to a simmer for 20 minutes

Add small hand-full of raisins or cranberries to each serving cup.

Serve with gingerbread.

This will take the bite off a cold winter's night—enjoy!

—THOR VOLKER

Poppets:

A Voodoo Doll by Any Other Name

MAKING POPPETS is a type of sympathetic magic dating back to prehistoric times. The gist of this kind of magical working is to direct energy onto an image or perform an action in order to create a desired result. For example, Stone Age hunters might have formed an image from the horns and skin of a deer, actually a primitive poppet, near a tribal fire while dancing around it pretending to "hunt" and "kill" the remains of the animal. The idea was that this drama would build an energy field to foreshadow a successful hunt in the future.

The first actual poppet might have appeared in ancient Egypt during the reign of Ramses III whose subjects detested him. Many hated this pharaoh enough to wish him dead and began to construct doll-like images of him which they could hang or burn. The intent, which has been consistent through the ages, was to use sympathetic magic. Thousands of years later in England, Guy Fawkes Day is celebrated to commemorate a failed plot to destroy the government by the infamous traitor. Images of that hated historical figure are still constructed of twigs and straw. These are then burned in large bonfires the night of November 5, the anniversary of his reprehensible act. The phrase "to burn in effigy" as a way of destroying someone in absentia reflects the sympathetic magic used to annihilate Guy Fawkes all over again. The destruction of his poppet suggests a wish that he burns on in the afterlife.

Usually linked with voodoo dolls, which are really poppets, the magical doll images have acquired a sinister reputation. Associated with mysterious Caribbean or African rituals, many believe they are used only to create a curse and cause harm. However this is far from the entire story. Poppets or voodoo dolls are used just as often for healing, prosperity and love rituals. The ancient Greeks created poppets called kollosos (pronounced 'caw law sauce'). When made in pairs and bound together the kollosos were intended to protect a love bond. The Greeks also used kollosos to bind and control dangerous ghostly spirits.

One thing is certain. Whether intended for good or not, poppets are extremely powerful tools for focusing spiritual energies toward a desired outcome. Poppets are portable. They can be made ahead of time, then carried easily by witches while on the move to be employed while at a comfortable distance from the intended target. These magical dolls can be fashioned from a variety of materials. Yarn, cloth, paper, sticks and straw, aluminum foil or clay are all good choices. Incorporating an appropriate stone, herbs or wax from a ritual candle burning into the poppet can further enhance the effectiveness of the sympathetic magic.

It's essential to concentrate on the intended subject while constructing the poppet. Speak its name aloud and talk to it. It isn't essential to be a great artist, just a basic figure resembling a human form will be fine. Some practitioners will incorporate a relic from the target into the poppet too. A relic is a personal physical link such as a hair, nail clipping, a scrap from an article of clothing or perhaps a small photograph.

A Witch from Germany once described how to make a protection poppet to halt an aggressive person. Her technique won't cause harm, but is merely intended to stop undesired contact. Once the image is complete, tie its arms close to the body, then place the doll in the freezer. Leave it there until the threat has passed. This puts the volatile situation "on ice," cooling the problem.

To make a love poppet, a piece of rose quartz might be inserted into the heart cavity of the doll. For healing try stuffing the poppet with a medicinal herb such as peppermint, which relieves pain and has been called the aspirin of the herb world. Green wax and a few coins or dollar bill would be appropriate for a poppet needed to attract money or improve a job related issue. Experiment, use colors and materials which feel comfortable and in harmony with the desired intent to you.

Once through with the doll, gently take it apart and bury or burn the remains. Don't use the same poppet for more than one person.

—SUE LEROY

278

Corpse Doors

OUR DISTANT ancestors employed numerous methods to keep the dead from returning to haunt the living. In Ireland, though a window was opened at the time of death to let the spirit leave, it was closed after a short time so the spirit could not re-enter. The Navajo didn't take any chances. They collapsed and abandoned the hogan in which a person died.

The Norse worried that if a corpse faced the house while being removed, it would see which house it came from and would be able to find its way back, so they carried corpses out of the house feet first.

They were especially fearful of the return of the dead, for it was believed they could return as draugar, undead creatures who possessed supernatural strength. Destroying a draug (singular) was nasty business. In addition to supernatural strength, the draugar possessed the ability to increase their size at will, making it a formidable opponent. Because the draugar was so hard to kill, they considered it wiser to prevent the transformation than to exterminate the result.

Sacred Rites

When a person died, the Norse followed strict protocol. They would lay a pair of open scissors on the dead person's chest and small pieces of straw crosswise under the shroud. The scissors, being iron or steel, would be imbued with the magical powers of the metal. In an open position they formed the shape of a cross, as did the pieces of straw. This invoked the protection of the Christian cross. The protocol contained a third invocation of the powers of Christian belief. Just within the threshold of the door, as the coffin was carried out, the bearers raised and lowered it three times in different directions, forming a cross.

To prevent the corpse from walking if it did wake, the family would tie the big toes together and also stick needles in the sole of the feet. The needles, also being of iron or steel, would have magical properties in addition to the practical value of causing pain to the revenant.

Yet the most effective way of preventing a draug was to use a corpse door. The family would open a hole in the wall of the house. With mourners standing close around the coffin to block the view, the bearers would carry the corpse feet first through this door. While the family processed to the place of burial, others would stay behind, bricking up the door so that the corpse could not use it to return, for they believed the dead could only return the way they left.

Hidden Portals

As late as 1907 there was still evidence of this practice. A folklorist returning to the west coast of Jutland reported seeing the outline of what he thought was a bricked-up oven door on the gable-end of a house. It didn't make sense to him since the wall was the outer wall of the house's "best room" or "company room" and one wouldn't be baking there. When he asked the inhabitants what it was, they told him it was a corpse door. Though not in use at that time, it was still alive in local memory.

Even now, the Draugr lives on in memory, though in video games, novels and graphic novels. Examples include The Elder Scrolls series of action role-playing games, The Morganville Vampire young adult urban fantasy novels from Rachel Caine, as well as The Corpse Door by Kris Sayer.

—MORVEN WESTFIELD

EASTER WITCHES

IN THE UNITED STATES, the non-religious and religious alike celebrate Easter by coloring eggs and setting up baskets to receive candy and gifts from the Easter Bunny. In Finland and Sweden though, you're more likely to find Easter Witches, and they're getting candy, not giving it.

Little girls dress up as witches (påskkärring) in a brightly colored kerchief, shawl and long skirt. Often they carry a broom. Their costumes may be either tattered or new, and some wear conical witch hats instead of the traditional triangular piece of cloth tied around the head. They rouge their cheeks and freckle their nose and face, making them resemble a Raggedy Ann doll more than a folkloric witch.

Like American children on Halloween, the Easter Witches go door-to-door gathering candy from their neighbors which they collect in wicker baskets or copper teapots. Carrying sprigs of pussy willow decorated with spring-colored feathers and crepe paper, they exchange the twigs for candy while reciting this traditional rhyme:

Virvon, varvon, tuoreeks terveeks,
tulevaks vuodeks;
vitsa sulle, palkka mulle!

The translation:

I wave a twig for a fresh and healthy year ahead;
a twig for you, a treat for me!

Pussy willow branches have long been

a symbol of spring and in some cultures where palms do not grow natively, pussy willows are blessed on Palm Sunday instead. In Sweden, twigs of birch, not pussy willow, are decorated with colored feathers at Easter.

The pussy willows that grow in northern Europe are the goat willow (*Salix caprea*), also called goat sallow and the grey willow (*Salix cinerea*), also called grey sallow. Like the American pussy willow (*Salix discolor*), the male catkins of these trees go through a fuzzy stage where they look like tiny kittens before they burst into flower, giving them the nickname pussy willow.

So why are there witches at Easter? Tradition says that in ancient times, witches travelled on Maundy Thursday (the Thursday before Easter) to Blåkulla, which was either a physical place (one tradition sets it on an island) or an astral destination, to worship the devil. Some even think that Blåkulla was the Brocken in Germany (see *Walpurgisnacht*, Issue 34, Spring 2015 to Spring 2016 of The Witches' Almanac).

One part of the tradition says that bonfires were lit to scare away the witches as they flew over land on their way to their destination and bonfires still play a part in the Easter celebration. The pussy willows and other signs of spring are to welcome the season and make light of what was feared (witches).

—Morven Westfield

The Sacred Acre
The Magic of the Land Between Low and High Tide

"Tell him to buy me an acre of land,
  Parsley, sage, rosemary, and thyme;
  Between the salt water and the sea sand,
  Then he shall be a true lover of mine."
    —*Scarborough Fair (Simon & Garfunkel variant, 1966)*

"Ye'll get an acre o gude red-land
  Atween the saut sea and the sand."
    —*The Elfin Knight (variant 2C around 1650, perhaps older)*

"One day the lad fared forth till he was on the brink of the sea - for the poets deemed that on the brink of water it was always a place of revelation of science."
    —*The Colloquy of the Two Sages (Druid teaching tale from around 800)*

THERE IS A PLACE called the Sacred Acre which is the land that lies between the marks of the low tide and the marks of the high tide. It is the land that belongs to both the spirits of the Sea and the spirits of the Land. The Sacred Acre, like the tides, is always in flux as it moves along the seashores of the world. As it shifts, its shape and size changes. As it moves, it travels through the hours of day and night, through all the phases of the Moon and seasons of the Sun. The Sacred Acre is the moving threshold, the walking crossroads, the liminal place where many realms and reali-

ties meet. As such it has been and will always be a place where magick can be wrought. This is a very powerful place. What would normally take many rituals, invocations, complicated preparations or convoluted sigils can often be done in an hour with no more than a driftwood wand. If you live near the sea, then you will have a task to perform. If you live far from the sea, a pilgrimage to make. If you cannot make it to the sea then the way is harder, but there is still a way.

If you have the good fortune to live near the sea, then begin by finding places on the shore that are quieter, less

crowded and private. Take time to explore the area you select and let the sense of the place seep into you through your senses. Pick up the local newspaper or go online and make it a habit to keep track of the local tides. When you are standing on the land between the boundaries of the tides, breathe in the salt air and feel how energy moves through you. Become aware of how the energy feels when the tide is coming in, when it is going out and in the quiet and churn that is the transition between tides. Open your subtle senses and become aware of the spirits of the sea and land that gather on the Sacred Acre. Come prepared to leave them offerings such as a pinch of soil from near your home, flowers, rainwater you collected or any other natural gift that means something to you. When you trust you are in alignment with the powers gathering on the seashore, then proceed with whatever ritual, working or divination you desire. Always offer thanks and a farewell to all the seen and

unseen that have witnessed and assisted your work before departing.

If you live far from the sea and your time at the shore will be brief, then it must be treated as an important pilgrimage. Before departing for the journey, take a purification bath. Choose clothing and jewelry that has a symbolic meaning for you. You need not wear robes or overtly occult jewelry, strangers around you do not need to know what you are doing. Though do not be surprised if other witches and pagans take notice of the symbolism of what you are wearing as a pilgrim to the sea.

When you get to the shore, as soon as your feet are upon the sand, pause and silently or aloud introduce yourself to the Sacred Acre and all the beings that dwell there. If you had more time, you could slowly build up a relationship with the place, but since time is short a formal introduction is quickest. Then, with whatever time you have for your pilgrimage, follow the same steps that were given for those that live close to the shore. Before departing, give one more offering and you may scoop up a small quantity of sand and salt water into a jar. Do not forget to offer thanks. When you return home place the jar upon an altar decorated with emblems of the sea. Study the tides of the place from which you took a piece of the Sacred Acre. Touch the sand and salt water at different tides and know you are touching the seashore however many miles away it may be. In time, your altar to the Sacred Acre will become imbued with power. Do not be surprised if you hear the cry of a gull within your home.

If life circumstances prevent you from going to the ocean, there are still ways to connect to the power of the sea and to tread upon the Sacred Acre. Through purchases or gifts brought by friends, collect and assemble an altar to the sea. Next acquire sea salt from a specific place. Sea salt with no specific provenance will not do. There are many gourmet shops that sell sea salt from particular locations. Pick a spot on the sea that provided the salt and look up its tides. If you can find photos of the seashore from the spot you picked, place them on your sea altar. Now the magic can begin.

All life on the land arose from the sea. You were formed in the salty water of your mother's womb whose cycles were called by the Moon. The salt in your blood remembers the sea. The sea is always with you. You just need to remember this and know it is true. When you believe it, put a grain or two of the sea salt on your tongue. Look at the tide charts and envision the Sacred Acre. Feel the sea breeze and hear the crash of the waves. Let the rhythmic pulse of the sea's power move within you. With practice, with time and tide, you'll be able to stand on the Sacred Acre within yourself.

The Sacred Acre is a place that is always changing yet very specific. It is found throughout the world, but is also between the worlds. The Sacred Acre is born of the dance of Sun, Moon and Earth and is motion made manifest. It is the place where sea, sky and land greet the fire of your spirit in the stillness and the roaring of eternal continuance. The Sacred Acre is like a cast circle, a great temple, a bubble of sea foam in the great sea of infinity. What can you do in the

Sacred Acre? The scope of what you can do in the Sacred Acre is the same as how much you can become it, a grain of sand or the whole of the ocean.

Whatever your path or tradition may be, it would be wise to visit the Sacred Acre. Whether it be to refresh your spirit and reconnect with the powers of nature, or whether it be the start of one of your regular ways of power, many a witch has come into their own on the seashore. Do not rush this work and do remember your offerings and gratitude. You will be rewarded by gifts that can only be given by this sacred portal.

–Ivo Dominguez Jr.

Making Powders

MANY OF THE POWDERS sold to practitioners of magic are composed mainly of talc, which is problematic because it is a known carcinogen. Another common ingredient in commercial powders is called wood flour, finely ground up wood of unknown source—so it could be "pressure-treated" wood (i.e., poison). Why mess with these ingredients when you can make your own powders? Moreover, since an excellent main ingredient for homemade powders—and a traditional use of plant material in old-fashioned pharmacy—is stalks, they demonstrate a Witches' thrift. You can strip off the leaves of a dried plant and reserve those for teas, strewings, stuffings, vinegars, waters, or even incense. But you can keep the stalks to make powders.

Stalks are the bones of a plant; this analogy appears as far back as the Greek Magical Papyri. Once Witchcraft practice distinguishes between Living and Dead Bones when it comes to plants; I find these categories useful. Living Bones are green stalks, those that are living when they are harvested. When dried and ground, Living Bones make powders embodying the plant's more positive or friendly aspects.

Brown stalks—those that have gone through a winter or have turned brown because the plant experienced drought or disease—are considered Dead Bones. Dead Bones evoke the plant's more negative aspects (hostility, aggressiveness) or may simply be used in more negative magic. To make your life a little easier, cut the plant bones up before you dry them. Use secateurs for Living Bones and an

anvil pruner for Dead Bones. Even though Dead Bones are already dried, they may have dew or rain on them and should be put through the dehydrator to crisp them up. Plant material is easier to grind when it's crispy dry.

You can take this further by "mortifying" Dead Bones in several ways. You can perform what is basically a Black Toad operation using decay. This was the first stage in alchemical transformation, during which most of the impure aspects of a substance are destroyed by rotting or fermentation. To do this, wet them and seal them up (the smell of such an operation can be pretty atrocious). Think of the possibilities of various liquids used in the wetting—wine for deadly intoxication, urine for destruction, vinegar for sharpening or souring.

Another way to mortify a plant's qualities is to heat the bones until the plant material is blackened, turned to ash, or even calcined (when the white, caustic, alchemical salt of the plant is all that's left). To mortify with heat, put the Dead Bones in a little roasting pan in the oven at 450°F for half an hour or so. This can also be done outside on a fire. Some people use a torch lighter or even a propane torch. You can then add the resulting mortified bones to other items like incense or oils. They also make a good foundation for a magical powder.

You can tweak a powder by adding other bones, Living or Dead, and also by tossing the powder with essential oils and/or perfumes to modify or amplify the plant's energy. You can also add any items that don't work well in incense because they are noncombustible or smell bad when burned, like mint or orange peel. And you can play with noncombustible ingredients like iron oxide (brick dust, for Mars energy), glitter, mica, metallic powders, mineral powders, rocks, dirt or pigments. You can see how wide a range of possibilities you have beyond the basic dyed sawdust you so often find being sold in foil packets as condition powders in occult shops. Better tools help make better magic.

A powder needs an appropriate vessel, even more than an oil, a water, or an incense. The vibration, if you will, of a powder is more subtle and more easily disarranged. Since only a fairy-sized pinch is necessary for dressing candles, clothing, tools or other objects, a small vessel is usually adequate. A used antique jar makes a good container—just cense it first with the purifier of your choice. Mugwort is nice for this—it's everywhere; it's a Witch's staple herb; and it's a traditional friend of flame in herbalism.

—HAROLD ROTH
Excerpt from *The Witching Herbs*
(See review on page 189)

The Sator Square

```
S A T O R
A R E P O
T E N E T
O P E R A
R O T A S
```

THE USE OF THE SATOR Square as a talisman of defense is buried in the annals of time, its origins being lost to antiquity. With the individual words of the Latin sentence SATOR AREPO TENET OPERA ROTAS each arranged to ccupy a single row of the square, an interesting phenomenon is observed. As you can see in the above illustration the text can be read top-to-bottom, bottom-to-top, left-to-right or right-to-left. Additionally it can be rotated 180 degrees with the results yielding the same word order.

The individual translations of the words shed some light on the meaning behind this talisman; Sator can be translated as "the founder or a divine progenitor." The meaning of word Arepo is a bit unclear, as it may simply be a proper noun or a shortening of the Latin word arrepo, meaning "to creep towards." Tenet is translated by some as "to have mastery over." Opera means "to work." Lastly Rotas meaning "wheel or rotating." A possible translation of the entire sentence being: The Great Sower holds in his hand all works.

Written in the Ink of Arte (such as dragon's blood or ink with other herbs), this talisman is a potent protection of the threshold not only of your home, but your magical working area.

The square can also be used as a focal point for astral journey during meditation.

—DEVON STRONG

TYPHON

Monster father, monster children

FEW MONSTERS have children for obvious reasons—mates are not readily to be found, especially for an entity described as "grisly." So indeed was Typhon, who embodied volcanic forces. All we know about Echidna, his spouse, is that she was "hideous" and that the couple begat brutish children. Typhon had a hundred horrible dragon heads that wriggled upward to the stars, lava and red-hot stones poured from his gaping mouths, and venom dripped from his evil eyes. He embodied deep volcanic forces, and like other monsters was a foe of deities and heroes. From his hundred mouths, Typhon hissed and roared as he hurled sizzling mountains at the Gods, who fled in terror.

"The whole earth seethed, and sky and sea: and the long waves raged along the beaches around and about, at the rush of the deathless gods: and there arose an endless shaking," the Greek poet Hesiod reports.

Only Zeus stood his ground even as Mount Etna was hurled at him, and terrible combat raged. Zeus struck the mountain with a black cloud of thunderbolts and the mountain fell back on Typhon, pinning him below. And there the monster remains to this day, sinister as ever, belching fire and smoke and rage. But he is also otherwise immortal.

During the battle, Echidna cowered in a cave to protect the couple's offspring, resembling their parents in eerie ways: Cerberus, the three-headed watchdog guards the Gate of Hell; the Sphinx, a winged lion with the head and breasts of a woman, the "Demon of Death"; the Chimera breathes fire and has the disparate parts of a lion's head, goat's body and dragon's tail; the Hydra lives in a swamp, has a hundred heads which can regenerate; Ladon, a hundred-headed dragon guards the golden apple tree in the Garden of Hesperides; the vast Nemean lion has teeth and claws like swords.

Zeus came to destroy Echidna and her atrocious brood, but the mother begged for their lives. Zeus spared the creatures for the most amazing of reasons—because future Greek heroes needed worthy challengers. And the monster siblings were destroyed by the most powerful of heroes. Hercules, the son of Zeus, prevailed over the beasts during the course of his legendary Twelve Labors.

—BARBARA STACY

The Tears of Frankincense

Six Millennia of Sanctity

The precious liquid emerges from the sacred tree when its bark is cut. This sap, the life force of the tree, hardens into small pieces which turn brittle and glitter. Carefully the dried resin is collected about a month after the cutting has occurred. These tiny golden-colored botanical bits and pieces, called the "tears," have been treasured for over 6000 years. Several different trees in the boswellia family will produce the desired resin. When burned, usually on a piece of pure charcoal, a supernatural power emerges. Frankincense is a superb natural incense, deeply symbolic and considered essential to ritual work by many

craft practitioners. Metaphysically, the high frequency of its fragrance creates an aromatherapy which connects directly to opening the crown chakra.

The sacred smoke is credited with soothing and calming a troubled mind, casting away negativity and karma while preparing the atmosphere to set desired intentions. Frankincense has been burned in temples, churches, yoga ashrams and craft circles to honor and invoke the favor of the Gods and Goddesses. Ayurvedic medicine uses it to drive away diseases and encourage improved health. It emits a precious essence as it burns which facilitates healing on many

levels. As an oil or when made into a salve, frankincense has been used to relieve the pain of arthritis.

The name frankincense hints at the role Frankish traders played in introducing it to the West, but it actually derives from an Old English phrase (franc incens) which refers to its quality. Sometimes the tears are diffused into oil for use in anointing or burning instead of the hardened resin or tears.

A few remote regions around the globe provide the right climate to grow the mystical and powerful trees which yield frankincense tears. Places where the trees can be found growing include areas around Oman in Ethiopia, Somalia and the Indian Himalayas. The resin from Somalia has a deep balsamic scent. Frankincense from other regions tends to be lighter and sweeter in aroma. This ancient and traditional incense is always a powerful aid in ritual work. The different varieties are all desirable and the selection of which to use is a matter of personal preference. Frankincense or its close cousin olibanum can be purchased at metaphysical and religious supply stores. In magical workings it is linked to the Sun.

An easy and powerful house blessing can be done using frankincense. This is especially good to do during times when situations just seem difficult. First open the doors and windows for a few minutes early in the day to invite in fresh air and sunlight while encouraging any negative energies or bad luck to disperse. It helps to follow this by thoroughly cleaning the premises. As sunset nears allow a few of the tears of frankincense to smolder on a burning piece of charcoal in a thurible or incense burner. Ring a bell three times then carry the fragrant burning incense around the inside of the premises. Give thanks to the Lord and Lady for inspiration, growth and improved good fortune. Once the charcoal has burned out allow intuition to guide you as to whether to cast any remaining ashes either onto the earth or into the wind.

—GRANIA LING

GREAT MULLEIN

The Witch's Taper

IN THE REALMS of Witchcraft and herbal medicine, few herbs are as well-used and well-loved as mullein (*Verbascum thapsus.*) An Old World plant found in most Medieval and Renaissance pharmacopeias, mullein was eventually brought to Australia and North America by European colonists, and was spread throughout US territories by no less a plant authority than "Johnny Appleseed" Chapman himself.

This easily-identifiable plant grows in a biennial cycle. In its first year of life, after months spent transforming underground through the winter cold, the plant first emerges in the springtime as an almost cabbage-like rosette of broad, fuzzy, pale green leaves. By its second spring, a tall stalk appears and climbs upwards, covered in small, green, cubic purses which eventually develop into the soft petals of yellow flowers. Certain plants can sprout multiple, tentacle-like stalks which curve toward the sky. Though most specimens won't grow more than four or five feet in height,

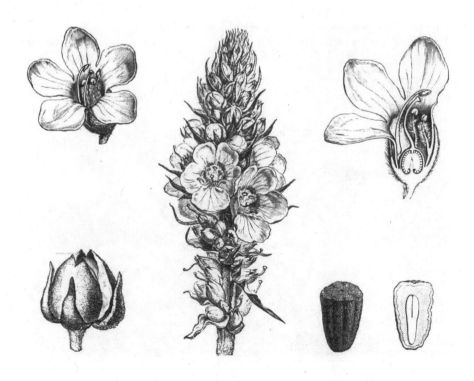

some exceptional plants can grow upwards of ten feet or more. It is said that seeds of the plant can remain dormant for decades—some studies claim over a century—and still be ready to germinate when conditions are right.

Medicinally, Mullein is used for a variety of lung and skin disorders. Both its inhaled smoke and a tea made from its leaves and flowers are said to help ease asthma and bronchitis symptoms, as well as aid general lung function, while an oil made by infusing the fresh flowers can be used to fight ear infections. For those hiking and in a bit of a pinch, one will be hard-pressed to find larger, more velvety leaves than those from the lower portion of a Mullein plant, should nature call at an inconvenient time.

Some nicknames of Mullein are "Hag Tallow" or "Witch's Taper," due to the herb's centuries-old use as a makeshift torch in the days before flashlights and electricity. After the second-year stalks died and dried out, many country folk—typically thrifty widows and wise women who preferred to not spend funds on more expensive light sources—would gather and soak the tops in oil, lighting them when needed, providing the perfect temporary illumination for a nighttime walk or herb-gathering session.

Mullein is most commonly found along roadsides and pathways, highways and overgrown spaces. In this way, it is a powerful ally for hedge magic and crooked path sorcery, thriving at crossroads, in graveyards and other places which represent the intersection of society and wild nature. Astrologically ruled by the planet Saturn, certain grimoires claim it to be highly pleasant to the spirits of the dead, with the dried leaves even capable of being substituted for graveyard dirt in certain conjurations, or burned in incense blends dedicated to sciomantic rites.

−ANTHONY TETH

Sigil Witchery

A SIGIL IS A SYMBOL, sign or design that is believed to have magickal properties. It can be carved, drawn, painted or inked on to any surface such as metal, clay, paper or skin. It does not have to make sense to anyone else who may see it as long as it holds meaning for the person who crafts and uses it.

What can you use a sigil for? It can be a mark of ownership, a symbol of protection, an aid in healing, a beacon for guidance, a tool for meditation, a call sign for deity, spirit and so forth. A sigil embodies a larger complex idea into a simplified image—essentially a kind of metaphysical shorthand!

Although certain magickal systems have evolved complex ways of making sigils, I would argue that sigilcraft is one of the oldest and simplest forms of magick, accessible to anyone willing to pick up a pen, pencil or brush. Lines, markings and carefully engraved designs on rocks, bones and shells found in ancient caves signify the start of humanity's capacity to picture time and space—to tell stories and mark ownership or clan. Our ancestors believed those simple lines, patterns and shapes had power. Thousands upon thousands of years later we still carry this core belief, evident from traffic signs to symbols of faith.

Visual artists who have been trained to interpret the world by translating it into lines, marks, shapes and colors, may find it very intuitive to carry those same skills into spellcraft and specifically the crafting of sigils. The right brain is known for seeing and understanding the world of images, and many of our most instinctual traits are also lodged in this realm. These skills also include visualization—a key tool for working magick. So whether you're more of a visual person or find you often get bogged down in analytical details and words, this approach may work exceedingly well for you.

Sigil witchery is not difficult to learn and is incredibly satisfying and useful. Essentially all you need is a basic understanding of magick and a way to make your sigil. So if you understand how to focus your intent and have some paper and a pen, you're well on your way.

To start, consider what it is you want to manifest. With what key words or phrases can you express it? Write down a short list that describes what you wish to accomplish. Next, consider what shapes and symbols have meaning for you. For example, what does a horizontal line mean to you? An arrow, star, circle, triangle or square? What about a heart or a spiral? Your astrological sign or the phases of the Moon? Do certain colors have personal meaning for you?

Now look at the list of words you have written and consider what shapes and marks can represent them. It is often best to start with the word that represents the key idea and put that shape down first. Then consider the rest of the words and their corresponding shapes, using them to build upon the base shape. If a shape or mark doesn't make sense you can erase it or start again, allowing yourself to brainstorm through the process.

Many work out sigils with a ball point pen, creating a worksheet for each. That way one can evaluate all of the designs made once they're done, instead of getting bogged down with overthinking each mark. The most important thing is that you are putting pen to paper, activating the eye-hand-brain coordination that helps you remember better than anything you could type or digitally create. The page should also have the word list, the date and who the sigil is for, if creating them for other people.

Once you have finalized your sigil, it's time to put it to use! You can mark your cubicle with it on a post-it note or marker it underneath your chair. It can be etched onto a talisman necklace. The sigil can be drawn with chalk on the floor or painted on a wall. You can tattoo it or burn a marked paper in a cauldron. You can design a complex ritual around it or just start using it. Where, how and when all depend on what works best for your purpose.

The most important thing in sigil crafting is finding a method that works best for you. We've been creating symbols and giving them power since the dawn of humanity, so there's a lot of options and variations. Allow yourself some room to practice and you'll be making your own marks in no time!

—LAURA TEMPEST ZAKROFF

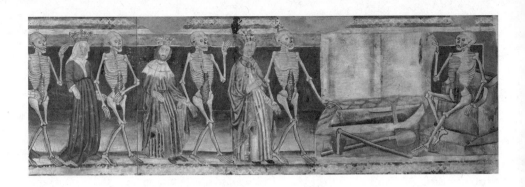

COFFIN RINGS

MEMENTO MORI, Latin for "remember that you must die," refers to a practice of reflecting on death and mortality. It's an admonition to seize the day and not fritter away your existence on things that do not matter.

One also contemplates the lives of others. Not only is your own life fleeting, but also the lives of those we love. Too soon they are gone, yet we should keep them in our thoughts. From this desire springs memento jewelry.

One example from the early 1700s is the coffin ring. Taking its name from the coffin-shaped crystal at the top, the ring was a gold band with a skeleton inlaid in black enamel. Around the ring there might be other symbols of death: a pick and shovel, a crown to indicate that death is the master of all, a tablet upon which the words "memento mori" have been inscribed.

Under the coffin-shaped crystal, which was mounted in line with the band, would be a tiny painted gold skeleton on a black background. Sometimes a single strand of the deceased's hair would be placed between the skeleton and the crystal. In an early example of a coffin ring, the face of the crystal was carved in the shape of a skull.

In England, memento mori jewelry enjoyed a revival during the reign of Queen Victoria (1837–1901).

She lost her mother and then her beloved husband Prince Albert in the same year (1861). When the Queen mourned, the country mourned, and followed her expressions of grief when mourning their own losses. In America, the mourning jewelry trend experienced its height in popularity after the Civil War, which ended by proclamation in 1865.

Coffin rings today often contain a stone, but it's much larger and mounted across the band. Instead of a clear crystal, you're more likely to find a precious or semi-precious stone. Ruby, emerald and onyx are common. Those without stones are often similar to poison rings; that is, they have a compartment that would have been used in the sixteenth century to hold poison.

Though we remember that nefarious use for the compartment, it was also used for holding locks of hair, messages and even tiny portraits of a loved one. When this compartment was made in the shape of a coffin, the ring was referred to as a funeral ring.

Slim band or large fashion accessory, the coffin ring reminds us of the universality of death, and of our loved ones, whether living or beyond the veil.

—MORVEN WESTFIELD

298

Transgender Questions
Among Witches and Pagans

Western European Pagan beliefs and practices have survived centuries of deadly persecution and abuse to arrive at last in a time when we can enjoy worshiping the Old Gods in relative freedom. Even in modern times, though, many Pagan people still report experiencing discrimination in societies dominated by mainstream religions, and while oppression serves to strengthen bonds among the victimized, transgender Pagans suffer additional discrimination within the Pagan community itself.

Multiple and complex issues affect transgender Witches and Pagans. The dichotomy of gender-specific events and the dilemma of inclusion or exclusion are keenly felt by those who already feel ostracized in their daily lives. Transgender individuals attending large, public Pagan festivals

and gatherings have found themselves barred from some women's or men's rituals and events. Although many Craft groups welcome Pagans and Witches regardless of their gender identity, some accept only cis-gender (genetic) people to participate in their rites. The division that ensues is a thorny problem for the Pagan community at large. Do the rights and desires of either group supersede those of the opposing position?

We cherish our freedom to enjoy the company of kindred souls, to associate and work with others of like mind. This very human need for fellowship with a select group with whom we are comfortable is the foundation of friendships, social circles, clubs and covens. The flip side of the closed-group coin is the exclusion of non-members—the element of exclusion defines a closed group. Private groups

299

have convened throughout human history, and are generally accepted as a normal part of life. At large events, however, which are billed as "public" and "open," attendees may expect featured activities to be open to all, and exclusivity can become a divisive issue. Those attending a restricted event feel they are in their rights to meet with whom they wish while specific exclusion is felt by transgender attendees as transphobic prejudice, sexism and rejection.

In Traditional Witchcraft, the binary division of roles in rituals and initiations can be problematic for transgender Witches. Everything from casting the Circle to the alternating male-female order of Witches in the Dance is defined by gender in Traditional Witchcraft. A Priest initiates a female Witch, a Priestess initiates a male Witch. What happens when a Witch transitions to the gender they identify with after initiation? In Traditions that emphasize the legitimacy of descending lines in rigid terms, some may question the letter-of-the-law validity of roles a transgender Witch filled before their transition. If the transgender Witch was always really the opposite gender, was it actually a priest or was it a priestess who performed that role in a given event? The real question is, of course, does it matter? One perspective adheres to the written rule "once a Witch, always a Witch" regarding initiations; the permanence of the transformation being legendary—it cannot be undone. Another view questions the validity of an initiation if all required elements were not exactly provided: was that Witch really "Witched?"

Some transgender Witches are comfortable with their personal magickal history as it is. If they are in a supportive group or groups that accept their personal experience and assessment, harmony prevails. Other transgender initiates of Traditional Craft choose to go back and repeat the steps of initiation with priesthood they feel appropriate to their corrected gender. After all is said and done, it is up to the Witch.

Rising from the Burning Times, Witches have survived centuries of oppression, violence and death, but in today's world Pagan folk of all walks have the opportunity to forge bonds with each other and build a strong, vibrant alliance. Working together with respect, love and trust, the Pagan community has the strength and solidarity to overcome fear and discrimination and become a place of peace and understanding where we can all come home.

—RHIANNON MCBRIDE

The Vain Jackdaw

JUPITER DETERMINED, it is said, to create a sovereign over the birds, and made a proclamation that, on a certain day, they should all present themselves before him, when he would himself choose the most beautiful among them to be king.

The Jackdaw, knowing his own ugliness, searched through the woods and fields, and collected the feathers which had fallen from the wings of his companions, and stuck them in all parts of his body.

When the appointed day arrived, and the birds had assembled before Jupiter, the Jackdaw also made his appearance in his many-feathered finery.

On Jupiter proposing to make him king, on account of the beauty of his plumage, the birds indignantly protested, and each plucking from him his own feathers, the Jackdaw was again nothing but a Jackdaw.

Moral: Hope not to succeed in borrowed plumes.

Dαrk Lɵrδ ɵf τhε Fɵrεsτ

THE DAY WOULD be peaceful and calm with a soft breeze whispering in the treetops, and the whole wood alive with bird calls. The woodland floor would be carpeted with bluebells in the spring; or summer sunlight filtering through the overhead canopy; crisp, dry leaves crackling underfoot in autumn; or the frozen quiet of a late winter afternoon as a fiery sun began to sink in the west, casting long shadows beneath the trees. Then, almost imperceptibly, there would be the sound of muffled footsteps following quickly in the undergrowth. Your pace quickened and so did that of your stalker. A sudden flurry of old dried leaves would be picked up by a passing zephyr and flung into the air like a mini-whirlwind. All the hair on the back of the neck would be standing on end, heart thundering in the chest, breath almost impossible to take. Then you turned to confront this persistent intruder only to find . . . nothing. The wind died away, carrying with it the faintest sound of laughter and a voice in your head saying: "Gotcha!"

The Wild Wood, however, is the dark, untamed part of natural woodland where unearthly and potentially dangerous beings are still to be found. This is not everyone's favourite place and many urban Witches never get over an "atavistic fear of Nature uncontrolled"... On a magical level, the Wild Wood refers to those strange, eerie places that remain the realm of Nature and untamed by man. Ancient gnarled oaks, festooned with ferns and draped with lichen, carry an air of solitude and remoteness that is deeply unnerving—here birdsong and the trickle of running water are the only sounds to break the stillness. It is the Otherworld of the "unearthly and potentially dangerous." It is the realm of Pan and the Wild Hunt. In modern psychology, it refers to the dark inner recesses of the mind, the wild and tangled undergrowth of the unconscious. Here, among the trees, we are never sure that what we see is reality or illusion.

Excerpt from *Pagan Portals: Pan, Dark Lord of the Forest and Horned God of the Witches*

—MELUSINE DRACO

RAIN SPELL

RAIN: OUR BODIES need it, animals need it, the crops need it. Without precipitation, dry vegetation makes the land vulnerable to wildfires. Search the news reports for the last two years and you'll see what happens when large swaths of countryside become combustible.

Weather magic can bring needed precipitation. Traditional spells often employ imitative magic, magic that works by mimicking the desired results. To bring rain, a village shaman or witch doctor would sprinkle or spit-spray water while chanting the appropriate words and drumming to mimic the sound of thunder.

With one small modification, modern Witches can help bring drought relief to areas thousands of miles away. The following is a simple spell that anyone with good intentions and the power of visualization can perform.

What You Need

Assemble the following items:

Container full of water—Traditionally, this is a bowl or a cauldron. The water can come from your faucet or from a stream, pond or well. Purists prefer natural sources, but work with what you have.

Aspergillum—An aspergillum is something used to sprinkle water. You might have read recent reports of a Mexican priest using a water gun to dispense holy water, but you don't want anything as directed or forceful. Remember that you're doing imitative magic and using too much force is asking for a deluge. Consider using a feather or a sprig of an evergreen tree.

Map—This is the modern addition mentioned earlier: a map showing the location in need of rainfall. Using your own drawing skills, a map site like Google Maps or an illustration from a newspaper, create a paper map.

Rain chant—Using your local library or Internet, look for a rain chant used by the indigenous people of the area. If you feel it would be better to invoke the aid of your own deities, find or write one that suits your pantheon or try this: Rewrite that old nursery rhyme "Rain, rain, go away" to call the rain. "Rain, rain, come today / Sprinkle down a gentle spray / Make the drought go away." If the area is being ravaged by wildfires, change the last line to "Make the fires go away." Resist the temptation to make the rain come down too hard in a burned area— with no vegetation to hold it, the runoff can cause flash floods.

The Spell

1. Cast your circle or do whatever creates sacred space in your practice. Ground and center yourself.

2. Pick up the container of water. Consider what you are doing: bringing gentle rain to a place that needs it. Keep that image in your mind—gentle rain. You don't want floods and you don't want to rob surrounding areas of the rain they need.

3. When you have the intent and image firmly in mind, pick up your aspergillum and dip it in the water. Shake some of the water off so that you're not spraying a downpour. Gently shake it onto the map while chanting the words of your spell. Visualize a gentle rain falling steadily over the area.

Continue to chant and sprinkle until you feel the spell taking effect. Know that the rain will appear, but it may take time.

—NEVROM YDAL

 # TALISMAN

Wedjat—The Eye of Horus

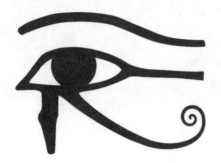

THE WEDJAT EYES ARE two of the most recognizable icons of the ancient Egyptians. The single eye was connected to many different roles throughout Egyptian mythology and as a result had many uses as a talisman. Just as there are two eyes to every human, so too are there two Wedjat eyes—either right or left.

We will concern ourselves with the left eye, known as the *Eye of Completion,* considered to be lunar in nature and associated with the mighty falcon-headed deity Horus. It was Horus who came to the defense of his father Osiris when he was murdered by his brother Set—the jackal-headed God of the night. In the battle to avenge his father, Horus' left eye was lost. The God of wisdom, Thoth, restored his eye, after which Horus was able to provide for the ascendency of his father.

Because of the regeneration of the eye of Horus, it was thought that the likeness his eye had healing powers and could bring safety, healing and protection. It was thought that as Horus was able to guide Osiris into afterlife, allowing him to become the Lord of the Dead, the eye constructed as a talisman would be placed in mummies to help the dead through the tribulations they would face.

For the land of the living, wearing the Eye of Horus was believed to protect the wearer from adversity as well as provide for good health, endurance and wisdom. It is also certain that it would protect the wearer from an untimely death.

In constructing the Eye of Completion, today's talisman maker might want to add an accent color of significance as the ancients did. They were often painted green or a blue-green, the color of fertility and rebirth. Accents of red were sometimes added to contribute significance. The Eye could very well be painted onto vellum/parchment or fashioned out of clay or sculpey.

—DEVON STRONG

Purple and Pleasure

The Folklore and Magic of Amethyst

AMETHYST IS one of the best known and most popular members of the quartz family—silicon dioxide coloured by iron giving the distinctive purple colour. Its popularity may be due to its attractive colour, with amethyst charms being found at sites going back to 25,000 BCE, making it one of the earliest crystals used by man in his attempts to engage with and control the unseen worlds.

In ancient times amethyst was frequently used for protective amulets. Heart-shaped amethyst amulets were often placed in the mummy wrappings of the pharaohs, and Egyptian ambassadors would carry an amethyst on them when travelling abroad for protection from treachery and surprise attacks. The Persians

believed that two amethysts engraved with the names of the Sun and Moon together with baboon hairs and swallow feathers worn around the neck would protect against spells; they also believed amethyst would keep away hail and locusts, as well as assist in approaching people of high station (for business or political matters). To the Romans an amulet of amethyst would protect against spells, hail and locusts, and amethysts were commonly cut into intaglio gemstones set in rings for such purposes. It was sacred to Neptune and worn by Roman sailors to ensure safe journeys.

In an allegorical Greek myth written by the sixteenth century poet Remy Belleau in 1576, the story was

suggested binding one into the navel to restrain the "vapour of the wine."

The Pope's Fisherman's ring is made of amethyst, an amusing irony in that the stone is usually attributed to Pisces, whose vice is intoxication (hence "drunk as a fish"), which amethyst is supposed to prevent. A bishop's ring of rank bears an amethyst, unsurprising considering the association since ancient times of the colour purple with power and prestige—the purple of the Caesars became the purple of the Catholic Church. In early Christianity the purple of amethyst was considered a symbol of purity, associated with Christ. This was sometimes associated with his suffering and wounds on the cross, resulting in amethysts being applied to bleeding wounds to attempt to heal them. To the early Christians it symbolized the constant thought of the heavenly kingdom in humble souls. In the Bible amethyst is the twelfth foundation of New Jerusalem and the ninth stone on the High Priest's Breastplate, representing the Tribe of Dan, being placed at the centre of the breastplate. Amethyst was also symbolic of the apostle Matthias, whose attribution replaced Judas. Saint Valentine was said to wear an amethyst ring engraved with a figure of Cupid.

told of how Bacchus was annoyed at having been neglected by mortals, and he swore to have his tigers tear apart the next mortal he came across. The nymph Amethyst was on her way to the temple of Artemis to worship, and she was the next mortal he met. Amethyst cried out to Artemis to save her from being torn apart, and Artemis responded by turning her into a pillar of quartz. Bacchus then felt remorse for his actions and libated wine over the stone in atonement, which absorbed the wine giving it the distinctive colour. This is an interesting tale which explains the name of the stone *amethistos* (Gr), *"that which pushes away drunkenness,"* but the name predates this to the ancient world. This tale (*L'Amethyste, ou les Amours de Bacchus et d'Amethyste*) may well be rooted in the belief that amethyst protected the bearer from drunkenness, mentioned by Greek writers including Pliny, and the fact that amethyst was considered sacred to Artemis in ancient Greece. Following on from Belleau's work some sources

Amongst the many virtues attributed to amethyst in the Middle Ages were the ability to repress negative thoughts and to give good understanding, to help neuralgia and insomnia, to expel poison, to make one vigilant in business, to treat toothache and headache, to treat gout, to protect from poison and plague and perhaps most curiously to prepare an easy capture of wild beasts and birds. An amulet of a bear engraved on an amethyst was thought to put demons to flight and protect the wearer from drunkenness. Soldiers also carried amethyst into battle to keep them safe and give victory over enemies.

In contemporary magic and Paganism amethyst is considered particularly useful for spiritual growth and protection, purification and mental healing. It is commonly seen as one of the prime magickal stones. It is particularly associated with the throat and third eye chakras, hence its use for inspiration, intuition and as a good seeing stone. The throat chakra is the centre of dreaming and amethyst is a good dreaming, stone. Placing one under the pillow may help with insomnia and aid lucid dreaming. When being used in such a manner the amethyst should be carried close to the skin for a period of time of at least a lunar month.

Other popular uses are for developing clairvoyance and astral/psychic vision. Amethyst is thought to work on the immune and endocranial systems, and it may influence the pineal and pituitary glands. Amethyst is used to help ease headaches, including migraines, for which it should be held whilst repeating three times *"Gabriel bind Barisfael"* (the demon of migraines, constrained by the archangel Gabriel). It is a good stone to work with if trying to overcome addiction due to its history of being used against intoxication.

—DAVID RANKINE

Senbazuru

One Thousand Origami Cranes

The origins of origami have been lost in the annals of time. It is likely that it followed shortly on the heels of paper arriving on the shores of Japan circa 105 CE. While present day origami is an arts and crafts recreation activity, initially it was a ceremonial act.

The iconic origami crane has a special place among the many items that can be fashioned by folding paper. The crane is a mystical creature in Japanese, Korean and Chinese cultures. It was believed that cranes lived for a thousand years and have been held in high esteem. They represent good fortune and longevity.

The folding of 1,000 origami cranes is called Senbazuru (*sen* meaning 1,000, *orizuru* meaning cranes.) Legend has it that any who would make one crane for each of its years of life will be blessed with one wish by the crane. There are also legends that folding 1,000 cranes can grant luck, long life or recovery from an injury or illness. Many of the legends advise that the cranes must be made and strung in a period no longer than a year.

The gifting of Senbazuru to the sick is a common practice. There is also a tradition of gifting them to newly married couples. In any case the cranes are usually made in a variety of colors. Instructions for construction of cranes can be found at TheWitchesAlmanac. com/almanac-extras/.

–DEVON STRONG

GODDESS OF NO ESCAPE

ON A LONELY STRETCH of Attica coastline, a mere 40 miles northeast of Athens, is the ruined temple of the long-forgotten Goddess whose cult would surely merit revival today. Originally a rural deity, worshiped as a local variation of the huntress Artemis, she became widely known as Nemesis, Goddess of just retribution and persecutor of the excessively rich and proud. She was sometimes called Adrasteria, meaning "one from whom there is no escape."

Patroness of gladiators, worshiped in Rome by victorious generals, Nemesis was known to everyone in ancient times for taking particular care of the presumptuous and especially punishing

hubris—the unpardonable crime of considering oneself master of one's own destiny.

But Nemesis of Rhamnous was how she was known; and the once-flourishing Rhamnous, a busy fortress town protecting the grain cargoes shipped across the narrow straits of Euboea, is now as abandoned and deserted as a Goddess herself. Overgrown by the prickly scrub that gave the place its name, it is unreachable save by car or on foot, visited by less than one in 10,000 tourists, and accessible by bus only as far as Grammatiko or Ayia marina, both several miles away.

Rhamnous' best-known native son was the orator Antiphon (c. 480 BCE)

311

whose school of rhetoric included Thucydides among its illustrious pupils. Built in 436 BCE by the same (unknown) architect responsible for the Poseidon temple at Cape Sounion and the temples to Hephaistos and Ares in Athens' Roman Agora, the Nemesis temple ajoined an earlier—and smaller—one on the site shared by a similar Goddess, Themis. Her special responsibilities were law, equity, and custom. Thus the Goddesses of "Just Order" and "Righteous Vengeance" would seem to be a harmonious match.

Originally measuring about 35 feet by 66 feet with twelve columns, fluted top and bottom, with gilded cornices bearing lotus decorations and lions' heads along the roof gutters through which rain escaped, the Doric temple was constructed from nearby marble whose workings still bear ancient tool marks. Sometime between being rededicated to Augustus' late wife Livia who died in 29 CE, and its excavation in 1813, the temple was ravaged and remained that way. It was the custom of the Greeks to leave in their ruined state and not restore temples that had been destroyed by "barbarians."

Nobody knows what Nemesis really looked like. Fragments of a large head discovered in the ruins (and now in the British Museum) were said to have been part of a statue of Aphrodite entered in a contest and renamed when not chosen, later to be sold by the sculptor, Agorakritos of Paros on condition it not be exhibited in Athens. Pausanias, writing about all this 600 years later, said that the actual sculptor was Agorakritos' famous teacher,

Phidias, and that the Nemesis statue was carved out of a block of marble brought a cross by the Persians in 490 BCE and intended for a "victory" statue when they had won the battle of Marathon in the nearby marshes. The Persians, of course, lost that one and as an example of hubris this story of the statue's origin is perhaps too good to be true.

Certainly was true that Nemesis was being worshiped locally well before that celebrated battle and even before the temple was built. It was the custom in those days for a year's garrison duty outside Athens to be served by all youths of military age; and at Rhamnous the recruits participated in torch races in honor of the Goddess, while in Athens itself an annual Nemesian festival was held.

Herodotus, born a half-dozen years after the Greeks' glorious victory at Marathon, made much of the Nemesis cult, as can be seen by his writings which refer constantly to the theme of some power that brought retribution. And, of course, the Goddess has the usual colorful history common to her kind. Pursued by Zeus but unwilling to mate with him, she kept changing her shape until, caught while she was disguised as a goose, she gave birth to a hyacinth-colored egg which, under the guidance of Leda, was hatched as Helen: that same Helen over which the Trojan war was subsequently fought.

At the base of the statue found in the temple of Nemesis, this tale of her encounter with Zeus was told in relief sculpture. Seen (and described) by Pausanias in its entirety, it remains today only as disconnected fragments.

The *Queen of the Night* Relief
Identified by some as Lilith

Mount, water, to the skies!
Bid the sudden storm arise.
Bid the pitchy clouds advance,
Bid the forked lightnings glance,
Bid the angry thunder growl,
Bid the wild wind fiercely howl!
Bid the tempest come amain,
Thunder, lightning, wind, and rain!

As she concluded, clouds gathered thickly overhead, obscuring the stars that had hitherto shone down from the heavens. The wind suddenly arose, but in lieu of dispersing the vapours, it seemed only to condense them. A flash of forked lightning cut through the air, and a loud peal of thunder rolled overhead.

Then the whole troop sang together—

Beat the water, Demdike's daughter!
See the tempest gathers o'er us;
Lightning flashes—thunder crashes,
Wild winds sing in lusty chorus!

The Lancashire Witches,
by William Harrison Ainsworth (1848)

Witch Windows

WHILE VISITING the state of Vermont in winter, either for a ski break or to see the sugar makers tapping sugar maples (*Acer saccharum*) for their delicious sap, keep an eye out for something unusual in this northern New England state. Though the blazing colors of the autumn foliage have long gone, this fascinating feature of the Green Mountain State is visible year-round.

Typically located in the gable-end wall of a house and rotated approximately 45 degrees from vertical, some windows are hung so that the long edge is parallel to the roof slope. More common in farmhouses from the 19th century, they are found almost exclusively in or near the U.S.

state of Vermont, though some were found as far south as Westborough, Massachusetts. These oddly placed windows were called *Witch Windows* or *Coffin Windows*.

Why Witch Windows?

Why were they called Witch Windows and why were they positioned at such an odd angle? Local folklore posits they were installed to keep Witches from flying into the house. Popular lore held that a Witch in flight would not be able to turn sideways quickly enough to make it through the window. This explanation doesn't make sense, however. Ignoring the fact that Witches don't really physically fly on brooms, why couldn't they turn in time? It's just as impossible as the flying itself. And why couldn't they simply enter through a window hung in the traditional manner?

Coffin Windows

Another tradition holds that the windows were installed to make it easier to remove a body from the upper floors of the house. At face value, this might seem to make sense; after all, in the 19th century in rural Vermont, hospitals were rare, and the custom was for sick and dying individuals to be treated at home. Once again, though, logic slices through this flimsy justification.

The slanted window opened out to a sloped roof. It would be hard and perilous work to push a coffin out this window, catch it from the other side and lower it to the ground. Wouldn't it just be easier for two farmhands to carry the body alone gently down the stairs inside to a coffin waiting on the bottom floor? And why would you carry an empty coffin upstairs to the body in the first place? That means an extra trip.

Lazy Windows

Another name for these slanted windows is *Lazy Windows*. It assumed the person installing the window was just too lazy to measure and frame a new opening. This is closer to the truth than the other beliefs, but the builder was not being lazy. Instead, the worker was being frugal and resourceful. When a house was enlarged by adding to an attic, the space at the gable end—where an opening was needed for light and ventilation—was usually not tall enough for a window to stand upright.

Were They Really There to Prevent Witches?

So now we return to the original question: Why "Witch Windows?" Did people ever really believe they were necessary to prevent Witches from flying in? Probably not. But it made a good story, didn't it? And once told, it was passed on to each young child who asked, "Why is that window like that?"

—MORVEN WESTFIELD

316

Saying Witch in European Languages

Language	Ways to say Witch
Albanian	magjistare
Basque	sorgina
Bosnian	vještica
Bulgarian	ьещица (veshtitsa)
Catalan	bruixa
Croatian	vještica
Czech	čarodějnice
Danish	heks
Dutch	heks
Estonian	nõid

Language	Ways to say Witch
Finnish	noita
French	sorcière
Galician	bruxa
German	hexe
Greek	μάγισσα (mágissa)
Hungarian	boszorkány
Icelandic	norn
Irish	cailleach
Italian	strega
Latvian	ragana

Language	Ways to say Witch
Slovak	čarodejnice
Slovenian	čarovnica
Spanish	bruja
Swedish	häxa
Ukrainian	відьма (vid'ma)
Welsh	wrach
Yiddish	מעכשײפֿע (mekha sheyfe)

Language	Ways to say Witch
Lithuanian	ragana
Maltese	saħħara
Norwegian	heks
Polish	czarownica
Portuguese	bruxa
Romanian	vrăjitoare
Russian	ведѣма (ved'ma)
Serbian	вешТица (veshtica)

The Evolution of the Magician

MAGIC in its primitive stage appears crude to present day ceremonialists. The use of stones and twigs in a ritual for crop fertilization, or the use of sacrifice in a healing rite seem totally unnecessary to us.

With the medieval European concept of the elements, brought to us by the alchemists of the times, came a whole new view of magical ritual based on the quartering of a whole. The four quarters of the universe, having the four elements as attributions, became the new setting for the temple. The use of the cardinal cross became more common, lending itself as a doorway to an infinite number of attributions ranging from colors to Godforms. The use of the double-cubed altar and the black and white checked floor of the temple are external reflections of the psychological base of the magician. The Cup, Wand, Sword and Pentacle represent the body of the magician as the universe. The microcosm becomes the macrocosm through the vibration of the four.

The Piscean age represents sacrifice for the sake of the whole. The family (being a reflection of four; Mother, Father, Child and Family unit) is a Piscean concept having its roots in the element of water. Members of society sacrificed themselves for the sake of others. The sense of working for the whole and the ignoring of the individual was, and still is, a very common attitude.

We are moving into the age of Aquarius, but few of us are willing to lay down our Piscean tools and beliefs and take that leap into a new home. The Aquarian age will bring a sense of individualization on the physical plane along with a true feeling of union on a higher plane. The mixed energies of Saturn and Uranus can lead to some difficulty in breaking away from old structures, but freedom will become an obsession with society, and people will make a move into the tide of air.

The magician will find that the concepts and methods employed in the Piscean ritual of yesterday will seem as crude as the primitive magician using stones and twigs. The obsolete employment of the four tools will be replaced by the use of color and sound vibration. The senses will play a much more important role on the path to transcendence. The sense of hearing (being attributed to Saturn) will be of the most importance. Secrets long forgotten from the age of Gemini will be rediscovered as the use of sound waves becomes the tool for the magician of tomorrow.

–From *The Emerald Star*,
volume 2, no.1, ©1980

Awake, Awake O Sleeper

of the Land of Shadows.

Wake! Expand!

Wm. Blake

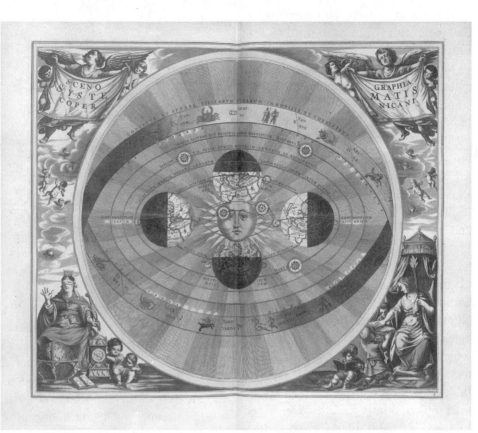

THE SOLAR SYSTEM
Heliocentric Astrology

EARTH, along with the other planets, revolves around the Sun. In astrology's lengthy history, which stretches back to the dawn of recorded time, this fact is relatively recent news.

The heliocentric, that is the Sun centered universe, was discovered by Nicholas Copernicus, who lived from 1473–1543 C.E. Copernicus was a Polish-German physician, astrologer and mathematician who is remembered as the father of modern astronomy.

Previously the geocentric, that is the Earth centered view of the universe, was accepted as the truth about the cosmos. The geocentric was described by Claudius Ptolemy and had the Sun and stars revolving around planet Earth. Ptolemy was an Egyptian-Greek mathematician, astronomer and astrologer who lived from 100–170 C.E. He drew upon much earlier Babylonian observations to determine how the celestial patterns in the heavens above correlated with the patterns of life and destiny on Earth below.

Most modern astrologers continue to calculate horoscopes like Ptolemy, from the perspective of Earth. Horoscope charts still continue to place Earth at the center of the universe because people who follow astrology seriously agree that the Ptolemaic universe works.

Despite being bombarded by critics and naysayers with the obvious fact that Copernicus accurately described the heliocentric over 500 years ago, astrology continues to follow the earlier model. Planets, such as Uranus, Neptune, Pluto and Chiron, and other celestial bodies, such as the asteroids, which were discovered in modern times are included in the ephemeris tables used by astrologers just as if they too are orbiting Earth. Why? The reason is simple: Ptolemy's geocentric Earth centered universe works for us because we live on planet Earth. From the earthly perspective the magnetic energies traveling toward the planet through outer space do impact Earth as if it is the center of the universe.

Most astrologers would agree that for the purpose of horoscope calculation Copernicus' heliocentric universe would only be valid if somehow it would be possible to reside on the Sun. In fact, the astrologers of the future will probably have to develop separate zodiac systems. Eventually, if Mars and other planets are colonized the dome of the surrounding space will have corresponding energy variances, and Earth centered horoscopes probably won't work.

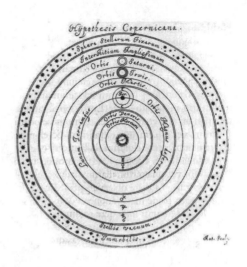

There are exceptions, however. There are a few recent astrologers who do prefer to use charts calculated using the heliocentric ephemeris. Benjamin Franklin, often praised as the greatest astrologer who ever lived, made references to using heliocentric astrology, although he followed the more familiar geocentric astrology in calculating his almanacs. Some contemporary astrologers emulate Dr. Franklin and actually consult both types of charts. One heliocentric astrologer who does this type of dual analysis calls it a twofold Gemini-like practice, alluding to the twins.

Those who would like to experiment with Sun-centered astrology will find that this kind of horoscope is quite different in several ways:

• There is no retrograde motion. Even though it is very influential, retrograde motion is an optical illusion viewed from the perspective of Earth.

• The placements of Mercury, Venus

and Mars are radically different.

- The planets from Jupiter out also have different placements, but they will vary less than the inner planets .
- There are no nodes of the Moon. Instead planetary nodes might be included.
- There are no Sun or Moon placements.
- Earth will be added instead of the Sun. The Earth sign opposes the familiar Sun sign. They are placed 180 degrees apart, exactly across the zodiac.

Some astrologers use the familiar house placements and zodiac in heliocentric astrology. Other practitioners use a plain circular wheel with only the planetary placements, but this creates a very blank and empty looking diagram.

A good way to take a look at heliocentric astrology is to start with considering the Earth sign. Determine whether what it indicates seems to hold true. If so, then further studies can be easily pursued. Here are some keywords to offer a quick glance at how the Earth sign, the single most significant factor in a heliocentric horoscope, might be interpreted. The sun sign in the geocentric chart is listed in bold with the description of the corresponding Earth sign in the heliocentric chart .

- **Aries** Your Earth sign is Libra. You seek a shield from the harshness of life, always looking for better options.
- **Taurus** Your Earth sign is Scorpio.

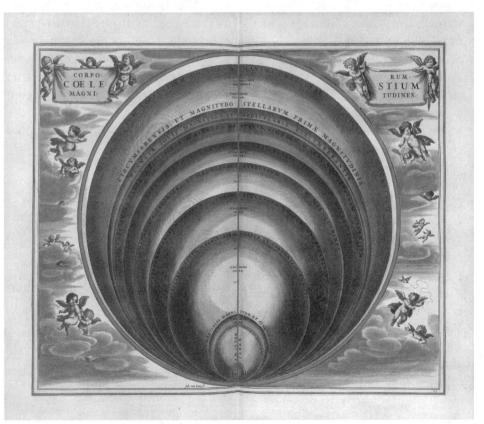

Secretive, grounded and possessive, your strong opinions invite controversy.

- **Gemini** Your Earth sign is Sagittarius. Planning where to go and what to do next, the dynamics of change exhilarate you.
- **Cancer** Your Earth sign is Capricorn. Serious and reserved, you value reliability. Highly motivated, you are a catalyst.
- **Leo** Your Earth Sign is Aquarius. Friendly and group oriented, you like to consider broad perspectives and wider viewpoints.
- **Virgo** Your Earth sign is Pisces. Fanciful and creative, you seek beauty. Charitable, you empathize with those in need.
- **Libra** Your Earth sign is Aries. An eternal rebel, you act quickly when faced with a challenge.
- **Scorpio** Your Earth sign is Taurus. Possessive and systematic, you prefer to develop proficiency in all you attempt.
- **Sagittarius** Your Earth sign is Gemini. Curious and fluid, to avoid being trapped you leave an exit open, a way out.
- **Capricorn** Your Earth sign is Cancer. Vulnerable and sensitive, you are attached to traditions and memories.
- **Aquarius** Your Earth Sign is Leo. Authoritative and dignified, you are critical of the ordinary and inferior.
- **Pisces** Your Earth Sign is Virgo. You analyze concerns and challenges, correcting and organizing priorities.

Please see this year's Celebrity Horoscope featuring Dion Fortune. Read her biography and then compare it to the heliocentric version of her natal placements below for deeper insight.

Heliocentric Astrology For Dion Fortune, born December 6, 1890 at 2:11 am in Llandudno, Wales

- Earth at 13 degrees Gemini 56
- Mercury at 17 degrees Capricorn 55
- Venus at 15 degrees Gemini 04
- Mars at 2 degrees Aries 38
- Jupiter at 18 degrees Aquarius 29
- Saturn at 10 degrees Virgo 42
- Uranus at 27 degrees Libra 40
- Neptune at 5 degrees Gemini 26
- Pluto at 6 degrees Gemini 54
- Chiron at 29 degrees Cancer 44

A free heliocentric ephemeris is available online. See horoscope: astroseek.com/heliocentric-ephemeris. Many computer programs will offer heliocentric astrology as an option. Solar Fire by Astrolabe is an excellent choice. See www.alabe.com for details.

—DIKKI-JO MULLEN

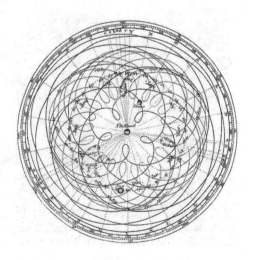

The Mystery of Mermaids in Mainstream Media

WHAT IS THE FIRST IMAGE that appears in your mind when you hear the word "mermaid"? Perhaps a red haired beauty singing of how she longs to be a part of the human world? Maybe you think of Daryl Hannah attempting to dry off her tail on the floor of a bathroom with a hair dryer. Instead, your mind might wander to the alluring sirens in Homer's Odyssey, Hans Christian Anderson's tragic fairytale, or even a simple two-tailed mermaid that graces the side of your coffee cup. While these creatures are all special in their own ways, each of them also allows your mind to conceive of different ideas of what a mermaid really is, as well as draws you in towards her. While her image has been drastically altered to make her fit into society's standards of beauty and intrigue, the modern portrayal of the mermaid has increased her popularity in recent years, introducing a figure of magic and mystery into day to day life.

Many stories and legends of mermaids persist from ancient times. The earliest European depiction of mermaids may in fact come from the sirens of Homer's *Odyssey*. The creatures that appear on Odysseus' voyage had the heads of women and the bodies of birds. The sirens' voices were so irresistible that sailors would jump overboard and attempt to swim to them, driven to the point of madness by the sound of their music. These men drowned or were otherwise killed attempting to reach the sirens, often colliding with the rocks upon which the sirens sat. Homer depicts the sirens as sinister and deceptive, painting them as one of the obstacles that Odysseus and his men must face on their journey. These femme fatales could not be resisted, being so desirable that men would die over them.

With the rise of the Christian era, an important shift occurred, as the bird-like woman became a fish-like woman. This more closely fit into the story of a sea voyage, illustrating why the sailors would jump overboard. Artistic interpretations also began to show the creature as a beautiful woman from the waist up with a fish tail from the waist down. It is from this shift that we arrive at the word "mermaid." The Christian era's new vision of the animal-woman hybrid is the origin of the European and American cultures' commonly accepted physical form of a mermaid, maintaining the overall tone of mystery and manipulative seduction.

In 1837, Hans Christian Anderson published his fairytale, entitled *The Little Mermaid*, in which a young, nameless mermaid falls in love with a human man and gives up her voice to a sea Witch in exchange for legs so that she might have a chance to win the man's heart. Although this story might seem familiar, it has a different ending than the one that today's culture is used to. The deal that the mermaid makes with the sea Witch is quite different. The mermaid has an unlimited amount of time to win the prince's heart, however, if she fails to do this she will turn to sea foam on the ocean waves and die. The prince ultimately falls in love with a human princess, and when the little mermaid is given one last chance to save herself by killing the prince, she cannot do it, showing that her love for him is pure, true and undying. She jumps off the prince's wedding ship and turns to sea foam. It is in this moment that readers sympathize with her because this mermaid's power to draw people towards her is enabled by pity.

This story somewhat changed the perception of how mermaids were viewed—no more were they all evil,

manipulative and seductive. Rather, some of them could be innocent, hopeful and morally good. This shift is the point at which not only the idea of good mermaids, but mermaids of all personalities came into play, painting them more like humans with distinct and varying traits.

In the 1984 movie *Splash* the mermaid Madison, portrayed by Daryl Hannah, comes to the human world for the first time. In this movie, the plot point of the mermaid being able to become a human at her own will arises. Touching water turns her into a mermaid, and when she dries herself she once again becomes human. Madison also states that she must go back to the sea in a certain amount of time, otherwise she will never be able to return. By giving the mermaid power over her own mythical abilities, this movie allows the mermaid to become a stronger character with more control over her destiny than earlier depictions.

The second characteristic of the mermaid in this movie is her naivete, showing her quite literally as a fish out of water. *Splash* shows Madison as innocently clueless—she does not know how to speak English or understand that she must wear clothes in public when she first arrives on land. A main part of Madison's growth is adapting to customs and traditions as she learns how to live like a human. As viewers go on this journey with Madison as she innocently experiences the human world for the first time, they become invested in her journey. Once again, the mermaid has proven her ability to draw people towards her. This movie along with all the previous incarnations of the mermaid paved the way for one of the most influential and iconic mermaids in the history of the big screen.

Ariel, the mermaid in Disney's 1989 animated feature *The Little Mermaid*, combines all the previous positive traits of the mermaid, but this version of her story also ends with her finding happiness in the human world. Disney's portrayal of this fairytale has become the primary version of the story. The plot follows Hans Christian Anderson's story closely, however the deal Ariel strikes with the sea Witch Ursula states that she will have three days to win the kiss of true love from the

prince. If she cannot achieve this, she will turn back into a mermaid and belong to Ursula, who is portrayed as an octopus-human hybrid. Like Anderson's mermaid, Ariel does not complete her goal and turns back into her original form. However, with the help of her friends, she eventually defeats Ursula and Ariel's father turns her back into a human so that she can marry the prince.

Like the mermaids before her Ariel is naive to the ways of the human world and has the traits of innocence and goodness, a beautiful and alluring voice and a fascination with a human man. Interestingly, the two qualities that mermaids possessed in earlier versions of the story but which Ariel lacks can be seen in Ursula. This sea Witch can become human at will and is manipulative and deceptive, using Ariel's stolen voice for evil—to bewitch the prince. The inclusion of all the past traits of mermaids between Ariel and Ursula pays homage to the earlier versions and creates two opposing and well rounded characters that audiences love to this day.

Different versions of her story have changed certain aspects of the mermaid, both giving and taking away her abilities. It is this very adaptability that makes her stand out from other mythical creatures and invokes such fascination from the public. Over time the mermaid has become a symbol for those who long for more than they have, as well as for those who are curious, optimistic and hopeful in life. Likewise she appeals to those who identify with the mysterious and the alluring, making her extremely likable and relatable. So the next time you see someone carrying a tote bag or wearing clothing with a mermaid on it, realize the impact that a magical figure has had over them. Even though she may only be a myth, her presence in any form still lures people towards her.

-NERITES

For bringing the Fairies back to house which they have deserted

Fairies!—whatsoever sprite
Near about us dwells—
You who roam the hills at night,
You who haunt the dells—
Where you harbour, hear us!
By the Lady Hecate's might we cry you to come near us!

Whether ancient wrong (alack!),
Malice, or neglect
Angered you and made you pack
With so drear effect,
Hearts you shall not harden:
Bathe your hurts and come you back again to house and garden!

For oak and ash and thorn,
By the rowan tree,
This was done ere we were born:
Kith nor kin are we
Of the folk whose blindness
Shut you out with scathe and scorn and banished with unkindness

We do call you, hands entwined,
Standing at our door,
With the glowing hearth behind
And the wood before.
Thence, where you are lurking,
Back we bring you, bring and bind, with your own magic's working.

Lo, our best we give for cess,
Having naught above
Handsel of our happiness
Seizin of our love.—
Take it then, O fairies!
Homely gods that guard and bless—O little kindly lares!

Punch JANUARY 1914

Epilogue to the Anniversary Edition

In the spring of 1973, I was 16 years old. Spending time in the local book-store was a favorite pastime. I would stand in the metaphysical section—about 20 titles in an obscure section of the store—and wait for someone interesting to come, possibly wearing black clothes and donning a sil-ver pentacle! As usual, I sat on the floor browsing through a book until the manager told me that I had to leave. I think this particular day it was Sybil Leek's *Diary of a Witch*. I nodded, stood and returned the book to the shelves. Head down, as I was sad to have not met anyone interesting, I slowly walked toward the front of the store. I found myself passing by a stand-up wire rack that spins around to display various magazines and small booklets. This particular visit, I saw *Dell Horoscope*, *Fate Magazine*, and *The Witches' Almanac*. Witches!

I immediately opened a copy, went straight for the Preface and read it through. It began "What is witchcraft?" And, it ended with:

> "Heard melodies are sweet, but those unheard
> Are sweeter; therefore, ye soft pipes, play on:"

Turn the page. Our music begins…

Well, I turned the page. And one dollar later—and that was a lot of money for me at the time—I was on my way home with the most influential book I was ever to lay my hands on.

I eventually contacted Elizabeth Pepper and we became good friends. She continued to publish *The Witches' Almanac* until 2004. In time, I ghost wrote a few pieces and eventually became her managing editor. When she passed in July 2005, she entrusted me with the care of her beloved life's work. Initially put on the correct path by the then editor, Barbara Stacy, I've done my best to uphold the legacy and tradition that is *The Witches' Almanac*. I hope that this 50-year *Anniversary Edition* will bring each reader insight and vision into the enchanted world of Witchcraft. I've also asked 13 people whose lives have been touched by *The Witches' Almanac* to give us their sentiments.

—ANDREW THEITIC

GERALDINE BESKIN

The Witches' Almanac has always been engaging and educating, and now, suddenly it seems, has been doing it for fifty whole years without aging a day! The *Almanac* is of immense historical significance as its voice of the moment has truly mapped trends, writers and practitioners in the very fast paced development of all aspects of the ever growing pagan scenes. I have a few copies going back to the 1970s when importing books from the States wasn't easy and magazines were a rarity for us to get our hands on here in London. I read every word! Many people have the *Almanac* to thank for publishing their first article, for the first ritual they actually performed, for giving them enough information to nod in agreement when someone who knew much more was speaking—but at least they had some idea what they were talking about. It is so familiar that it needs looking at with respect as well as interest when the new one comes out. Theitic is a second generation esoteric shopkeeper as am I and we both had mothers and grandmothers from whom we learnt SO much. We are members of a very small club as back in the day there were so few occult bookshops—The Atlantis Bookshop is 98 years old—so Bali, my daughter and my partner in the shop salute you and wish you and *The Witches' Almanac* well for another fifty years. Blessed Be.

—GERALDINE BESKIN

CO-OWNER THE ATLANTIS BOOKSHOP, LONDON, UK

IVO DOMINGUEZ

The Witches' Almanac has been a part of my journey as a Witch since I first put my foot on the path in the 1970s. For me, it feels as if it has always existed, is one of the few constants in the landscape of occultism in the US, and I expect it to continue for generations to come. I can and do praise the wide range of interesting articles, ads, and resources in *The Witches' Almanac*, but there are other characteristics that also merit applause. It fills in the small details of lore and practices, it speaks of customs, of history, of quirks, of ephemera and perennial truths, and these add up to a living, breathing culture of Witchcraft. This is particularly important for the many who practice alone or live in areas with sparse access to community events. In the ever-shifting fads, fashions, and schools of thought in the broader occult community, The Witches' Almanac remains unabashedly Witch positive and proud of who we've been and who we will become. Bless you Elizabeth Pepper for creating *The Witches' Almanac*. I will be offering her a cup of tea at my altar for the Mighty Dead for I think that she still watches, guides, and hopes for the future of Witches.

—IVO DOMINGUEZ, JR
AUTHOR

MELUSINE DRACO

The Witches' Almanac has become an institution in pagan circles and on an international level, too. Each edition contains a diverse selection of articles and builds into a valuable library over the years. A 50th anniversary is an impressive milestone to reach in the pagan publishing world and I am proud that I have been able to contribute to the publication in recent years—and hopefully will be able to continue do so for many more to come. Each issue contains a wealth of wisdom and information from a wide range of cultures and traditions, not to mention the writing of those who have grown long in the tooth in the Craft. There is a broad based theme to each issue, which all comes together as a cohesive whole of both folk and magical lore. Since we never stop learning, there are always gems of wisdom to take away and mull over. There is also a slightly old fashioned feel about the *Almanac*, which is no bad thing, and since this anniversary edition will be a collection of articles from editions printed prior to 2000, and many of those from the 1970s, it will be a valuable historical document indeed.

—MELUSINE DRACO

AUTHOR

PHILIP HESELTON

I first became aware of *The Witches' Almanac* when I was invited by Andrew Theitic to talk to a few friends in Providence, RI, a few years ago, and met such enthusiasm for what I had to say about the history of Witchcraft. How things have changed since Gerald Gardner wrote "there are no Witches' supply shops" in his *Witchcraft Today*, which was published in 1954. Although at first the Witches he knew had reservations about any sort of publicity, he finally convinced them because of his strong desire not to let something he had grown to value die out. The book achieved modest success, but I had no idea, after reading it in about 1959, how to make contact with any actual Witches. I eagerly searched for books on the subject, for it was my desire to become a Witch, something which I eventually achieved by picking up little hints here and there and was led to a coven and initiation. One of the last letters Gardner received before his death in 1964 informed him that the new initiates in the U.S.A. were taking to Witchcraft "like a duck to water." Gardner's great desire that it should not die out was achieved by the spread of that enthusiasm. And in those days before the internet, *The Witches' Almanac* was clearly a major player and helped Witchcraft grow in knowledge and wisdom, a role which it still plays today. May it continue to play such a role in the years ahead!

–PHILIP HESELTON
AUTHOR

JUDIKA ILLES

I vividly recollect the first time I ever saw *The Witches' Almanac*. Let me set the scene: it was the 1970s and I was a teenager who cared passionately about three things: music, divination and Witchcraft. I was in a Womrath's bookshop in New Jersey which was spread over two floors. The bestsellers were on the ground level, but if you ventured downstairs, you'd find shelves devoted to my passions. While looking at a shelf, I caught sight of a small, thin, mysterious book tucked between two big ones. I extricated the little book and there it was—*The Witches' Almanac*. I felt lightning struck. I had already read many books about Witchcraft, but I could tell at first sight that this book was magic. I also immediately knew that this book was for me. Its inclusive title indicated that it wasn't just about Witches, it was by them and for them. Although it can be a joyous path, an early call to walk the occultists' crooked path does not make for an easy life—I can see my fellow travelers nodding their heads. I sometimes wish I could time travel back to my young self in that 1970s bookshop with *The Witches' Almanac* in her hand and tell her that someday she would write and work for that publication and correspond with its founder, the magnificent Elizabeth Pepper. *The Witches' Almanac* opened doors of possibility for me, as it has for so many others. It has been my companion for decades and I feel unbelievably honored to be able to be associated with this 50th Anniversary Edition.

—JUDIKA ILLES

AUTHOR OF *Encyclopedia of Witchcraft, Encyclopedia of 5000 Spells,*
AND OTHER BOOKS DEVOTED TO THE MAGICAL ARTS

MICHAEL KERBER

Legacy. Tradition. Sustenance. This is what I think of when I think of *The Witches' Almanac*. The legacy is clear and very much alive. We are not just celebrating the past 50 years but the next 50. The tradition runs deep and while ever present it evolves and welcomes new readers and new generations. Each year a new *Almanac* emerges to guide and inspire. It feeds our curiosity, expands our knowledge of the seen and unseen worlds, and most of all provides sustenance to our practice, whichever form that may take. We at Weiser Books are proud of our association with *The Witches' Almanac* and to be part of its family. May this 50th Anniversary Edition inspire you as we have been inspired by the *Almanac* each and every year.

—MICHAEL KERBER
PRESIDENT, RED WHEEL/WEISER

PROFESSOR ROBERT MATHIESEN

A complete set of *The Witches' Almanac* has always held a special place on the shelves of my library of books on magic and Witchcraft, and I eagerly await each new edition every year. I think it is by far the most informative and interesting of all the magical almanacs published at any time in the 20th and 21st centuries. I had the pleasure of getting acquainted with its founding editor, Elizabeth Pepper, late in her life, and I remember her as one of the most delightful and wisest among all the magical people I have ever met. It is wonderful to see it reach the 50th year since it was first published.

—PROFESSOR ROBERT MATHIESEN
BROWN UNIVERSITY

CHRISTINA OAKLEY HARRINGTON

In a one bedroom apartment in West Philadelphia in the spring of 1987, on a sunny weekend I read my first ever copy of *The Witches' Almanac*. It couldn't be gotten from anywhere in Philadelphia, so I had procured it from New York City, from one of the several occult shops in existence then. It opened up for me a world to which I was seeking entry—the world of Witchcraft. I had just subscribed to all the magazines I could afford which had been listed in the back of Margot Adler's *Drawing Down the Moon*. *The Almanac*, however, had something nothing else had. It had the capacity to help me make my daily life a magical education, and indeed a magical experience. The almanac form had the effect of transforming the days of each month into occasions of astrological significance, days of Goddesses, opportunities for learning.

Almanacs were something my American mother had brought me up to love and understand, so a Pagan almanac was a coalescence of the enchantments of childhood with the mystery of the new world I was exploring. Some of the best and most memorable articles I've ever read are found in the pages of the *Almanac*—succinct, knowledgeable, engaged and engaging. It's remarkable to me that over thirty years later I can say that I have gotten to know its conservateur, and to thank him for his part in my journey, a journey that led to the creation of Treadwell's in London, whose aims are, like his, to spread the magic of the old ways. On this wonderful anniversary, I raise a glass to Theitic, the *Almanac*, and to all who tread the path.

—CHRISTINA OAKLEY HARRINGTON
TREADWELL'S'

CHRISTOPHER PENCZAK

Back when reliable information on Witchcraft was not so easily accessible, I remember having to go into the city bookstores, and hidden away not unlike the adult magazines on a high rack, you could find the occult section hidden under the stairs. Regularly and without fail, there would be a new copy of *The Witches' Almanac*. It was different, even then, from the majority of books available, pointing to a time in the past with its folklore and planting seeds in our present for a future generation of Witches. It was alive, and still is. You couldn't help but envision the authors of the article in the archetypal Witch house, gleefully practicing their craft as they have always done. And you couldn't help but want to be one of them, inspiring you to actually do it, even though any instructions were simple, like a friend or mentor passing on great tips from hard won experience. There were true nuggets of wisdom and hints to the practice. *The Witches' Almanac* was a shining gem in that otherwise dark section beneath the stairs.

—CHRISTOPHER PENCZAK

AUTHOR

DAVID RANKINE

The Witches' Almanac is 50 years old, a veritable elder in the pagan literary community! Significantly, it was created by Elizabeth Pepper in the same year that Greenpeace was founded and the first microprocessor created. How these events contributed to the chronological cauldron of its creation can be seen in the ethos embodied within *The Witches' Almanac*—the love of nature combined with the positive use of information technology to proliferate the spiritual diversity of Witchcraft and Paganism without being ruled or corrupted by it. Andrew Theitic took over the editorship of *The Witches' Almanac* in 2005, receiving the torch from Elizabeth Pepper as she passed through the veil and carrying it purposefully into the new millennium. Matching longevity with enduring quality is no easy task, and it is to their credit that the two editors have been able to do this consistently for half a century, providing an annual milestone and literary haven for Witches of all persuasions, ages and levels of experience. As Witches venerate their ancestors, so too do they evolve their craft through standing on the shoulders of the numerous giants who have gone before, and *The Witches' Almanac* stands tall amongst the titans that continue to inspire and teach all who encounter it with an open heart and mind.

—DAVID RANKINE
AUTHOR & MAGICIAN

SUMMANUS

When Elizabeth Pepper and John Wilcock introduced *The Witches' Almanac* in 1971, interest in contemporary Witchcraft was cresting in popular culture. In 1971 we saw Stewart Farrar's *What Witches Do*, Sybil Leek's *The Complete Art of Witchcraft*, Lady Sheba's *The Book of Shadows* and Raymond Buckland's *Witchcraft from the Inside*. June Johns' *King of the Witches* and Hans Holzer's *The Truth About Witchcraft* had come out in 1969, and in 1970 Paul Huson's *Mastering Witchcraft*, a new edition of Gardner's *Witchcraft Today* and Richard Cavendish's *Man, Myth and Magic* series appeared. Magic—and its exploitation in the popular press—was in the air and everywhere. But occasionally there was a truly admirable offering as well.

I still remember being charmed by *The Witches' Almanac's* 1970s editions, their tasteful covers modeled after an antique engraved title page, and the useful and informative content professionally presented within. Almanacs had been incredibly popular in both Britain and colonial New England, with American print runs reaching 60,000 copies. The second item printed in British North America was an almanac by William Pierce published in Cambridge in 1639. Yet this was something other than just another traditional almanac.

The Witches' Almanac integrated two historically competing astrological perspectives, the conventional annual almanac and the perpetual prognostication. The latter, commonly combined with the almanac proper, could also be a separate pamphlet like the *Kalender of Shepherdes* or the *Erra Pater*. Such "prognosticons" were for centuries the primary source among English speaking common folk for published astrological, medical and occult information. Generations later, the long missing elements of astral significance and arcane wisdom were finally reunited. Long may they prosper!

—SUMMANUS
AUTHOR

STEPHANIE TAYLOR-GRIMASSI

When I was a young teenager living in a sleepy Southern California beach community, I would often go to the Either/Or Bookstore owned by some "unusual" folks. There I would head to the cozy metaphysical section which was off by itself, full of all kinds of mysterious and exotic books. I would sit for hours and read and peruse as many as I could. This is where I discovered my first copy of *The Witches' Almanac*. I knew it was something special. The articles and illustrations were some of my first encounters with esoteric writings and images. I have no doubt that it influenced my pursuit on to my current path. I still have my first copies and treasure each and every one of them. I have since become a collector of *The Witches' Almanac* and look forward to every new season it reveals in its articles and imagery.

—STEPHANIE TAYLOR-GRIMASSI
PROPRIETOR OF HOUSE OF GRIMASSI

LAURA TEMPEST ZAKROFF

The Witches' Almanac is an indispensable tool and wondrous magical companion for anyone walking the path of the Witch. It was an exciting resource to me when I first started my practice decades ago, and it's still something I refer to daily today. Back then the *Almanac* was an extraordinary window to an esoteric realm, connecting voices from all over in one place long before the internet. Not just a collection of magical months and articles, the *Almanac* provided the means to find other practitioners, groups, shops and events. It was essentially a crossroads for finding like-minded people and hard-to-find materials without the aid of ethernet and search engines in a time when it was much harder to be out of the broom closet. Yet there it was, just sitting there on the shelf at the local bookstore!

While the internet has brought us together in many new ways, *The Witches' Almanac* still provides a magical experience that is unmatched in paper format. I still get a thrill every time I pick up the upcoming year's edition. Rich in folklore and metaphysical advice from a wide array of practitioners, it is one of my favorite tools to use for bibliomancy. Whatever page I happen to open to, there's always some drop of wisdom that's applicable to my needs. *The Witches' Almanac* is a must-have for every Witch who cherishes lore and having magic at their fingertips.

—LAURA TEMPEST ZAKROFF
Author of *Sigil Witchery & Weave the Liminal*

Ever a Keepsake

Collecting The Witches' Almanac is easier than ever. We offer various bundles covering the span of years that the Almanac has been available.

Bundle I—8 Almanac back issues (1991, 1993–1999)

Bundle II—10 Almanac back issues (2000–2009)

Bundle III—10 Almanac back issues (2010–2019)

Bundle IV—28 Almanac back issues (1991, 1993–2019)

Free bookbag and free shipping with each order
(free shipping US only)

https://TheWitchesAlmanac.com/search.php?search_query_adv=Bundle

MAGIC

An Occult Primer

David Conway

The Witches' Almanac presents:

- *A clear, articulate presentation of magic in a workable format*
- *Updated text, graphics and appendices*
- *Foreword by Colin Wilson*

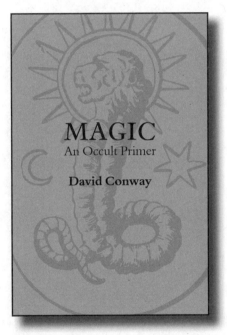

David Conway's *Magic: An Occult Primer* is a seminal work that brought magical training to the every-magician in the early 70s. David is an articulate writer presenting the mysteries in a very workable manner for the serious student. Along with the updated texts on philosophy and practical magic is a plethora of graphics that have all been redrawn, promising to be another collector's edition published by The Witches' Almanac.

384 pages — $24.95

For further information visit TheWitchesAlmanac.com/magic-of-herbs/

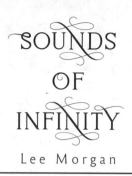

SOUNDS
OF
INFINITY

Lee Morgan

The Witches' Almanac presents:

• *Faeries explored from a global perspective*
• *A poetic understanding and exploration of Faery*
• *A modern grimoire of Faery workings*

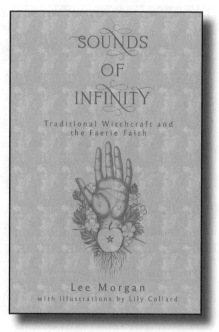

We are pleased to welcome Lee Morgan to our imprint. His latest tome, *Sounds of Infinity*, treats us to a comprehensive look at the world of Faery exploring geographical understanding, poetic understanding, and finally presents a very a workable grimoire. This book is about something so hidden it can never be the object of a direct gaze. For this reason this book aims to watch the faerie obliquely, off to the side a little, via a mixture of primary source study, ritual and art.

272 pages — $24.95

For further information visit TheWitchesAlmanac.com/SoundsofInfinity

DAME FORTUNE'S WHEEL TAROT

A PICTORIAL KEY

PAUL HUSON

The Witches' Almanac presents:

• Illustrates for the first time, traditional Tarot card interpretations unadorned by the occult speculations of Mathers, Waite or Crowley.

• Expounds on the meanings collected by Jean-Baptiste Alliette, a Parisian fortune-teller otherwise known as Etteilla

Based upon Paul Huson's research in Mystical Origins of the Tarot, Dame Fortune's Wheel Tarot illustrates for the first time the earliest, traditional Tarot card interpretations as collected in the 1700s by Jean-Baptiste Alliette In addition to detailed descriptions full color reproductions of Huson's original designs for all 79 cards are provided, including an extra Significator card as specified by Etteilla that may be used optionally. 200 pages $19.95

For information visit TheWitchesAlmanac.com/dame-fortunes-wheel-tarot-a-pictorial-key/

How to find

The **Witches'** Almanac

 TheWitchesAlmanac.com

 thewitchesalmanac

 thewitchesalmanac

 witchesalmanac

The Witches' Almanac, LTD.
P.O. Box 1292
Newport, RI 02840-9998

(401) 847-3388 (phone)
(888) 897-3388 (fax)

Info@TheWitchesAlmanac.com
Submissions@TheWitchesAlmanac.com

ORDER FORM

Each timeless edition of *The Witches' Almanac* is unique.
Limited numbers of previous years' editions are available.

Item	Price	Qty.	Total
2021-2022 The Witches' Almanac – The Sun: Rays of Hope	$12.95		
2020-2021 The Witches' Almanac – Stones: The Foundation of Earth	$12.95		
2019-2020 The Witches' Almanac – Animals: Friends & Familiars	$12.95		
2018-2019 The Witches' Almanac – The Magic of Plants	$12.95		
2017-2018 The Witches' Almanac – Water: Our Primal Source	$12.95		
2016-2017 The Witches' Almanac – Air: the Breath of Life	$12.95		
2015-2016 The Witches' Almanac – Fire:, the Transformer	$12.95		
2014-2015 The Witches' Almanac – Mystic Earth	$12.95		
2013-2014 The Witches' Almanac – Wisdom of the Moon	$11.95		
2012-2013 The Witches' Almanac – Radiance of the Sun	$11.95		
2011-2012 The Witches' Almanac – Stones, Powers of Earth	$11.95		
2010-2011 The Witches' Almanac – Animals Great & Small	$11.95		
2009-2010 The Witches' Almanac – Plants & Healing Herbs	$11.95		
2008-2009 The Witches' Almanac – Divination & Prophecy	$10.95		
2007-2008 The Witches' Almanac – The Element of Water	$9.95		
2003, 2004, 2005, 2006 issues of The Witches' Almanac	$8.95		
1999, 2000, 2001, 2002 issues of The Witches' Almanac	$7.95		
1995, 1996, 1997, 1998 issues of The Witches' Almanac	$6.95		
1993, 1994 issues of The Witches' Almanac	$5.95		
SALE: Bundle I—8 Almanac back issues (1991, 1993–1999) with free book bag	$ 50.00		
Bundle II— 10 Almanac back issues (2000–2009) with free book bag	$65.00		
Bundle III— 10 Almanac back issues (2010–2019) with free book bag	$100.00		
Bundle IV—28 Almanac back issues (1991, 1993–2019) with free book bag	$195.00		
Dame Fortune's Wheel Tarot: A Pictorial Key	$19.95		
Magic: An Occult Primer	$24.95		
The Witches' Almanac Coloring Book	$12.00		
The Witchcraft of Dame Darrel of York, clothbound, signed and numbered, in slip case	$85.00		
The Witchcraft of Dame Darrel of York, leatherbound, signed and numbered, in slip case	$145.00		
Aradia or The Gospel of the Witches	$16.95		
The Horned Shepherd	$16.95		
The ABC of Magic Charms	$12.95		
The Little Book of Magical Creatures	$12.95		
Greek Gods in Love	$15.95		
Witches All	$13.95		
Ancient Roman Holidays	$6.95		
Celtic Tree Magic	$7.95		
Love Charms	$6.95		
Love Feasts	$6.95		
Magic Charms from A to Z	$12.95		

Item	Price	Qty.	Total
Magical Creatures	$12.95		
Magic Spells and Incantations	$12.95		
Moon Lore	$7.95		
Random Recollections II, III or IV (circle your choices)	$3.95		
The Rede of the Wiccae – Hardcover	$49.95		
The Rede of the Wiccae – Softcover	$22.95		
Keepers of the Flame	$20.95		
Sounds of Infinity	$24.95		
The Magic of Herbs	$24.95		
Harry M. Hyatt's Works on Hoodoo and Folklore: A Full Reprint in 13 Volumes (including audio download) *Hoodoo—Conjuration—Witchcraft—Rootwork*	$1,400.00		
Subtotal			
Tax *(7% sales tax for RI customers)*			
Shipping & Handling *(See shipping rates section)*			
TOTAL			

MISCELLANY			
Item	Price	QTY.	Total
Pouch	$3.95		
Natural/Black Book Bag	$17.95		
Red/Black Book Bag	$17.95		
Hooded Sweatshirt, Blk	$30.00		
Hooded Sweatshirt, Red	$30.00		
L-Sleeve T, Black	$15.00		
L-Sleeve T, Red	$15.00		
S-Sleeve T, Black/W	$15.00		
S-Sleeve T, Black/R	$15.00		
S-Sleeve T, Dk H/R	$15.00		
S-Sleeve T, Dk H/W	$15.00		

MISCELLANY			
Item	Price	QTY.	Total
S-Sleeve T, Red/B	$15.00		
S-Sleeve T, Ash/R	$15.00		
S-Sleeve T, Purple/W	$15.00		
Postcards – set of 12	$3.00		
Bookmarks – set of 12	$12.00		
Magnets – set of 3	$1.50		
Promo Pack	$7.00		
Subtotal			
Tax (7% for RI Customers)			
Shipping and Handling			
Total			

SHIPPING & HANDLING CHARGES

BOOKS: One book, add $5.95. Each additional book add $1.50.

POUCH: One pouch, $3.95. Each additional pouch add $1.50.

BOOKBAGS: $5.95 per bookbag. **BRACELETS:** $3.95 per bracelet.

Send a check or money order payable in U. S. funds or credit card details to:

The Witches' Almanac, Ltd., PO Box 1292, Newport, RI 02840-9998

(401) 847-3388 (phone) • (888) 897-3388 (fax)
Email: info@TheWitchesAlmanac.com • www.TheWitchesAlmanac.com